The Psychology of Childhood

Contemporary Psychology Series

Series Editor: Professor Raymond Cochrane
School of Psychology
The University of Birmingham
Birmingham B15 2TT
United Kingdom

This series of books on contemporary psychological issues is aimed primarily at 'A' Level students and those beginning their undergraduate degree. All of these volumes are introductory in the sense that they assume no, or very little, previous acquaintance with the subject, while aiming to take the reader through to the end of his or her first course on the topic they cover. For this reason the series will also appeal to those who encounter psychology in the course of their professional work: nurses, social workers, police and probation officers, speech therapists and medical students. Written in a clear and jargon-free style, each book generally includes a full (and in some cases annotated) bibliography and points the way explicitly to further reading on the subject covered.

Psychology and Social Issues: A Tutorial Text
Edited by Raymond Cochrane, *University of Birmingham* and Douglas Carroll, *Glasgow Polytechnic*

Families: A Context for Development
David White and Anne Woollett, *Polytechnic of East London*

The Psychology of Childhood
Peter Mitchell, *The University of Wales College at Swansea*

Forthcoming titles:

On Being Old: The Psychology of Later Life
Graham Stokes, *Gulson Hospital, Coventry*

Health Psychology: Stress, Behaviour and Disease
Douglas Carroll, *Glasgow Polytechnic*

Food and Drink: The Psychology of Nutrition
David Booth, *University of Birmingham*

Criminal Behaviour: Explanation and Prevention
Clive Hollin, *University of Birmingham*

Contemporary Psychology Series: 3

The Psychology of Childhood

Peter Mitchell

 The Falmer Press

(A member of the Taylor & Francis Group)
London • Washington, D.C.

UK   The Falmer Press, 4 John Street, London WC1N 2ET
USA   The Falmer Press, Taylor & Francis Inc., 1900 Frost Road, Suite 101, Bristol, PA 19007

First published 1992

A catalogue record for this book is available from the British Library

Library of Congress Cataloging-in-Publication Data are available on request

ISBN 1 85000 954 6
ISBN 1 85000 950 3 (pbk)

Jacket design by Benedict Evans

Typeset in 10/11.5pt Garamond
by Graphicraft Typesetters Ltd., Hong Kong.

Printed in Great Britain by Burgess Science Press, Basingstoke on paper which has a specified pH value on final paper manufacture of not less than 7.5 and is therefore 'acid free'.

Contents

Series Editor's Preface

Childhood is a strange country to which all adults have been but about which we have few and distorted memories. We may just recall that golden sunny day when we picnicked with our mother and father by the stream and when everyone was happy and relaxed. Some may have darker and more depressing memories. But can any of us actually remember how we thought about those things when they were actually happening? When the lemonade was poured into two glasses, one for me and one for my brother, did I regard it as unfair because his glass was taller than mine, albeit also much narrower? I don't know.

I suppose we first develop self awareness, in the adult sense, at around 8–9 years of age and then we can semi-permanently fix our conscious thought processes by reflecting on them, or even writing them down. Before that it is unlikely we can recall our actual thought processes, or can be aware, except perhaps because of later retelling, of the parental, peer and other social influences which so deeply affect our later development and which make us what we are as adults.

Psychologists have to study early childhood as though they were studying the behaviour of another species – their own childhood experiences are not available for study as a reliable source of data. Indeed, they need to be quite ingenious to be able to get a handle on what is happening. They are denied the precise experimental control that is available to the student of animal behaviour, nor can they utilize the detailed introspection and self respect, or the completion of quantitive paper and pencil tests, that contribute so large a proportion of the data derived from studies of adult human behaviour. The magnitude of the ingenuity required to study the thought processes of young children is amply demonstrated in the first few chapters of Peter Mitchell's book. The work of the famous Swiss developmental psychologist Jean Piaget has been the catalyst for literally hundreds of other researchers who have committed themselves to finding more evidence to support his ideas or, equally productively, to trying to prove him wrong! Mitchell takes a balanced view of this enormous effort and aggregation of data (to which he has contributed in no small way) and at the same time provides a completely accessible route into the intricasies of research on the development of cognitive processes in infants and children.

The second half of this book is concerned not so much with how children think and behave during the time they are children, but the way in which childhood experiences and encounters permeate through the child's psyche as s/he grows up to create the adult personality with the attendant value systems, interpersonal skills and characteristic modes of interacting with others. Human psychological development is not like a train travelling along a track and stopping at various stations and then moving on to the next. Our trains carry bits of the stations, and some of the tracks we have passed over, on with us. We never escape our earliest social relationships, our earliest experiences, even if we cannot recall them. They form the template, the pattern, the stereotype of future relationships and understandings of situations.

There is probably no better way to begin the study of psychology than via the study of children. Although they are strange and alien in the way they think and behave, we know that they are going to grow up to be just like us. But how?

Raymond Cochrane
Birmingham
November 1991

Acknowledgments

The figures in this book were drawn by my wife, Rita Mitchell, and I thank her not only for the excellent art work, but also for all the encouragement and moral support she provided while I wrote the book. Raymond Cochrane's painstaking reading of a draft of the text has resulted in the omission of errors and also a final product which flows more smoothly. Any remaining blunders are, of course, my responsibility. I am also grateful to Raymond for suggesting that I write this book.

The book is a credit to those who taught me developmental psychology, particularly James Russell, who provided the inspiration during my first degree, and who then supervised my doctorate. Also, I am eternally grateful to my friend and colleague Elizabeth Robinson. In the three years I worked with Elizabeth at Birmingham University, my understanding of psychology truly took a quantum leap.

Last, but certainly not least, I am indebted to children, especially the thousands who participated in my studies over the years. My son, Andrew Mitchell, deserves special thanks for the patience he has displayed in being my most tested subject, and also for his highly insightful comments on the procedures I have tried to perfect. I need hardly add that it is the children above all who make developmental psychology such a fascinating topic.

Chapter 1

The Development of Thinking

The branch of psychology which studies the development of thinking is usually called cognitive developmental psychology. The word 'cognitive' refers to knowledge, but not in the general sense. When people talk about knowledge, they often mean the kind of information that it would be useful to call upon in order to answer questions in games such as *Trivial Pursuit* and *Blockbusters*, or in order to answer GCSE exam questions. In contrast, cognitive developmentalists think of knowledge as referring to understanding about things. So, for example, the finding that 5-year-olds are terrible at communicating on the telephone, because they seem to overlook the fact that the listener cannot see what they can see, or does not know what they know, might be taken as a symptom that the young child is incapable of putting himself or herself in someone else's shoes. Cognitive developmentalists look at particular difficulties children may have, such as poor communication ability, and then draw general conclusions about the child's immature understanding of the world. An example would be the conclusion that young children cannot take into account another person's point of view. An exciting feature of cognitive developmental psychology is observing some of the things children say and do in various situations, and speculating about the meaning of these things in terms of the child's understanding of the world.

Not everybody is in agreement about the way children understand the world, and how that understanding develops. This is mainly because what children say and do can be taken as symptoms of different underlying thought processes by different people. For example, a common-sense explanation for young children's difficulty in communicating on the telephone might simply be that their lack of experience in using telephones has not allowed them to develop a suitable 'telephone manner'. If this were true, the problem would not be attributable to the child's immaturity, but to lack of practice. The implication would be that an adult who had little experience of using telephones would be equally poor at communicating on them. Consequently, cognitive developmentalists look for independent evidence to support their suggestion concerning the child's immature understanding, in order to convince everyone that their idea about the child's immature understanding is correct. The result of this is that cognitive developmentalists who hold different opinions try to present evidence and argument to show that their idea is the correct one, and not their adversary's.

The most interesting aspect of cognitive developmental psychology is, of course, making discoveries about how the child understands the world. However, there is also an interesting subplot, which is the discovery process itself. The interest of this discovery process takes the form of some ingenious tasks which have been presented to children in order to assess their understanding, and also some brilliantly insightful arguments which have been developed in support of particular ideas about the nature of the child's understanding. The purpose of these arguments is to persuade us to accept one view of the child's understanding as opposed to a competing one.

In the pages which follow, we will begin by looking at some of the findings and ideas of the most brilliant cognitive developmentalist, Jean Piaget. We will consider some criticisms of Piaget's conclusions, and then examine contemporary findings and ideas which have been presented in this post-Piagetian era.

Piaget was born in Switzerland in 1896, and died in 1980. Piaget's early interest was in biology and his first publication, which was on that subject, appeared when he was aged ten. A few years later he was invited to be curator of shellfish at a natural history museum in Geneva. This was an offer he had to decline, since he was still attending secondary school! At the age of 21, Piaget was awarded a doctoral degree for a thesis he wrote about shellfish. It was at this point that the great man switched his attention to cognitive development, when he began working on the idea that a crucial ingredient in the relationship between creatures and their environment is intelligence. In order to acquire insight into this intelligence, he focused on the most intelligent creatures of all: human beings. Piaget believed that insight into the nature of intelligence could best be gained by studying its development. Hence Piaget became a cognitive developmentalist. At the time of his death, Piaget had written over forty books on cognitive development, and over a hundred articles on the subject. This was in addition to numerous other publications on shellfish, philosophy and education. Piaget also tried his hand at fiction: during the emotional turmoil of his adolescence, he expressed some of his feelings in a novel which was published in 1917.

Piaget suggested children pass through a series of stages on the way to cognitive maturity. His idea was that cognitive development is not a continuous process, dependent upon the accumulation of more and more information and skills; his view was that cognitive development proceeds not by gradual evolution, but by way of cognitive revolution. As the child shifts onto a new and more sophisticated plane of intelligence, she sheds many of the old cognitive limitations at a single sweep. Later, we will look at what, according to Piaget, it is that enables children to progress through the stages (i.e. the mechanism of development), but first we will examine Piaget's description of the stages, and some of the evidence he hoped would persuade us the stages are real.

Piaget indicated age ranges for the stages, but these were only intended as a rough guide. The more important point is that the order of the stages is supposed to be fixed and invariant. Piaget's idea was that each stage served as the foundation for the subsequent stage, so according to the theory, it would be impossible to miss a stage. To Piaget, missing a stage would be akin to building the second storey of a house without first building the first floor: impossible! To consider an example more relevant to the development of thinking, it is very hard to imagine how one could do long multiplication without first being able to do addition. Addition is necessary for carrying tens and also for subtotals in order to calculate the grand total. In this example, addition is a prerequisite for long multiplication. According to Piaget's theory, progressing through one stage is a prerequisite for shifting onto the subsequent stage. However, if one enjoyed the benefit of appropriate experiences, it might be possible to progress through the stages more rapidly than one who was less fortunate. We will consider what such experiences might be later.

Sensori-motor Stage: Birth to 2 Years

This is the stage of babyhood or infancy. The stage gets its name from the idea that the infant has sensory experiences (can see, hear, feel, taste, smell) and can move her limbs and other parts of her body (motor movements), but there is little cognition mediating the two. For example, Piaget's belief was that the infant has no conception of the permanent world which has an existence independently of the infant.

Piaget had a great many things to say about this stage, but we shall focus on his ideas about the development of the concept of object permanence. Piaget claimed that at birth we are in a state of solipsism. In other words, he was making the remarkable claim that babies cannot distinguish between self and not self. As a consequence, infants have no understanding of the permanent existence of things (i.e. objects) other than the self. However, after having passed through a series of substages, which we will take a look at in a moment, by the age of 24 months the infant will differentiate between herself and her surroundings, will be capable of mental imagery and will have an understanding of symbols.

In all, Piaget listed six substages of infancy, but we shall just examine those most relevant to the concept of object permanence. The first relevant one is Stage 3, which is approximately from 4 to 8 months of age. At this age, the baby is perfectly capable of grasping and picking up things such as a rattle. Given this ability, we can play a game with the baby, in which we take her rattle and put it in various places, just within the baby's reach. Providing the rattle is within reach (many babies of this age cannot crawl yet), the baby might enter into the game and retrieve it. However, if we put the rattle within reach but immediately cover it with a cloth, even though the covered object is in full view, the baby will not reach out. Instead she will switch attention to something else.

Piaget claimed that the baby does have the dexterity to remove the cloth, then grab the rattle. He claimed, therefore, that the baby's failure to retrieve the rattle from under the cloth was not due to a lack of skill. Instead, Piaget suggested that when an item is hidden from view, the baby no longer conceives of its existence. At this stage, when the infant can no longer directly sense an object, the object no longer exists as far as the infant is concerned. If we remove the cloth, the infant will then recognize the rattle and grasp it. So the infant can recognize objects she is familiar with, but when objects are no longer accessible to the senses, they no longer have any existence for the baby. According to Piaget, this is because the infant is unable to conjure up an image of the object in its physical absence. One implication of this radical claim is that although the infant recognizes and is familiar with her mother, when the mother leaves the room, from that moment to the mother's return, the infant no longer has any notion of the mother. To the young infant, the mother is just a picture which goes through a curious sequence of appearing and disappearing.

During Stage 4 of infancy (8 to 12 months), the baby's concept of object permanence develops to the point that the infant appears to possess a primitive notion that objects may exist even if they cannot be sensed directly. At this age, the infant will have no difficulty in retrieving a rattle hidden beneath a cloth. On the face of it, you may think that if the infant searches for something hidden from view, this must mean that the infant knows about that hidden thing even when it cannot be seen. However, Piaget would have us believe that the infant is still dominated by what she senses, and in particular, at this stage of infancy, her actions (i.e. motor movements). An older child, in contrast, would rely much more on mental imagery. According to Piaget, once the infant has retrieved the rattle from under the cloth, she then understands the existence of the rattle, in terms of her action in retrieving it.

Piaget demonstrated this with a simple test, known as the A-B task. Piaget spread out two cloths side by side in front of the infant. He then hid the rattle under the left cloth (cloth A), and, as expected, the infant pulled away the cloth and grabbed the rattle. Piaget repeated this a further two times. Then, on the fourth trial, in full view of the infant, Piaget put the rattle under the right-hand cloth (cloth B). The infant searched under the left cloth, as before, and on failing to find the rattle there, ceased searching and switched attention to something else! What makes this finding especially odd is that the shape of the rattle remains discernible under the right-hand cloth throughout.

In Stage 4, according to Piaget, once the infant has brought about the reappearance of the object by the act of searching, she then understands the reappearance of the object in terms of the specific actions involved in the search. In other words, the infant has little notion of the existence of the object independent of her own actions. To the infant, the existence of the object means a series of hand and arm movements.

Between 12 and 18 months, the infant progresses to Stage 5. The infant now has no problem with the A-B task, and searches under the right-hand cloth as soon as the rattle is hidden there, even if it had previously been hidden under the left-hand cloth on several occasions. Clearly, the infant no longer understands the object just in terms of her own actions. However, Piaget suggests that infants still have difficulty understanding the existence of objects they cannot directly experience, since they apparently have no notion of the movement of an unseen object. To demonstrate this, Piaget put the rattle under the left-hand cloth, and then, before the baby was given an opportunity to search, Piaget also put an upside-down bowl under that cloth, covering the rattle with the bowl as he did so. He then pulled the bowl from under the cloth, with the rattle hidden inside, and moved it under the right-hand cloth. He then removed the bowl, and placed it in full view, where it could be seen to be empty, having deposited the rattle under the right-hand cloth. The baby, who had been watching all this, was then allowed to begin searching. The baby searched under the left-hand cloth, where the rattle was put to begin with, but on failing to find it there, ceased searching and switched attention to something else.

During Stage 5, the infant is no longer dominated by her own actions in understanding the existence of objects. However, it seems the infant continues to have great difficulty in understanding objects which are not sensed directly, since she seems unable to comprehend the possibility of movement of the object when it is hidden from view. Older children presumably understand that if the rattle was not under the left-hand cloth, it must have travelled with the bowl to the right-hand cloth. This is an understanding which seems to be beyond a baby aged between 12 and 18 months. The reason, according to Piaget, is because the infant has difficulty in imagining the object to have its own independent existence; the infant struggles to understand that although the object is not directly experienced, it is possible for things to go on happening to it, such as moving from one place to another.

At 18 to 24 months, the infant enters the final of Piaget's stages of infancy, Stage 6. At this stage, the infant at last is able to conceive of the existence of an object independently of the self, and therefore is no longer in a state of solipsism. The infant now understands that on the one hand there is the external world, and on the other hand, distinct from that, is the self. The infant achieves this, according to Piaget, by acquiring the facility of mental imagery. The infant is able to generate a mental picture of things, and what might happen to those things, even though these events cannot be experienced directly. As a consequence, the infant no longer has difficulty locating an object which is hidden and then moved, providing it is easy to work out where it was moved to. That is, the child no longer has any difficulty with the task she failed during Stage 5 of infancy.

As you will discover further on in the book, there is some disagreement about Piaget's interpretation of the findings of his object permanence 'tests'. However, to my knowledge, no one disagrees about the way babies perform in these tests at roughly the ages Piaget indicated, and it is easy to replicate his findings. You can establish this for yourself, testing babies in your own family, providing you get the permission of the baby's parents to begin with.

The acquisition of mental imagery is a revolutionary point in the child's life, which heralds the transition to a whole new stage of development in the broadest sense. It is at this point that the child is viewed as progressing from the sensori-motor stage of infancy to the preoperational stage of early childhood. We will explore the preoperational stage in some detail later, but first, we will take a further look at the implications of being capable of mental imagery.

Perhaps the most important consequence of mental imagery is that it makes possible the use of symbols. A mental image need not be a mental replica of the thing it is concerned with. If the image is about something in the world, but is not a mental replica of that thing, then it is a symbol of that thing. According to Piaget, it is no coincidence that at the end of infancy the child begins to develop proficiency in that most powerful of human symbols, language. The intellectual achievements which become possible with the aid of language in its various forms are literally unimaginable. For example, consider some of the remarkable progress in technology and science this century. Most of this would have been impossible without mathematics and written language to work out and communicate the ideas responsible for this progress.

An important aspect of Piaget's thinking becomes clear at this point. Piaget stressed that intellectual development underpins language development in important ways, not the other way round; a capacity for mental imagery permits proficiency in use of symbols, one form of which happens to be language. It hardly needs to be stated that language enables more efficient problem solving. However, symbolic activity other than the use of a recognizable language may also facilitate problem solving.

Piaget tells of how his daughter, who was nearing the end of infancy, solved the problem of how to retrieve a chain hidden inside a matchbox. When given the matchbox, the girl made a clumsy attempt to open the box but failed. She then paused, opened and closed her mouth a few times whilst gazing at the matchbox, and then smoothly opened the box to retrieve the chain. According to Piaget, his daughter registered the way in which the matchbox opened symbolically in her mouth movement. After working out the problem in this way, she was able to proceed and open the box with no difficulty. This example shows that Piaget believed it is not the case that language makes possible symbolic problem-solving activity. The child can solve problems symbolically without language. However, no doubt Piaget would accept that, given the potential for symbolic activity, language then becomes a useful tool for this purpose.

Symbolic activity is most evident in young children's pretend play. Here we find children pretending that bananas are telephones, that chairs are cars, that shoe boxes are television sets, and so on. Watching young children engage in pretend play gives the impression that they are exercising their newly acquired symbolic ability purely for the delight of it. There is reason to suppose that the symbolic element of pretend play is not just a manifestation of having reached a developmental milestone. Some argue persuasively that pretend play actually promotes cognitive development in various ways (e.g. Leslie, 1987).

Preoperational Stage: 2 to 7 Years

As the child enters this stage, she is capable of solving problems with the help of symbolic activity, and is rapidly developing proficiency as a language user. You would be forgiven for thinking that most of the developmental milestones have been achieved, and that things are downhill from this point. However, Piaget argues vehemently that this could not be further from the truth.

According to Piaget, the young child is plagued with egocentrism. This term might seem a little confusing to begin with, because Piaget did not use the term according to its common meaning. In ordinary parlance, we might call someone 'egocentric' to mean that they are selfish and inconsiderate of others. Piaget's use of the word, in contrast, indicates a cognitive limitation which prevents the child from seeing things from somebody else's point of view. It is not really appropriate to say the young child is inconsiderate, since it is claimed that the young child is incapable of understanding that another person might have a viewpoint different from her own. In this case, 'different viewpoint' is used both in a literal sense, as in failing to understand that objects look different from different perspectives, and in a conceptual sense, as in failing to understand that people may hold opinions, beliefs, etc. different from her own.

Intimately linked with egocentrism is a profound inability to understand and apply principles to the world. The young child's grasp of things is intuitive and highly subjective, rather than logical and objective. Consequently, the child's thinking is dominated by surface appearance, rather than by underlying principles. The best way to illustrate this is with examples of tests which a preoperational child fails. We will consider this in a moment, but first a note on the name of this stage.

By 'operation', Piaget meant the following of a set of rules in solving a problem: in other words, a logical operation that is done mentally. According to Piaget, operational intelligence is necessary to rid the child of egocentrism, to rid the child of his highly subjective and overly intuitive view of the world. So the *pre*operational child is egocentric.

Perhaps the best known evidence of failure to understand and apply principles during the preoperational stage is in the failure to conserve. In this sense, 'conservation' has nothing to do with green politics, but rather is to do with the understanding that transformation of appearance need not result in alteration of the underlying reality. The underlying reality remains constant, and therefore is conserved, despite the transformation in appearance.

In the conservation of quantity task, the child watches as we fill two short wide jars with water to the same level. We then carefully pour all the content from one into a tall thin jar, and put this beside the remaining short wide jar. Of course, the level of water in the thin jar is much higher than that in the wide jar. Very few people above the age of 7 would say that the thin jar has more water in it, but nearly all children below that age claim that it does. Young children's incorrect judgments seem even more striking because Piaget always got them to agree initially that there was the same amount of water in the two wide jars. Also, he took pains to ensure that the child was watching carefully as he poured the water from one glass to another; the child could see that no water was added.

Apparently, instead of attending to a principle (i.e. operation), such as 'none was added or taken away, so the amount of water must be the same', young children were seduced by, and centred on (to use Piagetian terminology), the increased height of the water level in the thin glass. The child gives an intuitive answer instead of working out the correct answer on the basis of an underlying principle. That is, the child fails to 'decentre'.

Young children also display a failure to conserve on a variety of other tasks, some of which we will now take a look at. In the conservation of length task, we show the child two pencils of the same length, and begin by aligning the points so that equality of length becomes apparent. After the child agrees they are the same length, we move one of the pencils slightly, so that its point protrudes above that of the other by about a centimetre. We then ask, 'Are these two pencils the same size now, or is this one bigger or is that one bigger?' Preoperational children will judge they are no longer the same size, and point to one of the pencils, claiming it is bigger. In the conservation of mass task, we make two balls of plasticine the same size, and, after the child agrees that they are the same size, we roll one into a sausage shape. Preoperational children usually judge that the sausage shape is bigger and has more plasticine in it. In the conservation of number task, we spread out two rows of, for example, ten counters, in one-to-one correspondence. After the child has agreed there is the same number of counters in each row, we spread out one of the rows further, making spaces between the counters bigger. Pre-operational children now claim that the longer row has more counters in it.

Piaget documented many errors young children make which he claimed are symptoms of preoperational, non-principled, non-logical thinking. We shall consider just two more of these. First is the difficulty young children have with class inclusion. We spread out, for example, seven Lego bricks, five red and two blue. In this example, the overall class of bricks includes the subclasses of red bricks and blue bricks. The child knows that all seven items are in the class of bricks, because if we ask how many bricks there are, they have no difficulty in answering with 'seven'. We then ask, 'Are there more bricks or more red bricks?' Preoperational children answer with, 'More red bricks.' According to Piaget, the young child centres on the greater number of red bricks compared with blue bricks, and as a result fails to operate on the principle that the class of bricks must be bigger than the subclass of red bricks, because the class of bricks includes both red and blue bricks.

Finally, we come to transitive inference. This is the test that gives most of us a cold sweat as we hear the problem: Jane is taller than Susan; Jane is shorter than Mary; who is the tallest, Susan or Mary? Piaget presented a task which involves the same problem in principle, but which to adults and older children seems absurdly simple. We show the child two towers made of lego, one a little taller than the other. Just by looking, it is impossible to tell which is the taller, for two reasons. First, the towers are in different parts of the room, so they can't both be taken in at a glance. Second, they are on different levels, for example, one on a coffee table and one on the floor.

We present the child with a stick which is of intermediate length, and ask him to compare each tower with the stick in order to find out which is biggest. The comparison reveals that one tower is bigger than the stick, whilst the other is smaller. Preoperational children are very poor at this task. They seem to have no idea what to do with the stick, and even if we do the measuring for them, they do not reliably give the correct answer, that the tower taller than the stick is bigger than the tower shorter than the stick. According to Piaget, this is yet another example of young children failing to operate on a principle, which, in this case, would be 'if this tower is bigger than the stick, and that tower is shorter than the stick, then this tower must be bigger than that tower'.

It is very unusual indeed to find a young child who does not make the errors described in these pages, though some people, as you will discover later, disagree with Piaget's interpretation of the findings. The tests are very simple to carry out, and you can demonstrate the errors very easily by performing them on young children in your family. It is especially interesting to introduce modifications to the procedure of the tests to see if it helps children to get the correct answer.

I began this section with a definition of what Piaget meant by 'egocentrism'. Since then we have looked in some detail at preoperational errors but little at the way in which the young child's thinking is manifest in an egocentric manner. A classic example of egocentrism can be found in the 'three mountains task'. We sit the child in front of a model landscape of three mountains located side by side. On each of these mountains is a single distinctive feature, such as a man, a house and a cross. We then seat another individual facing the child, on the other side of the model, and ask the child to select a photo of what the landscape looks like to the other individual. In the set of photos would be a picture of the child's own view as well as the view from the other side of the model, in which the distinctive features on the top of the mountains are in left-right reversal, of course. Pre-operational children nearly always choose a photo of the model from their own vantage point, and claim that that is how the individual seated opposite sees the mountains. Piaget claimed that because young children are egocentric, they only conceive of their own viewpoint, and fail to recognize that from another perspect-ive things may look different; they have no notion of alternative views of the world.

Stage of Concrete Operations: 7 to 12 Years

Children suddenly appreciate that there is more to things than superficial appearances, and that their view of the world is only one of the many possible. They acquire a first grasp that an underlying more objective reality is accessible by operating on principles. When they do, they are described as entering the stage of concrete operations in middle childhood. We will take a look at some of these principles in a moment, but first a note on the name Piaget gave to this stage. In this context, the term 'concrete' means 'real or tangible'. Piaget's idea was that the child in this stage can solve problems in a principled way, in other words using logical operations, providing the problem is real or concrete. A child in this stage cannot handle imagined or hypothetical problems, according to Piaget.

The difficulties the preoperational child has, which we examined in the previous section, are not shared by the child in the concrete operational stage. The child gives the correct conservation judgment that there is the same amount of water, that length, mass and number are the same, following transformation. The child gives the correct class inclusion judgment that there are more bricks than red bricks, and can reliably give the correct answer to the transitive inference problem, indicating which of two towers is bigger after measuring both with a stick of inter-mediate length. Also, the child no longer selects his own view on the three mountains task.

Not only do children give the correct answer, they provide justifications which give the impression of being based on logical (operational) principles. Consider justifications which children give for correct conservation judgments. Piaget identified three:

> (i) Compensation – the child says that although the water in the thin glass is taller, the water in the wide glass is broader. The broadness makes up (i.e. compensates) for the tallness, so there is the same amount;
>
> (ii) Inversion – the child says that although the water in the thin glass is taller, if you poured the water back into its original container (i.e. the inverse transformation), it would look just the same as the water in the comparison container, so that shows that really the amount is just the same;

(iii) Identity – you never added anything or took anything away from the water in the thin glass, so it must be the same.

After these momentous achievements in thought processes, it might be difficult to imagine how the child's thinking could be refined much further. Although the concrete operational child has a radically different and better understanding of things than the preoperational child, chiefly because he is no longer seduced by surface appearances, the concrete operational child nonetheless is firmly ensconced in the real world. As a result, the child is no good at dealing with problems which cannot be located in reality. He cannot handle the 'just suppose ...' variety of problems. We will consider some examples of these in the next section.

Formal Operations: 12 Years Onwards

Before looking at these examples, as usual, a note on the name given to this stage. In no sense does 'formal' as used by Piaget mean well-mannered etiquette. Rather, it means systematic reasoning about things which take a hypothetical form and not necessarily a real, concrete form. The best exemplar of such systematic reasoning can be found in the procedures for scientific investigation. Piaget obviously upheld the scientific method as pre-eminent, and as the highest form of known intelligence.

During this stage, but not during the concrete operational stage, the child is able to solve the transitive inference problem on a purely mental level; no real items need be involved. The adolescent can work out that if x is bigger than y and x is smaller than z, then the smallest altogether must be y. These characters need have no value in the real world for the adolescent to find the correct solution. In solving the problem, the adolescent can mentally manipulate the symbols in a way that is purely formal and logical.

Another classic example Piaget gave, which better illustrates the 'scientific' aspect of formal operational thinking, is to be found in the pendulum problem. We show the adolescent a pendulum, and state the problem, which is to find out what determines how frequently the pendulum swings back and forth (i.e. number of oscillations per minute). We show the adolescent how to vary four factors which rightly or wrongly we may suppose would affect speed of oscillation: weight of the suspended object, length of string, force of initial swing setting the pendulum in motion, and the height from which the pendulum is released. In case you did not know, it is the length of string which is the important factor, but the correct answer to the problem is nowhere near as important as the way the adolescent goes about finding the solution.

A concrete operational child will approach the problem apparently with no plan, in a haphazard manner. For example, he may first test a long pendulum with a light weight and then compare that with a short pendulum which had a heavy weight. Whatever the result, it would be impossible to tell whether any difference observed was due to the difference in weight, the difference in length or a combination of both.

In sharp contrast, the formal operational adolescent will systematically compare a short heavy pendulum with a short light one, and so on. In other words, the adolescent will hold three of the factors constant whilst comparing the effect of different values of the remaining factor. Because of this, the result of the adolescent's 'experiments' can unequivocally be attributed to differences in values of just one of the factors.

To repeat what I said earlier, it is not getting the correct answer that is important. What is much more important is that the adolescent should approach the problem in a systematic and patterned manner. According to Piaget, this reveals something special about the adolescent's thought processes. It shows the adolescent understands that in order to make a sensible interpretation of the results, whatever the outcome, the experiment must be carried out in a certain systematic way. Therefore, the adolescent identifies the optimal conditions for interpreting the results before any results have been obtained. In this case, the adolescent anticipates, and therefore reasons in a hypothetical manner. Putting it another way, before acting on the pendulum in any way, the adolescent works out that altering the values of two of the factors simultaneously would yield uninterpretable results. The fact that when the adolescent eventually begins her experiment she takes a systematic approach shows that prior to this she must have reasoned hypothetically about how to get the best from her test.

Piaget suggested that not everybody achieves formal operational thinking, and added in characteristically arrogant fashion that such thinking may be scarce in some primitive 'concrete operational' cultures. According to Piaget, the ability to reason systematically in the hypothetical is a feat which is enjoyed by people who have been fortunate enough to have experiences that aid progression through the stages of cognitive development. We shall now turn our attention to what these experiences might be, and how development takes place. Our guiding question will be 'what is the mechanism of development?'.

Piaget's Explanation of Cognitive Development

Piaget identified the building blocks of thinking as mental units he called 'schemes'. At birth, we are equipped with a set of action schemes, which develop and multiply. The descendants of those early schemes come to form intelligent thought processes. The schemes provided by our genetic heredity are commonly recognized as a set of reflexes, such as the grasping reflex: from the moment of birth, the baby will close its hand around any item which comes into contact with the palm. This is quite likely to be the mother's finger, in the first instance. What we now need to know is how these simple reflexes could evolve into the dizzy heights of formal operational intelligence.

A clue to Piaget's view of this development is provided by the fact that young babies will grasp at things other than a finger. The infant generalizes the scope of application of the scheme in this way. Piaget called the exercising of a scheme in a novel context 'assimilation'. It gets its name from the idea that the new application is taken into the overall scope of the scheme. However, the scheme, which may be thought of as a set of mental instructions to the hand on how to grasp the object, inevitably will not be suited to every item the baby holds. For example, the first time the baby holds her rattle, it may be necessary for adjustments to be made to the position of the fingers and the extent to which the hand closes around the object. Information about these adjustments is fed back to the scheme, and as a consequence, the scheme is modified. Now the scheme is activated in one way if it is a finger that is being grasped, but in a slightly different way if it is a rattle that is being grasped. Piaget called the modification to the scheme 'accommodation'. Assimilation and accommodation work in conjunction as a scheme is activated; it would be peculiar for one to occur in the absence of the other.

Piaget suggested that the ideal is when assimilation and accommodation contribute equally. If either dominates, then there may be a problem. An example of over-assimilation is pretence. In this case the child displays little adaptation to the world, but instead interprets the world in her own highly idiosyncratic way. As I commented earlier, some take the view that pretence may be cognitively beneficial, but presumably pretence to the exclusion of any acknowledgment of reality would be disastrous. An example of over-accommodation is imitation. Here, the child parrots somebody else, with little understanding.

According to Piaget, we are intrinsically motivated to exercise our schemes, particularly when the schemes are newly acquired, and this process is not dependent on external reward. Therefore, there is plenty of opportunity for assimilation and accommodation to occur, and therefore plenty of opportunity for schemes to develop. In other words, there is plenty of opportunity for the growth of intelligence, given the way in which development supposedly takes place.

As the scheme's breadth of application increases, so the demarcation in each mode of application increases. There comes a point when the modes of application of a scheme are so diverse that it is no longer a single scheme but rather a series of schemes within a certain genre. For example, the scheme for holding a paintbrush is in some respects quite different from the scheme for holding the steering wheel of a car, yet both are descendants of the innate grasping scheme.

Schemes may also be coordinated, or brought together, into a giant scheme to perform complicated actions. Driving a car is a useful example of this: steering, gears, brake, clutch and accelerator, just to name some of the individual schemes comprising the overall scheme of 'driving'.

At this point things may seem reasonably straightforward, that schemes develop, and this is influenced in an important way by assimilation and accommodation. So how do the stages of development feature in all this? Piaget would have us believe that underlying each stage is a new category of scheme. In the sensori-motor stage, the only schemes are motor schemes as in throwing rattles, crawling and so on. In the preoperational stage, the child has schemes which are not just motor, but may involve mental imagery also. At the concrete operational stage, schemes may proceed through a series of mental actions perhaps in the way a computer runs a program, to arrive at the solution to a problem in a principled and logical way. In the formal operational stage, the same maintains, except the problem need have no physical reality.

How does a new category of scheme emerge? One of the main factors in this development is the internal motivational force Piaget called 'equilibration'. We shall examine the idea of equilibration in relation to the acquisition of understanding conservation of quantity. The non-conserving child entertains the belief that tallness and quantity are intimately linked, so she will think that a tall column of liquid contains more than a short one. That seems like a perfectly reasonable belief to hold, and no doubt most adults think in a similar way. However, the child is different, because she thinks tallness is all that counts. We adults know that width is also important. At the age of about 6 or 7 years, the child begins to recognize, perhaps through observation and experience, that attention to width might be useful in judging quantity. The trouble is that the child of this age does not bring together, or coordinate, these two beliefs, and so may vacillate when faced with a conservation judgment: after the contents of one of two identical glasses is poured into a tall thin glass, sometimes the child will judge that the tall one has more, and sometimes the same child will judge that the wider glass has more.

This situation gives rise to a state of cognitive conflict, because the tall glass cannot both contain more and contain less than the wide glass. The cognitive conflict activates the motivational process, equilibration, which functions to remove that conflict, and in the process generate new schemes which will be on a higher cognitive level. In the case of conservation, through equilibration, the child resolves the conflict by viewing the problem in a whole new way. The child achieves reconciliation between the old beliefs by appreciating that although it is fair to think the wide glass contains more due to its extra width, and that the tall glass contains more due to its extra height, the tall glass has a corresponding reduction in width which cancels out the increase in quantity that might be expected from the extra tallness. Therefore, quantity has remained constant, and the pouring from one glass to another was irrelevant.

In this case, the motivational force of equilibration, stimulated by cognitive conflict, pushed the child onto a higher and more flexible cognitive level. In the previous stage, the child had made judgments on the basis of single dimensions, such as width or tallness. In the new higher stage, the child can mentally handle both width and tallness simultaneously and compare the two in relation to the problem they were making a judgment about. Having achieved that, the child is then in a position to face novel tasks with this increased mental flexibility, and so development enjoys a quantum leap at around the age of 6 or 7 years. The child's mental processes are then reorganized, or restructured, to use Piagetian phraseology, to take on board the new flexible thinking capability. In the aftermath of mental reorganization, enormous potential for a mental growth spurt opens up. The child can now view the world in a new light. For example, the child now has the mental flexibility to view the world from another viewpoint, and therefore no longer suffers the egocentrism characteristic of the preoperational stage.

Traditional Learning Theory as a Contrasting Explanation of Development

At the time Piaget's theory first became widely known to psychologists, in the early 1960s, the 'establishment' view was that learning, including all the learning that takes place during childhood, can be understood purely by looking at external rewards and punishment. The prominent figure endorsing this view was B.F.

Skinner, who showed that any kind of behaviour that is followed by reward is more likely to occur again in the future, whereas any behaviour that is followed by punishment is less likely to occur in the future. On the face of it this claim seems absurd, but not so when we realize that Skinner meant something much more general than the common meanings of 'reward' and 'punishment'. Skinner's use of these words did not necessarily imply *money* or *spanking*. Rather, he meant that behaviour which has pleasant consequences is likely to recur, whereas behaviour which has unpleasant consequences is likely to be extinguished.

Statements like these would not be new to the circus trainers who have for centuries trained elephants to waltz. However, remarkable as it may seem, Skinner succeeded in persuading psychologists to accept his outrageous claim that all human behaviour can also be understood in terms of reward and punishment. For example, a child achieves literacy by being rewarded with praise from teacher and parent 'for doing the right thing', and by being punished with chastisement 'for doing the wrong thing'.

Piaget's ideas flew in the face of this mainstream psychology, because his findings strongly suggested that there is much more to development than reward and punishment. In particular, Piaget argued that we need to consider how receptive a child is to acquiring new information or a new skill primarily by reference to her particular stage of development. For example, a child in the operational stages may be receptive to understanding principles which require mental juggling and flexibility, whereas a child in the preoperational stage would not. Also, Piaget argued convincingly that development is partly driven by an internal motivation, with the idea that humans are such that they find learning and development to be pleasurable experiences. This was anathema to Skinner, who believed that all learning can be explained in terms of rewards independent of the learning process itself.

Piagetian psychology has now replaced Skinnerian psychology as the mainstream, and hence the discrepancy in the space given to the two approaches in this book. Nowadays, those who wish to revolutionize cognitive development do so by analyzing, criticizing and modifying Piaget's theory. One such modification to the theory, or perhaps it should be called an addition, is presented in the next section.

A Supplement to Piaget's Theory: Self-Centred Adolescents

Piaget's writing about adolescents was mainly concerned with their competence at solving problems. He seemed to revel in the adolescent thought potential. However, no doubt a random sample of middle-aged people would have many misgivings about adolescents, with comments such as 'lazy, vain, self-centred ...'. These negative features are not so obviously to do with cognitive development, but perhaps more related to personality characteristics. Yet many personality traits, such as extraversion, introversion, eccentricity and neuroticism, seem to endure, spanning much, if not all, of the individual's life. In contrast, vanity and self-centredness seem to have a peak in many people during adolescence, and therefore seem more to do with a stage of development rather than with enduring individual differences in personality.

Is it possible that the aberration in personality during the adolescent years can be understood by reference to Piaget's theory? It cannot be understood directly from his writings, but it can be explained by the ideas of one of Piaget's disciples, David Elkind, who supplemented Piaget's theory about adolescent thinking in order to embrace some of the more noticeable aspects of adolescent behaviour.

As already reported above, Piaget claimed that young children are unaware of other people's points of view. In a sense, young children seem to be unaware of other people's thoughts and cognitions. Elkind suggested that although adolescents know about other people's thoughts, they very often egocentrically assume that their own preoccupations will be shared by others. That is, adolescents recognize that others have the potential to think differently from themselves, but in the absence of strong evidence to the contrary, assume that their own interests, likes, dislikes, etc. are universally held views. For example, an adolescent who enjoys rock music to the exclusion of all other kinds of performing art, will find it barely comprehensible that their taste is not shared by others. If they find that a middle-aged person expresses a preference for classical music, the adolescent is likely to attribute this to snobbery, lack of energy and excitement and desire to uphold establishment values. If the middle-aged person expresses distaste for rock music, the adolescent is likely to interpret this not as a genuine feeling, but rather as a general attack on the values held by adolescents.

Elkind suggests that since adolescence is a period of radical physiological change, during that period it is no surprise that teenagers become preoccupied with their own appearance. For example, because an adolescent boy egocentrically assumes what is of interest to him is of interest to everyone, he wrongly thinks that everyone else is preoccupied with whether his facial hair is sufficiently prominent to require the use of a razor. Just as the adolescent spends long periods of time scrutinizing her own face, so she will assume others she meets will wish to examine her face in a similar way. According to Elkind, all this results from the adolescent becoming more sharply aware of others' thoughts, but failing to appreciate that her own interests would not necessarily be universally shared. The adult, in contrast, recognizes that she has idiosyncratic preoccupations, and that others have different personal preoccupations. The adult has more of a notion of being just one rather unexceptional person out of the billions who inhabit our planet.

In order to help describe the adolescent failure to distinguish between topics of interest held by the self compared with those held to be of interest by others, Elkind introduces the idea of 'imaginary audience'. The adolescent forever anticipates the reactions of others to herself, anticipations which are based on the wrong belief that others will be as admiring or critical as she is of herself. Therefore, the adolescent believes she will be the focus of attention, and hence the term 'audience' used by Elkind. However, this 'audience' is imaginary, because it is likely that people the adolescent encounters will have much more interesting things to be concerned with than contemplating whether a youth has skin problems. Of course, it might be that the adolescent engineers the situation so that she really does become the centre of attention, but that is a different story.

Elkind suggests, then, that the imaginary audience is responsible for the self-consciousness typical of adolescence. Due to the belief that the audience is concerned with, and enlightened about, the adolescent's cosmetic defects, the adolescent becomes overly shy and incessantly seeks privacy. This is an understandable reaction to a feeling of being under the eye of an audience. Therefore, Elkind claims that adolescents frequently experience a sense of shame, a characteristic reaction to a disapproving audience.

There is another side to this coin, which is that sometimes the adolescent plays to the audience, with the idea that others will find the adolescent's 'performance' terribly interesting. On these occasions, the adolescent actively takes a high profile by being loud, both in the sense of making lots of noise, and in wearing outrageous garments and hairstyles. The adolescent will spend extended periods of time preparing for an appearance before an audience, partly imagining how members of the opposite sex will find her features and qualities irresistible, and partly adding the final touches to those appearances by careful application of cosmetics. When adolescent members of the opposite sex eventually meet, in characteristically vain manner they are more concerned about being observed, and imagining the impact they make on the observer, than doing the observing.

Because the adolescent is the centre of her own attention, and also assumes she is the centre of everyone else's attention, she develops an inflated notion of self-importance. Elkind tells us that adolescents believe their feelings, experiences and ideas are especially intense and unique. They often believe that they have been specially chosen by divine decree, and as a consequence believe that they have a preferential relationship with a personal God. Altogether, these adolescent feelings lead the individual to think she holds a special, perhaps immortal, position on earth. To help describe this idea, Elkind used the term 'personal fable'. This is a kind of story the adolescent tells herself about her gifted special status, which might be that no matter what, the adolescent will always win through in the end. Thus the adolescent feels an inevitability that she can gamble and win, and can dice with death with impunity.

Elkind points out that imaginary audience and personal fable are concepts that can help us understand some deviant or delinquent adolescent behaviour. Consider the case of soccer hooliganism, which is an almost exclusively male adolescent phenomenon. Soccer violence is an activity which is guaranteed the attention of an audience in thousands if not millions in the case of televised events, and it is an activity which involves considerable danger. Perhaps the adolescent relishes the opportunity to display courage and skill in fighting to such an audience, believing that onlookers will be immensely impressed. A risk is that the ensuing physical combat could result in serious injury. However, the adolescent's personal fable leads him to think that he will be immune to harm inflicted by adversaries.

The personal fable also leads the adolescent to think that he will be able to avoid reprisal from the authorities. If he happens to be arrested, then he relishes the new source of attention from police, solicitors, jury, probation officers and so on. After the event he may perceive himself to have achieved legendary status with peers for going on official record as having committed an act of horrible brutality. He may believe that this earns him special respect and fear from fellow hooligans who have not graduated to star-status in this way.

Towards the end of adolescence, and during early adulthood, the imaginary audience begins to wane and eventually disappears. How does this development occur? Elkind suggests that imaginary audience is actually a prediction about how people will react, based on the adolescent's own preoccupations. However, the actual reaction is frequently different from the anticipated reaction, when others treat the adolescent as a rather boring person who presents as new and unique, things which everyone else already knows about and considers trivial. This reaction of the real as opposed to the imaginary audience enlightens the adolescent to her true position in the universe, which of course is usually that she is just another unremarkable person. Thus it is the adolescent's capacity for making hypotheses that is responsible for the emergence of the imaginary audience, and her subsequent testing of those hypotheses against real experiences which is ultimately responsible for the evaporation of the imaginary audience. A by-product of the imaginary audience is the personal fable, and as the former dissolves, so does the latter.

Elkind's ideas about imaginary audience and personal fable possess very strong intuitive appeal, and most of us can recognize aspects of our own behaviour encapsulated in these ideas. No doubt most of us would also acknowledge that these kinds of behaviours were prominent during adolescence. Critics of Elkind pay tribute to the appeal these ideas have.

Despite this, Elkind's critics question whether it is sensible to suggest that imaginary audience and personal fable are manifestations of egocentrism. Lapsley and Murphy (1985) draw attention to an anomaly in Elkind's account. Recall that Elkind suggested adolescents appreciate that other people have thoughts, but fail to differentiate the content of their own thought from that of others. That is what Elkind meant by egocentrism in this case. However, Lapsley and Murphy point out that even pre-adolescents are perfectly capable of differentiating the content of others' thoughts from their own. For example, concrete operational children have no difficulty in selecting the appropriate photo on the three mountains task, when asked how the model looks to someone sitting in the seat on the other side of the table. Clearly, these children can differentiate between the content of their own thought (how the model looks to them) and that of another individual (how the model looks to the person opposite).

Lapsley and Murphy argue that imaginary audience and personal fable are not so much to do with failure to differentiate between content of own thought and that of others, but on the contrary that they are to do with an acute enlightenment of the thought of others. During adolescence, the individual first becomes aware of others' thoughts on a big scale. Therefore, so far as the adolescent is concerned, a first awareness of others' views of oneself is akin to suddenly being thrown in the limelight. We all know from the well-documented cases of legendary pop and film stars about the effect overnight fame can have. Perhaps the adolescent experiences the same when she suddenly becomes aware of others' thoughts about her. This could provide a better explanation for imaginary audience and personal fable than the concept of adolescent egocentrism.

Lapsley and Murphy suggest that the disappearance of imaginary audience and personal fable could take place in the following way. Knowing that others think about us is quite harmless in most cases. As a result, young adults come to terms with the fact that they feature in the thoughts of others, and begin to pay less attention to the thought as a consequence.

Further Reading

There are several texts summarizing Piaget's theory. My favourite, for its detail coupled with easy prose style, is:

GINSBERG, H. and OPPER, S. (1979) *Piaget's Theory of Intellectual Development*, London, Prentice-Hall International, Inc.

Alternatively, or additionally, you may wish to look at Piaget's summary of his own theory. Piaget's writing is notoriously difficult to understand, and is usually targeted at a highly specialized audience. However, the following book was written for people new to the subject, and as such is not quite so difficult:

PIAGET, J. and INHELDER, B. (1969) *The Psychology of the Child*, London, Routledge and Kegan Paul.

Chapter 2

An Assessment of Piaget's Theory

Einstein once said that theories should not only be assessed in relation to how well they can explain and predict things, but also according to how beautiful they are as theories. Some take the view that Piaget's theory has beauty. His ideas about cognitive conflict stimulating complete cognitive reorganization certainly embody qualities which have excited many people. Also his discoveries about infant behaviour and children's judgments on such things as conservation tasks are undoubtedly fascinating, whatever the status of the theory produced to explain them.

In some respects, though, there are serious misgivings about Piaget's theory. The eminent American developmentalist John H. Flavell, who was responsible for popularizing Piaget in the early 1960s, has recently expressed some of these misgivings. Flavell (1982) argues that Piaget did not clearly or consistently define the mental activities which constitute the thinking involved in such things as conserving quantity. He goes on to suggest that the thinking required to solve conservation problems may bear no resemblance to that suggested by Piaget. Flavell further points out that findings obtained by others indicate that young children may have cognitive limitations which would be completely unexpected on the basis of Piagetian theory. Also, it seems the logic Piaget developed as he formulated his theory could be seriously flawed. Braine and Rumain (1983) analyzed the components and structure of the theory, and concluded on logical grounds that it simply does not hold water and moreover that it does not hang together properly. If these critics are right, we may find that we are left with some interesting findings on the way children answer questions about certain problems, but with an incomplete or inadequate account of what these findings mean. However, the validity of Piaget's findings are also now being questioned. We turn to this next.

Recall that Piaget proposed that infants are in a state of solipsism, meaning that they fail to distinguish between self and surroundings. An implication of that claim is that infants do not understand that objects have an existence independent of self. Consequently, so the story goes, all the infant is aware of is a series of images, and the infant has no notion of the continued existence of things in their perceptual absence. The development of an understanding of object permanence, and therefore an understanding that the self is just one of many relatively permanent items in the world, progresses through a series of stages during infancy. In

Stage 4 of infancy, which occurs roughly between 8 and 12 months, the infant fails on the A-B task. Recall that we hide the rattle under cloth A three times, and the infant retrieves it with no difficulty, but when we hide the rattle under cloth B in full view, the infant perseveres in searching under cloth A.

Studies carried out by other researchers suggest that Piaget underestimated infants. Bower (1965) reasoned that if Piaget is correct in claiming that infants perceive the world as a series of images, and are ignorant about the stable permanence of things, then they would have no notion of size constancy. That is, they would not understand that an object moved into the distance is the same object, and that it is merely the apparent size of the object which changes. That would require understanding that things have underlying enduring qualities which remain stable despite changes in appearance. If they understand this, presumably we could argue they understand object permanence.

Bower trained 1- and 2-month-old babies to suck on a pacifier only when he showed them a box of a certain size. Bower trained the babies to do this in much the same way that circus trainers train elephants to stand on their hind legs: by giving a reward for doing the right thing. Bower trained the infants to suck only when a box of a certain size was placed in front of them, by *not providing reward* when boxes of other sizes were present. Bower then moved this box into the distance and found that the babies continued to suck on seeing it. In contrast, when he presented a box of different size, babies did not suck, even if the new box was strategically placed so that its image striking the eye was the same size as that of the original box. This suggests that these young babies could recognize the original box, despite changes in its apparent size with changes in distance. Bower argues that this shows that even young babies understand that objects have stable and enduring properties which remain despite changes in appearance.

Butterworth (1981) goes further than this, and argues that not only do infants know that things have a stable and enduring quality, they appreciate that there are other people in the world who hold perspectives different from their own. Following earlier work by Scaife and Bruner (1975), Butterworth arranged for the infant, aged between 6 and 8 months, to sit facing her mother. At a certain moment, as arranged with Butterworth, the mother was to break eye-contact with her baby and look to a specific point in the room. When the mother did this, the infant promptly looked to the same point. It was not that the infants were just imitating the mother's head-turning, failing to look at any point in particular. A detailed video analysis of the babies' eye movements revealed that they were accurately fixating on the same point the mother was fixating on. Butterworth argues that this shows the infants understood something might be going on that the mother could see, but that they could not yet see, and turned their heads to find out what it was. If this interpretation is correct, it implies the infants did know about a stable enduring world that was not always perceivable.

Do these findings indicate that the 'Stage 4 place error' is unreliable or unreal? The answer is that the place error is real and reliable. Indeed, the tendency to continue searching in location A when the object is hidden at B is so strong that infants continue searching at A even when no covers are involved. Harris (1974) arranged two ramps 'back-to-back', each of which terminated in a toy garage. On the first three trials, he rolled a toy car down ramp A, and the infant retrieved it without difficulty each time from garage A. On the fourth trial, he rolled the car down ramp B, and the infant continued searching in garage A, at least initially. Amazingly, the infant searched in garage A even though the garage was more like a carport, with open sides, and therefore was visibly empty. To begin with, the child seemed to ignore the visual presence of the car in garage B. This finding shows that the tendency to search in location A is so strong that the child continues to do this even when the search is in an empty space.

Bremner and Bryant (1977) succeeded in prompting infants to search in location B in a study which nonetheless further demonstrated how reliant infants are on their past hand movements. After three trials with the rattle at A, Bremner and Bryant swiftly moved the infant to the opposite side of the table, and placed the rattle at B. This time, infants always succeeded in searching at B, but note that the infant searched at B making the same hand movement s/he had made whilst searching at A on the first three trials. In another test, Bremner and Bryant did the same, except after shifting the infant round the other side of the table, they once again, for a fourth time, hid the rattle at A. The infants searched wrongly in location B, using the same hand movement as they had previously!

These findings strongly suggest that when infants aged 8 to 10 months handle an object, they subsequently understand that object in terms of their previous hand movement. They only searched in location B if that could be achieved with the same hand movement involved in searching at location A on the first three trials. These findings suggest, then, that Piaget was partly right and partly wrong. It seems that infants have a potential to show that they can distinguish between themselves and other things in the world, a potential which is demonstrated by findings suggesting they do not think things are just a series of changing pictures, but recognize that things have a stable and enduring quality. This is evident in their understanding that an object is the same object even if it moves nearer or further away. It is a potential which is demonstrated in that they seem to be aware that other people may be privy to things going on that they cannot see, which prompts them to gaze in the same direction as another person.

Nevertheless, it seems that infants are dominated by their own actions: if a hand action leads to retrieval of an object, then no matter what goes on outside in the world, they repeat that hand action when they want to retrieve the object. That the object is visibly absent seems not to be as important to an infant as it would be to an adult. This finding suggests that in some respects the infant has not come to terms with the idea that the world exists independently of self. The infant seems to assume that the existence of things in the world, such as a rattle, depends largely on her own actions. In this respect, Piaget seems to have been right.

We shall now turn our attention to the errors made by children Piaget would judge to be in the preoperational stage. Margaret Donaldson and her colleagues investigated many of the findings reported by Piaget concerning the inabilities of young children. In a very readable book entitled *Children's Minds*, Donaldson (1978) argues that Piaget's findings tell us next to nothing about children's immature or absent logical abilities, but instead tell us simply that children misunderstood what Piaget was asking them. She argues that Piaget's tasks made no *human sense* to the children, so they imposed their own sense and answered according to what they thought Piaget wanted to hear. The unfortunate consequence, according to Donaldson, was that children gave 'the wrong answer' as defined by Piaget, but not for the reasons Piaget suggested. In a nutshell, Donaldson claims Piaget concluded that the young children he tested were incompetent, whereas in fact they were highly competent. Apart from being a complete rejection of the importance of Piaget's findings, and, by implication, his whole stage theory, Donaldson's account represents a terrible indictment on Piaget's ability as a researcher. We shall examine Donaldson's claim by looking at the studies she either carried out, or cited, in support of her argument.

Let us begin with conservation, using conservation of number as an example. We show the child two rows of seven counters, one above the other, arranged in one-to-one correspondence so the two rows are the same length. We ask, 'Is there the same amount of counters in these two rows, or is this one more or is that one more?' Children reply by saying that each has the same amount. We then say, 'Now watch,' and further spread out the counters in the top row. We then repeat the question we asked at the very beginning: 'Is there the same amount of counters in these two rows ...?' Most 6-year-olds answer by saying that the rows do not have the same amount, and that the longer row has more. According to Piaget, the child's lack of a logic of conservation is responsible for this error, just as it is in the case of quantity, length and mass non-conservation, described in the previous chapter.

Donaldson argues that the repetition of the question makes the young child think that she is supposed to give an answer that relates to the alteration we made to one of the rows. That is, the child thinks: 'He asked me that question before, and I gave the answer. Since he's asking me the same question again, he must want me to say something different. What shall I say? He spread out the counters to make the row longer, so he probably wants me to say that the longer row has more; why else would he spread out the counters and then ask the same question?' That is, Donaldson argues that the repetition of the question, coupled with the change the experimenter makes to the length of one of the rows, makes the young child think that the answer to the repeated question has to be about that change. Donaldson reasoned that if either the first question was omitted, or if the change to one of the rows was accidental, and done by someone other than the experimenter, the young child would give a correct conserving judgment that the two rows still had the same amount of counters in each.

Rose and Blank (1974) presented a conservation test which excluded the first question, resulting in no repetition; children were asked about equality only after the experimenter had made the superficial change. Just as Donaldson expected, under this condition more 6-year-old children gave the correct answer that the two rows were the same, even though the counters in one of them had been spread out. The occurrence of correct answers under this condition stands in stark contrast to the procedure used by Piaget, involving repetition of the question.

Donaldson, in collaboration with her colleague James McGarrigle, carried out a study which also supported her argument. McGarrigle and Donaldson (1975) repeated the question, but made the change in length of one of the rows of counters appear to be accidental. In their study, they introduced a character called 'naughty teddy'. They told the children that naughty teddy was always trying to spoil games, and that he might mess up the game the experimenter was playing with the child. The experimenter spread out the two rows of counters in one-to-one correspondence, and the child agreed that there was the same amount in each. Then the experimenter said, 'Oh no! Look, here comes naughty teddy, and he's going to try and spoil the game!' The experimenter moved the delinquent teddy over the counters and made him kick those in one row, resulting in the counters being spread out more compared with the row not disturbed by naughty teddy. Naughty teddy then returned to his base, and the experimenter asked if there was the same amount of counters in each row, thus repeating the initial question.

Under the 'naughty teddy' condition, the great majority of children aged between 4 and 6 years gave the correct conservation answer, that the two rows had the same amount of counters in each. Under the standard Piagetian condition, the great majority of children this age gave an incorrect non-conserving answer. Donaldson argued that because it was naughty teddy, and not the experimenter, who disturbed one of the rows of counters, the child no longer felt compelled to answer the repeated equality question by focusing on the change in length of one of the rows of counters. In this case, the experimenter's repeated question made 'human sense', Donaldson claims, because the experimenter wanted to establish whether naughty teddy had messed up the game to the extent that the two rows no longer contained the same number of counters.

Donaldson's argument, therefore, is that in fact young children can conserve, but Piaget's failure to get down to the child's level resulted in the child answering incorrectly. If Donaldson is right, then Piaget's idea that cognitive development progresses through stages, from non-logical to logical thinking, is all wrong.

Some believe that Donaldson was a little hasty in claiming Piaget to be wrong about non-conservation. Moore and Fry (1986) repeated the naughty teddy experiment, using two rows with only a few counters under one condition, and two rows with lots of counters under another. Under the 'few counters' condition, the findings were much the same as those reported by McGarrigle and Donaldson. In contrast, under the 'lots of counters' condition, children gave incorrect non-conservation judgments, even though the counters had been disturbed by naughty teddy. This finding cannot be explained by Donaldson's suggestion that non-conservation is due to a simple failure of the child to understand what the experimenter means.

Moore and Fry argue that when the naughty teddy condition produces correct conservation judgments, these are not genuine ones. They claim that naughty teddy distracts the children, resulting in them no longer paying attention to the issue of conservation. What they do instead is *count* the counters. When two rows containing lots of counters are involved, children find it too difficult to count all of them, and so answer on the basis of appearance, judging that the longer row contains more. This is just what Piaget claimed. He argued that instead of answering about the underlying quantity which remains unchanged, young children answer about appearance as though failing to understand the underlying reality. Quite simply, Moore and Fry's findings cannot be accounted for by Donaldson's explanation of non-conservation.

Light, Buckingham and Robbins (1979) conducted an experiment similar to McGarrigle and Donaldson's, and obtained consistent results. Instead of 'naughty teddy' bringing about an accidental change, the change appeared to be incidental. In a conservation of liquid task, after the child agreed that there is the same amount in the same-shape glasses, the experimenter 'noticed' that one of the glasses had a crack in it. He therefore had a legitimate reason for pouring the liquid into another glass, which just happened to be taller and thinner. The experimenter then asked the child if the two glasses contained the same amount, one being an original glass and the other a tall thin glass. Again, the question seemed a reasonable one to ask. Children were more likely to judge that the two glasses contained the same amount, compared with a standard Piagetian condition. However, Light *et al.* proposed that often children were not answering the question as a question about conservation. Their argument seems to be that because the change and question were incidental, the children were giving the answer in an incidental way, rather than in a serious and reflective way. In sum they suggested that the disruption in the procedure of the task resulted in children saying that there was the same amount whilst really believing that there was not the same amount.

So what are we to make of all this? Perhaps we should conclude, as did Light *et al.* that Piaget's procedure resulted in some children making non-conservation judgments when really they could conserve, and that McGarrigle and Donaldson's procedure resulted in some children making conservation judgments when really they could not conserve. In other words, what Piaget said about conservation may be right. It may be that young children are incapable of the logical thought required for conservation, but that children come to acquire such thought at an earlier age than Piaget had supposed. Piaget said that children come to conserve at the age of about 7. Perhaps the truth of the matter is that children one year (but not two years) younger than this may be able to conserve.

Let us now consider the status of Piaget's findings about the three mountains task. Recall that Piaget showed children a model of three mountains, each with a distinctive feature at the summit. The child's task was to select a photo of what the mountain looked like to a doll sitting at the opposite side of the model. Children below the age of 7 tended to select a photo of their own view, rather than a view showing the mountains in left-right reversal. Piaget claimed that children made this error because they are egocentric, and fail to imagine that other people have different points of view.

One of Donaldson's colleagues, Martin Hughes, challenged this claim with a study which seemed to have the same ingredients as the three mountains task, yet young children usually gave a correct judgment. On Hughes' task, young children apparently acknowledged that others do have views different from their own. The task drew on the child's knowledge of the hide-and-seek game, which the experimenters assumed children know about and enjoy. Hughes prepared two intersecting walls from a doll's house, forming four quadrants, which we will label A to D to aid description (see Figure 2.1). Hughes introduced two 'policeman' dolls, overlooking quadrants A and B and B and D respectively. The child overlooked quadrants C and D. The child was told that a naughty boy doll was trying to hide from the policemen, and the child was instructed to hide the boy doll where he could not be seen by the policemen. Ninety per cent of children aged between 3 and 5 placed the boy doll in quadrant C. That is, the children recognized that a quadrant they could see was one that the policemen could not see.

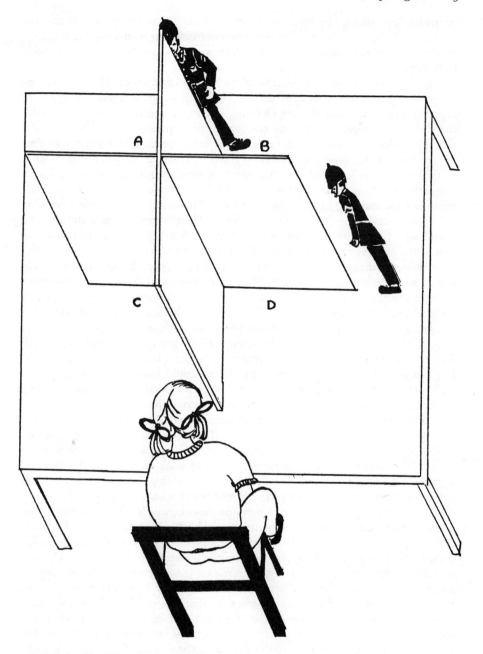

Figure 2.1: The hide-and-seek policemen experiment

As such, these young children seemed to understand that others, in this case the policeman dolls, have a view of things different from their own view. On this task, children displayed no sign of the egocentrism we have come to expect on the basis of Piaget's theory.

Donaldson explains the success of the young children on Hughes' task by suggesting that it made 'human sense'. The children knew about the game of hide-and-seek, and about the aim of trying not to be seen by the seeker. Donaldson claims that young children are not egocentric, contrary to Piaget's claim, and that this is demonstrated by the finding that they appreciate that something they can see themselves may not be visible to another person. So why is it that children of this age would have failed on the three mountains task? Donaldson acknowledges that the three mountains task not only involves understanding someone else's point of view, but also involves performing a difficult mental left-right reversal of the appearance of the mountains in order to identify what somebody opposite would see. That is, the policeman task involves determining what someone else cannot see, whereas the three mountains task involves working out how a scene viewed from a different vantage point will appear, presumably by a complex process of mental rotation. Despite acknowledging this potentially important difference between the tasks, Donaldson argues that the difference that really counts is that the policeman tasks made sense to the children in that they could understand the motives and intentions of the protagonists involved. Also, Donaldson asserts that young children have considerable knowledge of the game of hide-and-seek, which they can call upon in order to comprehend the problem Hughes presented to them. She suggests that in contrast, young children would have no experience of an eagle's-eye view of mountains from differing perspectives, and made wrong judgments (selecting their own view) for this reason.

With the wisdom of more recent research, we are now in a better position to assess the implication of Hughes' finding. There is little doubt Hughes' study poses a serious challenge to Piaget's idea, and it cannot be dealt with quite so easily as with the naughty teddy experiment. Light is shed on the issue by Flavell's suggestion about Level 1 and Level 2 perspective-taking abilities. At Level 1, the child thinks about viewing objects, but not about views of objects. There is a subtle but very important difference between the two, which is best illustrated with a simple test Flavell and his colleagues (e.g. Flavell, Everett, Croft and Flavell, 1981) presented to children. They had a double-sided picture of a turtle, which showed the creature's back on one side, and its underneath on the other. The task began with the experimenter laying the turtle on the table on its back and then on its feet, to make sure the child was acquainted with the two sides of the picture. Flavell then oriented the turtle in space so that the child could see its back, whereas he, Flavell, could see its feet. Children then had to describe what they themselves could see, and also what they thought the experimenter could see. The picture was then turned round, so the child could now see the the turtle's feet, and they had to answer the same questions. The findings were that children as young as 3 years had no difficulty reporting their own view. Children of this age also judged correctly that the experimenter could not see what they could see. That is, they understood that the experimenter did not share the same view (Level 1). However, a majority of children below age 4 were unable to specify what the experimenter could see instead. For example, children judged correctly that they could see the turtle the right way up but failed to judge that the experimenter could see it upside down. In contrast, nearly every child above age 4 years judged correctly that the experimenter could see the turtle upside down even though they themselves could only see it the right way up (Level 2).

There is an obvious resemblance between Level 1 ability and success on Hughes' policeman task, and Level 2 ability and success on the three mountains task. Strictly, Piaget's account is wrong. Young children do know something about others' points of view in that they can recognize when another person can or cannot see something. Therefore, young children do not necessarily assume that others can see what they themselves can see, and perhaps in this respect are not so egocentric as Piaget had supposed. However, young children do have great difficulty in imagining what it is another person can see if that person is viewing something different from what the child can see. In this respect, Piaget's interpretation of the children's failure on the three mountains task seems to have some truth. However, Piaget again seems to have underestimated children. Flavell's Level 2 ability is achieved by many 4-year-olds, which is much younger than Piaget would have expected, given that he had attached a great deal of significance to the finding that a great many 6-year-olds have difficulty with the three mountains task. Perhaps Donaldson is correct to argue that part of the reason children failed the latter was because they had difficulty interpreting what the experimenter wanted them to say.

We shall now turn our attention to young children's difficulty with class inclusion. An example of this task involves wooden beads, say four red and two blue. Piaget asked, 'Are there more red beads or more wooden beads?' Most children aged 6 years and below say there are more red beads, apparently comparing subclass (red beads) with subclass (blue beads) instead of comparing subclass (red beads) with total class (wooden beads, which includes both red and blue ones). As usual, Donaldson claims that children's problem is not with the logic of class inclusion, but is due to misunderstanding what the experimenter means. Donaldson presents the case of failure on class inclusion as another example of Piaget intending one thing and children interpreting him to mean another, which wrongly gives the impression that young children are logically incompetent.

Donaldson supports her argument once again by citing the work of McGarrigle. McGarrigle supposed that children ignore the literal meaning of the words when presented with the class inclusion problem and focus on what they think the experimenter means: a comparison between the two sub-classes. This seems like a sensible argument when we consider that when we ask children a question, and specify alternatives, the alternatives are usually mutually exclusive. In other words, one alternative usually does not include the other: for example, 'Are you a boy or a girl?' Therefore, in order to give children a fair chance to demonstrate their competence, McGarrigle saw it as essential to make it clear to the children exactly what the problem was. He attempted this by laying out four counters, which he called 'steps', to a toy chair and a further two beyond this to a toy table. The steps to the chair were coloured red, and those to the table were coloured white. McGarrigle then asked children either 'Are there more red steps to go to the chair or more steps to go the table?' or 'Are there more steps to go to the chair or more to go to the table?' Only 38 per cent of 6-year-olds answered the first question correctly, whereas 66 per cent answered the second correctly. Donaldson argues that in the case of the first question, which is very similar to the question Piaget asked, because it mentions colour of items in the subclass, it makes children think that colour is the important feature: are there more red steps or more white steps? When colour is not mentioned, as in the second question, even though the problem still concerns class inclusion, children tune in to the correct way of thinking about the problem, so revealing that they can handle class inclusion. According to Donaldson, this is because the emphasis on subclasses as the focus of interest is reduced.

In order to deliver the *coup de grâce* to Piaget, McGarrigle carried out a further demonstration to show that young children thought Piaget wanted them to do a comparison between subclasses, rather than between subclass and total class. He arranged four cows facing four horses situated either side of a fence. There were two black and two white cows. There were three black horses and one white horse. McGarrigle asked 6-year-olds, 'Are there more cows or more black horses?' The correct answer, of course, is that there are more cows. However, 86 per cent judged that there were more black horses, presumably meaning 'There are more black horses than there are *black* cows'. As before, children were performing the comparison on subclasses (black cows/black horses), except this time the comparison was not between a subclass which was included in a total class, unlike the classic class inclusion problem used by Piaget. According to Donaldson, this shows that really the child's problem has nothing to do with class inclusion, but rather is to do with the sense they try to impose on the question the experimenter asks.

In the case of conservation and the three mountains task, it seemed that although Piaget had underestimated young children, it was also the case that Donaldson had *overestimated* their abilities. However, it seems that in the case of class inclusion, Donaldson is correct in judging the child to be competent, or at least not to have the kind of problem Piaget suggested they have. This has led one eminent developmentalist, Howard Gardner (1982, p. 403) to conclude that 'the class inclusion question does seem more of a trick than most other Piagetian puzzles'.

The final phenomenon we shall look at relating to young children's suggested lack of logical thought is that of transitive inference. Transitive inference is where, for example, you work out the relative length of two sticks, not in a direct comparison, but by employing a stick of intermediate length. Stick A is smaller than stick B. Stick C is bigger than stick B. Therefore, C must be bigger than A. There is no need to compare A and C directly. We know that C must be bigger on the basis of the preceding information. In other words, we can solve the problem logically, and as such no practical comparison between A and C is required. Piaget claims that children of 7 years and below do not yet possess the logic to do this. Recall that Piaget showed children two towers, and asked them to use a stick he supplied, which was of intermediate length, to work out which tower was tallest. Children of 7 years and below failed, but older children succeeded. This finding is not in dispute, but the interpretation of it is.

We may ask what it is that develops at age 7 that allows the child to solve the transitive inference problem. Is it, as Piaget claimed, acquisition of logical thought, or is it improved memory retention of the important information provided in the transitive inference task? Regarding the second possibility, consider this: suppose someone says, 'John is heavier than Fred; John is lighter than Joe. Who is the heaviest, Joe or Fred?' You may think, 'What did he say? John is lighter than Fred, or was it John is heavier than Fred? What did he say about Joe?' The point is that when we hear these problems, the panic we experience is usually concerned with trying to hold in mind all the important information we have to juggle with in order to arrive at the correct answer that Joe is heavier than Fred.

According to Piaget, children fail because they cannot grasp the logic that Joe *must* be heavier than Fred if John is lighter than Joe but heavier than Fred. However, how can we be so sure this is the case, given that the problem does not just require understanding of logical relations, but also puts a massive demand on conscious space? What if it is limited conscious space that really prevents young children from giving the correct answer? Of course, the measuring problem Piaget presented to children seems a little more user-friendly than the verbal version of the problem, as presented above. Nevertheless, it may be that young children find it difficult to give joint consideration to the facts that the measuring stick is bigger than tower A, but smaller than tower B. If so, error on Piaget's transitive inference task may have a lot to do with memory weakness in children, but little to do with lack of logical thought.

Bryant and Trabasso (1971) tried to devise a 'pure' transitive inference test, one which could be used to assess understanding of the logic without putting a big demand on conscious space. They used five rods of different length and colour, held in a special box. The box had holes drilled in it to different lengths, so that when the rods were placed in the holes in the appropriate sequence, each protruded above the surface of the box by one inch. The rods were in a left-to-right sequence, from big to small, though that was not obvious just by looking at the visible tops of the rods. The experimenter then went about training the children that the red rod (at the left end) was bigger than the white rod next to it, that the white rod was bigger than the yellow rod to the right of it, and so on. The experimenter questioned children about the relative size of pairs of rods situated next to each other, and then lifted the pair out of the box to show the child whether she was right or wrong. The experimenter continued with this laborious procedure until the child always stated which rod was the longer in any given pair situated side by side.

At this point, Bryant and Trabasso could be sure that children retained all the relevant information, because they had 'over-learned' which rod was biggest in each pair situated side by side. They then asked children which was biggest in a pair not situated side by side. Bryant and Trabasso claimed that this time children had to perform a transitive inference to work out the correct answer, of the kind 'if the red one is bigger than the yellow one, and the yellow one is bigger than the white one, then the red one must be bigger than the white one'. They found that children even as young as 4 years could give the correct answer on this task.

Bryant and Kopytynska (1976) conducted another study which also indicated that young children may be capable of transitive inference. They presented children with a block that had two holes bored in it, one to a depth of four inches, and the other to a depth of six inches. Children had to work out which hole was deeper, and were provided with a measuring stick for the purpose. The stick was not of a length intermediate between the depth of the two holes, for obvious reasons. However, the stick did have a yellow band round its middle section. When the stick was dropped into the shallower hole, the yellow band was in view at the top of the hole. When the stick was dropped in the deeper of the holes, the yellow band was submerged beneath the surface of the hole, and not in view. Bryant and Kopytynska found that a majority of children who had already failed on the Piagetian tower measuring task succeeded in working out which hole was deeper by using the measuring stick.

According to Bryant and Kopytynska, the main difference between hole measuring and tower measuring was that in the case of the towers, since their heights were always in view, children may have formed a wrong impression, just by looking, as to which was the taller. In the case of the holes this could not have been so, and children had to rely solely on the stick to arrive at the answer. When this was the case, children succeeded in giving a correct answer.

Impressive reasoning has been elicited from 4-year-olds using a completely different procedure. Pears and Bryant (1990) showed children four towers, each made up of two coloured building blocks. For example, red on top of green, green on top of blue, blue on top of yellow, and yellow on top of white. The child's task was then to make a tower out of blocks of five different colours used in the sample towers: red, green, blue, yellow and white. Pears and Bryant had previously trained the children to build towers maintaining the relationship between colours in the sample towers. In other words, we can infer that the tower the child had to construct would be red at the top, followed by green, blue, yellow, and finally with white at the bottom. In other words, from the sample towers we can make a transitive inference that in the tower the child was to construct, green would be at a higher position than yellow. Before commencing with the construction, Pears and Bryant asked the children which brick would be higher, the green one or the yellow one. Remarkably, a substantial majority of the 4-year-olds tested answered correctly with 'green'.

In that case, can young children do transitive inference? It certainly seems they can do some problems which appear to require transitive inference reasoning. However, perhaps we ought to give further consideration to children's failure on the Piagetian version of the problem, which requires a judgment about the relative height of two towers using a stick of intermediate height for measuring. Why is it that most children below age 7 years fail, but most above this age succeed? To my knowledge, there is no suggestion in this case that children misunderstood what Piaget was asking them, unlike the cases of conservation, class inclusion, and the three mountains task. Is it, then, that increasing success with increasing age is simply to do with a corresponding increase in the capacity of conscious space, as Bryant and Trabasso suggest?

On the face of things, it seems rather odd that at around the child's seventh birthday there is a sudden and dramatic increase in conscious space. To some, it seems so odd as to be unbelievable. For example, Russell (1978) suggests that the more sensible explanation is, as Piaget claimed originally, that young children do not have the requisite logical thought to grasp that if tower A is bigger than the stick, and tower B is smaller than the stick, A must be bigger than B. Russell (1981) made this argument seem highly convincing when he showed that about a third of those who failed to give the correct answer had no difficulty in recalling that the stick was shorter than tower A, but taller than tower B. Indeed, those who gave the correct transitive inference answer were not much better at remembering this information! This suggests that those who failed did not have a problem in holding in mind the relevant information. The onus was then on Russell to explain how children succeeded on Bryant's tasks, if it was not by transitive reasoning.

Piaget's idea was that young children understand things in terms of how they look, or how they can imagine them looking. Older children have a cognitive advantage over younger ones, because they can reason in a logical way, a way that goes beyond mere images, which allows them to do transitive inference, amongst other things. Russell suggested that children could solve Bryant's tasks just by the appearance of things, or by imagining the way they appear. In the Bryant and Trabasso task, in which children thoroughly learned the lengths of all the rods, Russell suggests they became so familiar with the rod lengths that they developed a mental image of all the rods. When faced with the transitive inference problem, all they had to do was a direct mental comparison of the two rods in question. As such, the problem did not require any logical understanding of the kind 'A is bigger than B, B is bigger than C, therefore, A must be bigger than C'. The same argument can be applied to the Pears and Bryant findings. Perhaps a correct judgment of relative heights of differently coloured bricks in a tower yet to be constructed could be achieved by a non-logical process of imagining how the tower would look.

As for the Bryant and Kopytynska task, which required children to determine which of two holes was the deeper, again children could short-circuit the problem by looking at how deeply the stick is submerged. Certainly the child has to remember how deeply it sank into the first hole when assessing the depth of the second hole, but once again the task does not seem to require the kind of logical reasoning that we call transitive inference.

The general picture to emerge from these recent studies investigating Piagetian phenomena is that young children are far more able than Piaget gave them credit for. However, it seems that there is also a danger of overestimating the abilities of young children, and that perhaps they lack the requisite mental flexibility or perhaps the logic for solving certain problems, such as conservation. Even in the case of conservation, though, it seems children younger than Piaget had supposed are able to give the correct judgment if the problem is presented in the right way. Collectively, then, studies investigating Piaget's claims have served to blur the distinction between preoperational and concrete operational thinking. So although we can argue that young children do appear to have difficulty with the logic of certain problems, it now looks very unlikely that these errors all fit together neatly to suggest an overarching complex of thought process we could call preoperational intelligence as described by Piaget.

Now we shall examine the validity of formal operational thinking. This time the moot point is whether Piaget *overestimated* rather than underestimated the abilities of adolescents and adults. If Piaget underestimated the abilities of children, and overestimated the abilities of adults, then this would substantially undermine his stage theory of development, that development consists of a series of distinct cognitive stages, each of which is characterized by its own special way of thinking. Instead, it would suggest that the thought of children and adults has much more in common than Piaget had supposed.

Piaget's claim was that a feature of adolescent reasoning is that it is formal and scientific. Is that really true, or do people have more of an intuitive and practical intelligence? Everyday experience certainly seems to suggest the latter, but let us take a look at the evidence on this matter.

We shall begin by considering Karl Popper's (1972) idea on the philosophy of science. At first sight, this seems highly irrelevant to adolescent reasoning, but it will become apparent that Popper's idea hits on something central to Piaget's belief about formal operations. One of the key facets of formal operations as described by Piaget is an ability to test ideas. That is, it is not so much whether the problem is solved correctly or incorrectly, but whether the adolescent displays a formal operational strategy in solving the problem. In other words, does the adolescent display any understanding about a scientific way of thinking? This is where Popper comes in, because he had a great deal to say about the way scientists should go about solving problems.

Consider the example of a glass beaker which we are told is made of a special new kind of glass that is indestructible. Let us say that because of knowledge of the composition of the glass, we have the firm expectation that a beaker made from this material literally could not be broken. So our theory is that the beaker is unbreakable. To test this, we situate the beaker next to an A-bomb, and then detonate the device. After the smoke has cleared, we search the area and eventually find the beaker intact. Does this mean the beaker is unbreakable? Probably, but what if we tried an H-bomb instead, a device with the strongest known blast? We repeat the test with an H-bomb, and find the beaker is still intact. Does this mean the beaker is unbreakable? Again, probably, but we could never be certain that a future device, let us call it a Z-bomb, with an even stronger blast, would destroy the beaker. If this came about, we would demonstrate that the theory that the beaker is unbreakable is wrong. All this goes to illustrate, according to Popper, that it is possible to prove a theory wrong, but impossible to prove it correct. For that reason, he continues, there is no point in trying to prove a theory, but only in trying to disprove one. More generally, perhaps we can say that if we want to assess the truth of something, we should not look for evidence suggesting it is true, but look for evidence for suggesting it is false. In essence, we have to engage in negative reasoning.

Piaget's adolescents who succeeded on the pendulum problem, described in the previous chapter, appeared to adopt a negative reasoning approach. Given that they avoided varying the values of two factors simultaneously, such as varying both the weight of the suspended object and the length of the string all in one move, they must have realized that had they done this, the results would have been uninterpretable. That is, the results would have been uninterpretable in principle, no matter in what form they appeared. Therefore, it seems Piaget's adolescents' testing strategy was influenced by a negative reasoning process: they avoided tests that would have yielded meaningless results.

Although the pendulum problem may have prompted negative reasoning of the kind held as being fundamental to science, it now seems that in the great majority of situations adults are very poor at this. Wason and Johnson-Laird (1972) demonstrated this in their excellent book, *The Psychology of Reasoning*. They tested university students. If these people do not display proficiency in the negative reasoning we suppose is at the heart of formal operations, we can assume that formal operations are not a central feature of adult intelligence, contrary to Piaget's claim. Wason and Johnson-Laird presented what is known as the selection task in which they showed students four cards, each of which displayed a letter on one side and a number on the other:

E   K   4   7

The students were given a rule, and had to find out whether or not it was true:

If a card has a vowel on one side, then it has an even number on the other.

The students were allowed to turn over two cards to test the rule. Before reading further, spend a few moments choosing which cards you would turn over. Think very carefully because the problem is not quite as simple as it seems!

We are not concerned so much with whether the students gave the correct answer, but with which cards they chose to turn. This reveals how they go about solving the problem. Now, remember that the correct approach, as discussed above, is to engage in a negative reasoning process, and thus treat the problem as 'find out whether the rule is *false*'.

Most intelligent adults wrongly choose E and 4, but in fact the correct pair is E and 7. If it turned out that E had an odd number on the reverse side, that would show the rule was false; likewise if it turned out 7 had a vowel on the reverse side, that would also show the rule was false. So if there is an even number on the other side of E, and a consonant on the other side of 7, so far as we know, on the basis of these few cards, the rule has not been violated.

As you have probably gathered by now, most of Wason and Johnson-Laird's intellectually able students chose the wrong pair of E and 4. Especially surprising was the finding that when professional logicians had a go at the problem, even some of them, to their great embarrassment, chose the wrong pair of E and 4.

Everybody can recognize immediately that E is a correct card to choose, but why is 4 incorrect? The reason is because whatever is on the reverse side of 4, as Popper could have told us, it is totally uninformative. You may feel that if there had been a consonant on the reverse side, it would show that the rule was wrong. In fact, that is not true. Remember, the rule only says 'if a vowel on one side, then an even number on the other'. For all we know, and this is irrelevant to the rule just presented, there may be another rule that says 'if there is a consonant on one side, then there is *either* an odd or an even number on the other side'.

Why did the students choose the wrong pair of cards? It seems that they were looking for instances of vowels being paired with even numbers in order to show that the rule was true. This erroneous strategy Wason has called a 'confirmation bias', which is characteristic of adult thinking in very many diverse instances. What the students should have asked themselves is, 'Supposing the rule were wrong, which pair of cards would show that to be the case?' If students thought along these lines they would realize that if 7 had a vowel on the other side, the rule must be wrong. In other words, the students did not adopt the classic scientific-problem solving attitude as described by Karl Popper.

Wason and Johnson-Laird's selection task neatly demonstrates that most intelligent adults do not meet the ideal of effective scientific reasoning proposed by Piaget. That is a blow to the status of Piaget's stage of formal operations, but a more damning finding has emerged over the past two decades. Namely, it has now emerged that people have far less difficulty at solving certain versions of the selection task. Cheng and Holyoak (1985) demonstrated this in an envelope version of that task:

Sealed   Unsealed   20 cents   10 cents

Subjects saw four envelopes, two with their back in view and a further two with their front in view. Looking at the two with their back in view, subjects could tell whether the envelope was sealed or unsealed. Looking at their fronts, the subjects could see either that a 20-cent stamp was attached or that a 10-cent stamp was attached. They then heard the rule 'if the envelope is sealed, it must have a 20-cent stamp on it', and had to choose two of the envelopes to turn over in order to test the rule.

The subjects were from America, where in fact no postal rule of this kind is in operation. Presented like this, most subjects committed the error we have come to expect, choosing the wrong pair of 'sealed' and '20 cents' (the correct pair, of course, is 'sealed' and '10 cents'). However, under a slightly different condition, nearly all subjects succeeded in choosing the correct pair. The crucial difference responsible for the dramatic improvement was a simple justification, explaining why sealed envelopes should have 20-cent stamps on them. The reason given was that the mail company knew that personal mail is nearly always posted in a sealed envelope, and that the company sought to improve its bank balance by demanding higher revenue from personal mail. Thus, if the sender has a personal message and therefore wishes to seal the envelope, then he should pay an extra ten cents.

Now the subjects could easily recognize that the rule would be violated if an envelope with a 10-cent stamp was sealed. In other words, providing the subjects could grasp a good reason for the rule, and particularly the implications for viol-ation of the rule, they no longer exhibited the confirmation bias described by Wason. To borrow a phrase from Donaldson, when the selection task made 'human sense', the subjects could engage in the appropriate reasoning required for a successful choice.

The finding that some versions of the selection task are easy, whereas others are hard, poses a serious problem for Piaget's stage of formal operations. Piaget proposed that formal operational reasoning is not entrenched in specific tasks. Logical reasoning entrenched in specific tasks is concrete operational reasoning. The whole point behind Piaget's idea of formal operational reasoning is that it is a general reasoning strategy, which works much the same no matter what the nature of the particular problem in question. Cheng and Holyoak's findings clearly suggest that in the great majority of cases, adult reasoning is context-specific and therefore context-bound. The clear implication is that a stage of formal operations does not exist, and that perhaps there is no real difference between the quality of a 9-year-old's thinking and a 16-year-old's thinking.

We should now take stock of the situation, and consider the status of Piaget's theory. Recall Einstein's comment that the beauty of a theory ought to feature in the way we assess it. I think Piaget's theory, or at least the part I understand, is in some ways beautiful, but evidence compels us to accept that the theory requires modification. Indeed, the evidence suggests that perhaps some aspects of the theory deserve to be rejected. For example, the idea that cognitive development heads towards formal operational thinking patently seems wrong, and, for that reason, perhaps the whole idea of formal operations as a typical feature of adult cognition should be dismissed.

Studies on infants suggest that babies may well be sensitive to the existence of a stable and enduring world, contrary to Piaget's claim. As for young children, it seems that some things Piaget claimed they could not do, in fact they can do. Class inclusion is an example of this. Also, many conceptual difficulties young children have may not be quite so severe as Piaget had supposed. Conservation and three-mountains perspective taking are examples.

Nevertheless, it seems wrong to argue that babies and young children are like mini adults, with the main difference being that they have less knowledge. Studies continue to suggest that babies and young children may think in a way different from that of adults. In that case, although we may accept that some of the details of Piaget's account are wrong, is it still possible that young children and babies are egocentric in a certain sense? For example, do they know about their own views, feelings and so on, and fail to imagine other points of view? In the next chapter, we shall touch upon this very important issue.

Further Reading

Margaret Donaldson's book is excellent in many respects. It is highly readable, outlines many educational implications of her ideas, and provides a neat summary of Piaget's theory in the appendix into the bargain.
DONALDSON, M. (1978) *Children's Minds*, Glasgow, Fontana/Collins.

You may also be interested to take a look at the following text:
GRIEVE, R. and HUGHES, M. (1991) *Understanding Children: Essays in Honour of Margaret Donaldson*, Oxford, Basil Blackwell.

As for reasoning in adults, particularly reasoning on the selection task, the following book provides an excellent summary of the important experiments:
EVANS, J.StB.T. (1989) *Bias in Human Reasoning: Causes and Consequences*, Brighton, Lawrence Erlbaum.

Chapter 3

Theory of Mind and Autism

Piaget took a biological view of human cognitive development. In this case, the biology is not so much concerned with the physiology of the brain responsible for intelligence, but rather with the place of intelligence in the evolution of our species. We all know about *Homo habilis*, our technological tool-making ancestors. Perhaps Piaget fixated on this, believing that the special quality of humans is a scientific and technological potential. On the face of things, given the enormous scientific and technological advances over the past few centuries, this idea seems correct. However, is that potential the only highly developed human quality? Perhaps not.

As well as being technological and scientific, humans are also social creatures, just like their ancestors and animal cousins. Piaget focused on technological abilities in an attempt to understand human cognition, but perhaps we should also focus on the social side of things. Being social creatures, humans live in groups and communities: they work and play together. How is this possible? We know how social coordination is possible in the case of social insects. Soldier ants work together in building nests and transporting food as though there is some overall group aim they are striving towards. Despite the appearance, there is no overall group aim, and these creatures are controlled almost entirely by instinct. For example, one ant leaves a trail in the form of a special chemical, and another, detecting this, will follow. Events in the world, such as the presence of a chemical message, trigger instinctive behaviour in the ants. In a sense, they are just like mini computers or robots, simply responding in a set way when a program is activated. In contrast, humans do not function in such an automatic, rigid and instinctive manner, and what goes on in human groups is nothing like what goes on in ant colonies in that respect.

What do we have instead of the ants' instincts that enables us to be such proficient social creatures? We have a 'theory of mind', and this could be the most important feature of human cognition. The idea of 'theory of mind' is that ordinary people are natural psychologists, requiring no degrees or other qualifications to engage in contemplating the mind. They collect evidence about other people and then on the basis of this construct a theory which can be used subsequently for predicting and explaining others' behaviour. For example, suppose we have an acquaintance called Bloggs who we judge is seriously lacking in self-discipline, given that we have noticed Bloggs is frequently late for work, or absent altogether. We also observe that Bloggs' room is a tip, and that he is prone to a variety of vices, such as drinking and smoking. From this evidence we might formulate a 'theory' that Bloggs is a slave to his hedonistic impulses, which results in his life being rather disorganized. Suppose, then, that we hear Bloggs has been found guilty of possession of drugs. This would come as no surprise, and our theory of Bloggs' personality (that he is a slave to his hedonistic impulses) would explain it. In addition to an explanatory capability, our theory of Bloggs can be used to predict his future behaviour. For example, suppose Bloggs is asked to present a talk to his peers about an aspect of his work at a set time and date. From our 'theory' of Bloggs, we could predict it would be unlikely that he would turn up at the specified time. In sum, from observations of Bloggs, we come to formulate a theory which can then be used to explain and predict his behaviour. In this respect, our theory of Bloggs is similar to scientific theories, such as the theory of gravity.

It might be that Piaget tackled the problem of human cognition from too narrow a viewpoint. Instead of asking how it is humans come to be scientists, perhaps he should also have asked how it is humans come to be so effective at social feats, such as diplomacy and discretion. It is obvious that the ability to develop accurate theories of mind is important to survival and reproduction, and therefore it must have played a part in natural selection. In combat, it helps if we can acquire allies and influence them to fight alongside us. The more accurately we know how others' minds work, the better equipped we are to do this. Similarly, the better we understand the enemy's mind, the better we are able to predict his behaviour and deploy an evasive, defensive or offensive strategy accordingly. In terms of reproduction, the better we can understand a potential partner's mind, the better equipped we are to do things to please that person, and so become attractive to him or her.

The human preoccupation with the mind could account for the popularity of games, sport and fiction. In a game like chess the success of a player will depend partly on her ability to assess accurately what her opponent is up to, and to assess accurately what her opponent thinks she is up to. Similar processes operate in sports such as soccer: 'I'm going to dribble the ball this way, but I want the defender to think I am going to go the other way'. Also, consider Shakespearian plays. These are full of intrigue about people being influenced and deceived. Such examples of contemplating other's minds have parallels in the everyday experiences of ordinary people, and that is something which makes games, sport and literature so exciting.

A central component of a theory of mind is being able to appreciate that sometimes people entertain false beliefs. If we understand that people can have false beliefs, then we know that the way people's minds represent the world can be different from the way the world is really. In other words, we would know about the mind as distinct from the world. In contrast, if we were unable to grasp that people can have false beliefs, then our judgments about others' behaviour would be restricted to the way the world really is. For example, suppose we take a Smarties tube, and replace the familiar confectionery with pencils. We could then predict that someone who had never seen that particular tube before would say, on first seeing it, that it contained Smarties. So we would judge their behaviour on the basis of their false belief. If one judged wrongly that the other person would say the tube contained pencils, then one would be judging another person's behaviour according to the way the world really is, and therefore we would have little reason to suppose that the person being asked knew about the mind as distinct from the world. In that case, the person who wrongly judged 'pencils' would lack a central requirement for the possession of a theory of mind.

On the face of things, it seems bizarre to think that anyone might fail such a simple test as that posed by the Smarties tube with the usual content replaced with pencils. Yet we find that the great majority of children below 4 years of age do fail. Perner, Leekam and Wimmer (1987) carried out the test as follows. They showed the child a Smarties tube, and asked her to say what was inside. Children nearly always answer correctly with 'Smarties'. The child was not given an opportunity prior to this point of looking inside the tube to check the contents, but the box is so familiar, that she was confident just by looking at the exterior that there were Smarties inside. The experimenter then opened the tube to reveal that really it contained pencils. Finally, the experimenter returned the pencils, closed up the lid, and then told the child that next she was going to show the tube to little Johnny who had never seen it before, just as it was, all closed up. The experimenter explained that she was going to ask Johnny to say what was in the tube. Finally, the experimenter asked the child being tested what she thought Johnny would say. The great majority of children above the age of about 4 years correctly said 'Johnny will say Smarties'. The great majority below that age answered incorrectly with 'Johnny will say pencils'! Providing you have the parents' consent, this is an easy demonstration you can carry out. There is no doubt that the results of your 'experiment' will be the same as those of Perner *et al.*

Let us first consider the older children, who give the correct answer of 'Smarties'. Without hesitation, we can say that these children have a fundamental basis for theory of mind. They understand that although the tube really contains pencils, someone who has never seen the tube before will wrongly think it contains Smarties. Apparently, they understand that another person will be misled by the nature of the tube into thinking that it contains something other than it really contains.

In contrast, because younger children give the wrong answer of 'pencils', this is consistent with them being seriously lacking in a theory of mind. Apparently, they do not make a distinction between the way things are and the way people think they are. They are happy to make judgments about people's thoughts, but the judgments are always based on the way things really are. Young children seem to have no notion of people holding beliefs that are distinct from reality. If they have no idea about beliefs distinct from reality, then we can say that they have little basis for theory of mind.

Is this any different from Piaget's claim that young children are egocentric? Certainly there is a difference in detail. For one thing, theory of mind research suggests that children have a conception of others' beliefs from about age 4 years, whereas Piaget claimed children are egocentric until about age 7 years. Also, there is a difference in the testing techniques for assessing theory of mind and egocentrism. However, isn't it the case that the claim that young children have no theory of mind is the same as the claim that young children are egocentric? The answer is 'no'.

Piaget's idea about egocentrism was that young children know about their own experiences, and fail to consider that another person's experiences might be different. Consequently, they just assume that their own way of looking at things is the only way, and therefore is shared by everyone. There is a similarity between this and claiming that young children are unaware of others' beliefs, and have little theory of mind as a consequence: both accounts deny that young children are capable of an accurate assessment of others' minds. However, there is also a very important difference. The idea of egocentrism is specific to ignorance about other people, whereas the idea that young children lack a theory of mind is much more general. It is the idea that young children know nothing about minds, including their own.

In that case, how can we show that young children have no notion of their own minds? The test to demonstrate this is very simple. As usual, we show the child a Smarties tube and when we ask him what is inside, he replies with 'Smarties'. We then reveal that really it contains pencils. After returning the pencils to the tube and closing the lid, we ask the child, 'When you first saw the tube, before we opened it, what did you think was inside?' Once again, the great majority of children above about age 4 answer correctly with 'Smarties', whereas the great majority of children below that age answer wrongly with 'pencils'. Moreover, the children who give this wrong answer are usually the same ones who give the wrong answer when judging about another person's false belief (Gopnik and Astington, 1988). Again, you can try this test on children in your family. You will be surprised to discover that no matter how you word the question, quite simply young children seem to find it almost impossible to judge that someone (themselves or another person) has had a wrong belief.

Let us not be so hasty, though. Perhaps there are trivial reasons why young children wrongly judge that they had thought the tube contained pencils. Whenever I talk to teachers of preschool children about the Gopnik and Astington (1988) experiment, they always say that youngsters say they had thought the tube contained pencils because they are loath to admit they had got it wrong. In other words, these preschool teachers suggest young children engage in a face-saving tactic. This alternative explanation of the results was investigated by Wimmer and Hartl (1991) with a group of Austrian children. On Austrian children's television there is a well-known glove puppet called Kasperl, who is notorious for getting things wrong and general misunderstanding. Presumably, the TV producer thinks this is why Kasperl is such a popular character. Wimmer and Hartl borrowed the Kasperl glove puppet and presented the Smarties test to him. They showed him the tube and asked him to state the content. He said 'Smarties'. They then revealed the pencils, returned them to the tube and closed up the lid. Meanwhile a child subject had been watching Kasperl being tested, and the experimenter now turned to the observing child and asked, 'What did Kasperl think was inside the tube when he first saw it?' Most children below age 4 answered wrongly with 'pencils', whereas most above that age answered correctly with 'Smarties'.

Wimmer and Hartl (1991) set up the Kasperl test so that it would be similar to the test conducted by Gopnik and Astington, except instead of having to judge what they themselves had thought, children had to say what Kasperl had thought. Although children may have experienced a loss of face in admitting they themselves had thought the wrong thing, surely they would not feel that way in judging Kasperl's wrong belief. Indeed, children could expect Kasperl to think the wrong thing, even putting aside the deceptive nature of the Smarties tube, for the simple reason that Kasperl is renowned for his errors. What we find, however, is that young children fail to acknowledge Kasperl's false belief, just as they fail to acknowledge their own. Therefore it seems that young children's wrong judgments result from a fundamental difficulty in reasoning about beliefs rather than from a desire to save face.

Another explanation advanced to account for children's errors in a trivial way is that they have very weak memory, and as a consequence are prone to forget what they had thought was in the tube to begin with. If this explanation is correct, then young children's primary difficulty is not with false belief and therefore perhaps they do have a theory of mind potential. This alternative explanation was tested by Gopnik and Astington (1988). They placed an apple into a doll's house and allowed the child to peep inside and take a look at it. They then replaced the apple with a doll in full view of the observing child. Finally, Gopnik and Astington asked the child what was in the doll's house now, and what was in it before. Very many children even as young as 2 years succeeded in answering the two questions correctly with 'doll' and 'apple' respectively. Apparently, they had no difficulty in remembering what they had thought was in the doll's house to begin with. This differs from the Smarties test in a crucial respect: in the doll's house test, what the child had thought was in the house to begin with was true, whereas in the Smarties test, what the child had thought was in the tube to begin with was false. In other words, perhaps children can succeed with the doll's house test because it does not require an acknowledgment of false belief. Yet the doll's house test and the Smarties test are equally demanding on memory, so memory weakness does not seem a good explanation for young children's difficulty with false belief.

It genuinely seems the case, then, that young children have difficulty acknowledging false belief, whether the belief in question is their own or another person's. Therefore, contrary to an idea advanced by Piaget, it is not that young children know about their own mind and simply attribute their own thoughts to others in an act of egocentrism. Rather, they don't acknowledge thoughts distinct from the world, no matter whom those thoughts belong to.

Young children's difficulty in acknowledging false belief could be an example of a broader difficulty in acknowledging any false representation – any representation which purports to be about the world, but which in fact misrepresents the world. Photographs which depict an outdated scene that no longer maintains are representations which, because of their obsolescence, misrepresent that scene. What do young children know about this state of affairs? A simple study conducted by Zaitchik suggests that 3-year-olds have just as much difficulty acknowledging the image on an outdated photo as they do in acknowledging false belief. She obtained the kind of camera which, once the film has been exposed, issues from the front a blank card on which, after a period of a few seconds, the photographed image begins to appear.

While a 3-year-old watched, Zaitchik photographed a doll sitting beside the television set, and immediately after the blank card issued forth, she repositioned the doll so it was now sitting beside the fireplace. Zaitchik then promptly asked the observing child where the doll would be located in the scene which was about to emerge on the photo: by the television or by the fireplace? Very many 3-year-olds judged wrongly that the doll in the photo would be by the fireplace (where it really was at the time the question was asked), whereas older children judged correctly that it would be by the television set (where it was at the moment the film was exposed). It thus seems that young children fail to acknowledge photographic misrepresentation just as they fail to acknowledge belief misrepresentation. In both instances, they wrongly judge representations, whether beliefs or photos, according to what they know maintains in reality. In that case, young children's difficulty is not specific to understanding how the mind represents, but rather is more general, and extends to a failure to understand how anything represents things. The failure takes the form of an inability to recognize misrepresentation.

Why do young children have difficulty acknowledging misrepresentation, if it is not due to egocentrism? One idea is that 3-year-olds lack the mental capacity to give joint consideration to two things (e.g. Gopnik and Astington, 1988): the way the world is really (pencils in the Smarties tube) and the way the mind represents the world (Smarties in the Smarties tube). However, research I have carried out in collaboration with Hazel Lacohee (Mitchell and Lacohee, 1991) suggests that really young children do know about false belief, but that they are loath to acknowledge anything which does not have an anchor in reality.

I need hardly remind you that a false belief is something which does not have a counterpart in reality. Just suppose it were possible to endow a false belief with a reality basis, yet preserve its 'false' status: perhaps then children would acknowledge it. This is precisely what we endeavoured to achieve in our study. We showed 3-year-olds a Smarties tube, and asked them to mail a picture of what they thought was inside into a special postbox. They all posted a picture of Smarties, and the picture remained in the postbox out of sight till the end of the procedure. Next, we revealed that really the tube contained pencils, returned them to the tube, closed up the lid, and then asked a modified question: When you posted your picture what did you think was in this tube?' Tested under this procedure, a good majority of 3-year-olds gave a correct judgment of 'Smarties'.

We wondered whether children's dramatic success was because they thought we were asking them what was in the postbox. To check on this, we carried out a very similar procedure, except instead of posting a picture of Smarties, children had to post a picture of their favourite cartoon character. If it were the case that children gave the 'correct answer' because they interpreted the question to be about the content of the postbox, we should find they would state the name of the cartoon character they had posted. The finding was that none of the children we tested did this, and that the majority answered wrongly with 'pencils'. The main difference between these two versions of the postbox procedure is that in the first, children's false belief had an anchor in reality in the form of the picture of Smarties mailed into the postbox. This was not so for the cartoon version of the procedure.

The postbox experiment is consistent with the idea that young children have difficulty acknowledging false belief because they seek a reality basis when conceptualizing things. If we endow a false belief with a reality basis (as we did by getting children to mail a picture of their false belief into a postbox), they succeed in acknowledging belief about the content of the Smarties tube as distinct from its real content. This shows that they are capable of the mental elaboration required for contemplating misrepresentation, contrary to the claim made by Gopnik and Astington (1988).

Returning to the business of egocentrism, another study demonstrates directly and more powerfully that young children are not egocentric, and it also indicates that development of a theory of mind is not something which is complete at 4 years of age with the acknowledgment of false belief. The study was conducted by Sodian and Wimmer (1987), and it demonstrated that 5-year-olds fail to attribute knowledge to another person who has had opportunity to infer the knowledge in question. In this study, child subjects observed another child called Susan apparently being tested on her knowledge of the contents of an opaque bag. The scene the observing child subject watched is as follows. The experimenter showed Susan a red and a blue ball. She then asked Susan to look away while she, the experimenter, placed one of the balls in the bag. Susan was allowed to look once again, but could not see directly into the bag which had now been closed. However, on the table was the blue ball, so we can suppose Susan would infer that the ball in the bag must be the red one (given that she knows *one* of the two balls has been placed in the bag). Would the observing 5-year-olds make this supposition? It turned out they did not, and when asked, they judged that Susan did not know the colour of the ball in the bag. In contrast, 6-year-olds judged that Susan did know the colour of the ball in the bag.

So the 5-year-olds refused to attribute knowledge to Susan even though Susan had opportunity to infer the knowledge in question (the colour of the ball in the bag). It was not that 5-year-olds assumed Susan, being a child, was incapable of inference: their judgments were just the same whether the character playing Susan was a young child or an adult. Neither was it because the 5-year-olds were unable to make an inference for themselves. When they were asked to state the colour of the ball in the bag, they had no hesitation in saying 'red'. That is, they could make a simple inference that if one of the balls has been transferred to the bag, and the one left out is the blue one, then the ball in the bag must be red.

These 5-year-olds made an error, which demonstrates two things. First, the kind of error they made is incompatible with the idea that they were egocentric. If they had been egocentric, they would have judged that Susan knew the colour because they themselves knew the colour. They did not do this. The second thing it shows is that although these children were old enough to have a fundamental basis for theory of mind, namely they were old enough to acknowledge false belief, they lacked understanding about the mind in another respect. Apparently, they failed to understand how information can enter the mind via inference. As such, their theory of mind was incomplete.

Theory of mind research is important in various ways. First, it suggests that Piaget's idea about cognitive development progressing through stages could be correct. Although the stages may not be quite as Piaget had imagined them, nevertheless we can identify at least three stages to development: no conception of false belief and no conception of inference as a means of knowing; conception of false belief but no conception of inference as a means of knowing; both conception of false belief and conception of inference as a source of knowledge. It may also be the case that we can identify more advanced stages, as children's theory of mind develops. Perhaps it is useful to think of the research so far carried out on the development of theory of mind as being rather crude (though of course this is not meant in a disrespectful sense). Perhaps future research will reveal a much broader picture of the way one's theory of mind develops, and why it develops in that way.

The second reason why it is important is because it draws attention to the possibility that a very important feature of cognitive development could be the developing understanding of people's minds. This conflicts with Piaget's idea, that the central feature of cognitive development is a technological and scientific understanding. It could be that in our societies we now value understanding of scientific issues more than we value understanding of psychological ones, but in order to get to the bottom of human cognition, it might be useful to focus on the latter.

This discussion raises a whole new question: is 'theory of mind' a special feature of human cognition, or is it something shared by other species, particularly our closest cousins? Premack and Woodruff (1978) set out specifically to address this question. They trained chimpanzees to deceive each other whilst playing a game. The task was such that in order to apply deception successfully, the chimpanzees would require some grasp of how their actions could bring about a state of false belief in their opponent. If they succeeded, then we could argue that chimpanzees are capable of developing a theory of mind.

Premack and Woodruff found that their chimpanzees did succeed in deceiving each other, but only after very extensive and laborious training. They could have trained the chimpanzees to do much more complex things with far less effort. Although the authors claimed that chimpanzees are capable of developing a theory of mind, perhaps we ought to consider how difficult it was to train the chimpanzees to succeed at deception. Perhaps the difficulty arose because chimpanzee cognition is not well suited to theory of mind. If so, this suggests that theory of mind could be a uniquely human capability.

If we are not born with a theory of mind, and that is something we have to acquire, surely there would be cases of unfortunate individuals who have an aberrant development, one in which a theory of mind does not emerge. What would these individuals be like? How would we identify them? Is there already a group of individuals in this category, consisting of people who are identified as abnormal, but who are not recognized as having a theory of mind deficit? These are questions we shall look at in the next section.

Autism: A Failure to Acquire a Theory of Mind?

Autism is a developmental disorder which occurs at a frequency of about 2 per 10,000 of the population, first identified as a substantive syndrome in the middle of this century independently by Leo Kanner and Hans Asperger. Mild forms of autism are often called Asperger's syndrome. In a marvellously readable book, Uta Frith (1989) gives an exposition of her theory of autism.

Many people with autism also have severe learning difficulties, and few have above average IQ scores. Autism seems to result from a physical abnormality of the brain, rather than from social causes such as bad parenting. As Frith puts it, 'Theories that consider Autism as emotional maladjustment ... are obsolete. We now know that Autism is a type of mental handicap due to abnormalities in brain development.' (1989, p. 186).

Autism is an enigmatic disorder. Despite Frith's claim, the strong impression one gets from interacting with a person with autism is that he or she does have some kind of emotional maladjustment, and no doubt this led Leo Kanner in his original description to suggest that autism is a consequence of failure to understand expressions of emotions, which impairs the ability to form affective relationships.

Interacting with a person with autism is a curious experience. On the one hand, it is patently obvious that the individual is abnormal. This is evident in that normal children very quickly identify a child with autism and then cruelly make fun of him or her. On the other hand, it is profoundly difficult to specify what the abnormality is. Comments that people typically make are that the person with autism looks right through you; he always has an expressionless face; he always takes things literally to the point of absurdity, and has no common sense. For example, if I say 'Can you pass me the salt?', a normal child would pass the salt, taking this as a request for action, whereas a child with autism might simply reply 'Yes', taking it as a request for information!

More able people with autism often display special abilities. Some are advanced at reading, drawing, memorizing bus timetables, and so on. However, many of these special abilities turn out to be useless in practice. For example, some people with autism can rapidly work out the day of the week a particular date will fall on at almost any point in time. This is a remarkable cognitive feat, but it is difficult to envisage how it could be utilized in any practical way. In contrast to the few pockets of exceptional cognitive functioning bright people with autism enjoy, when it comes to comprehending text, or understanding the implications of things, they perform very poorly.

Frith's theory is that people with autism do not suffer from an emotional disorder, but from a cognitive one. She suggests that it is the nature of normal people to try to impose sense and meaning on things, to look for patterns in our experiences, and interpret them. This can be seen in the case of the 'gambler's fallacy'. If we toss an unbiased coin, 50 per cent of the time it will be heads. In other words, the probability of heads on each toss is .5. There is no pattern to be found in the sequence of heads and tails, it is purely chance. However, the gambler's fallacy is that there is a pattern. So if the last five tosses have yielded heads, the gambler may fallaciously believe that the probability of the next toss resulting in tails is increased. This is not so, and the probability of tails remains .5. This goes to show that we, as gamblers and in other aspects of life, have a strong tendency to look for sense, meaning and patterns in the world. Frith's view is that people with autism, in sharp contrast, have no such tendency. The point Frith makes is that autism is not primarily an emotional disorder, but rather is a cognitive deficit in the form of a failure to try to make sense of things.

We try to make sense of all sorts of things, such as the weather, the movement of the planets, and the failure of the car to start when we turn the ignition key. Perhaps the most ubiquitous attempt at imposing sense does not relate to physical things but rather to the psychological or intentional. For example, when someone asks 'can you pass me the salt?', the sense we impose on this is, 'she wants me to hand her the salt'. Indeed, the tendency to look for intention in making sense of things could be so engrained in our nature that our ancestors supposed an invisible intention is behind certain physical events. They thought that thunderstorms were God expressing his wrath, and likewise for earthquakes.

Here we come to Frith's most radical claim. She points out that having a theory of mind is all about trying to understand and interpret people's intentions. She goes on to suggest that because people with autism do not do that, or at any rate are poor at doing it, they are seriously lacking in theory of mind capability. If that suggestion is true, people with autism ought to fail on the 'Smarties test'. Perner, Frith, Leslie and Leekam (1989) conducted a study to find out.

Perner *et al*.'s (1989) study involved presenting the 'Smarties test' to children with autism. As in the test presented to normal children, described above, Perner *et al*. showed the tube to children with autism, and asked what was inside. All replied with 'Smarties'. The researchers then opened the tube to reveal that really it contained a pencil, returned the pencil to the tube and closed the lid. Then they asked what another person, who was about to be tested next, would say was inside. The findings were dramatic: 80 per cent of children with autism gave the wrong answer, saying 'he will say pencil'.

The high frequency of error could not simply have been due to mental immaturity of the children with autism. Prior to doing the test, the children with autism had their mental age assessed, to ensure that it was well above 4 years, the age at which most normal children succeed on the task.

One thing Perner *et al*. (1989) wished to establish was whether failure to attribute false belief is something exclusive to normal young children and children with autism, or whether we would find the error in anyone who has severe learning difficulties caused by abnormal brain development. To find out, they tested a group of children suffering from Down's syndrome. This is a disorder due to genetic aberration which gives rise to abnormal brain development and psychological handicap as a consequence, but which is quite unlike autism in terms of the behaviour exhibited by the individual. The Smarties test posed no difficulty for the children with Down's syndrome, and they correctly judged that another person would wrongly think the tube contained Smarties. The good performance of these children was all the more interesting given that they had a lower mental age on average, compared with the children with autism. This finding suggests that failure on the Smarties test does not result from a general difficulty in developmentally handicapped children, but rather might be specific to a deficit children with autism have. According to Frith, the deficit in question is that people with autism are unable to acknowledge false belief and therefore are lacking in a fundamental basis required for the development of a theory of mind. To put it more strongly, perhaps the symptoms of autism are the symptoms of having no theory of mind.

That said, it does not necessarily follow that the person with autism has a cognition just like a normal 3-year-old. Indeed, Leekam and Perner (1991) discovered that the deficit of the child with autism might be more specific to understanding the mind compared with the normal 3-year-old. They presented the misrepresentation photo task, devised by Zaitchik (1990), described above, to a group of children with autism and to normal 3-year-olds. Their 3-year-olds performed just like those tested by Zaitchik, and judged wrongly that the image which was about to appear on the developing photograph would depict a scene in its present arrangement, rather than as it had been at the moment the film was exposed. In sharp contrast, the great majority of children with autism judged correctly that the developing image would be the scene at the moment the film was exposed, and not as it was at the moment the child made his judgment. It was not that this was an extraordinary group of children with autism, since they judged wrongly that the next child to see a Smarties tube would say it contained pencils, thereby failing to acknowledge false belief.

This intriguing finding suggests that although in some respects the mind theorizing of children with autism resembles that of a normal 3-year-old, in other respects it could be quite different. In particular, children with autism may not have a general difficulty with misrepresentation, unlike normal 3-year-olds, as revealed by their success in performing on the misrepresentation photo task. Instead, it seems that their difficulty could be restricted to acknowledging that the mind is distinct from the external world, with failure to recognize false belief serving as a symptom of this.

At the end of the previous section, I posed some questions regarding what a person who lacked a theory of mind would be like. The possibility that a central feature of autism is the possession of an inadequate theory of mind is very new, and as yet there has been little opportunity for the possibility to be assessed critically. Consequently, we must proceed with some caution. However, it could well be the case that if we want to know what a person who fails to develop a normal theory of mind would be like, we need look no further than the group of unfortunate individuals with autism. These people take meaning on a very literal level, they look straight through you in conversation, are profoundly lacking in common sense, and, perhaps most of all, appear unable to empathize. These symptoms are all consistent with the person with autism having no notion of other people's meanings, intentions and feelings. In this decade we could see the emergence of a finer understanding of autism, as we take on board the important and revolutionary ideas advanced by Uta Frith and her colleagues.

Further Reading

Because 'theory of mind' is such a new topic, there are no introductory texts on this subject. There is a high-level collection of writings, however, which is aimed at a specialized audience. Only look at this if you have a very strong interest in the subject, and don't be surprised if it is extremely heavy going.

ASTINGTON, J.W., HARRIS, P.L. and OLSON, D.R. (Eds) (1988) *Developing Theories of Mind*, Cambridge, Cambridge University Press.

In contrast, thanks to Uta Frith there is an excellent text on autism, which is suitable for beginner and specialist alike:

FRITH, U. (1989) *Autism: Explaining the Enigma*, Oxford, Basil Blackwell.

Chapter 4

The Role of Heredity and Environment in Intelligence

What is Inherited?

By this question, of course, I mean behaviour, personality traits, intelligence and so on, and not family heirlooms. In other words, what part of the way we are, and the way we behave, is determined by the genes passed on to us by our parents? At a glance, this may seem like a simple question to answer: all we have to do is watch newborn babies, who have had no opportunity to learn anything, and whatever they can do is obviously determined genetically, and therefore likely to be inherited from the mother, father or both. From the observation of the newborn we could compile a long list of behaviours: crying, swallowing, blinking, defecating, sucking, yawning, sneezing, coughing, grasping, etc.

However, while we can be confident that these behaviours are genetically determined, how can we be sure that behaviours which emerge later in development are learned – that is, a consequence of exposure to the environment? What about walking? Are we genetically programmed to do this, or do we have to learn to walk? What about riding a bicycle, a skill which seems similar to walking on the face of things? These are both behaviours which emerge sometime after birth, yet only one of them is genetically programmed.

Babies begin to walk at around 12 months. There is little learning involved in this, and babies 'know' before they begin to walk how to move their legs and balance. We can show that a baby knows how to walk from birth by suspending the newborn from its arms. It will make characteristic 'walking' leg movements. This demonstrates that the newborn has a latent knowledge, that is, a knowledge about how to walk which is not cashed until it is approximately 12 months of age.

In contrast, riding a bike is something we have to learn to do. I can be completely confident about this fact for the simple reason that bikes are a relatively recent invention. Our ancestors, except for our very close ones, had no opportunity to ride bikes. Therefore, there has been no evolutionary pressure for bike-riding genes to emerge in the population, perhaps until recently. As such, we can ride bikes only in so far as this skill falls within the scope of our general capability, and we are not genetically endowed with specific bike-riding knowledge.

Although we can make a clear distinction between walking and bike riding in the extent to which genetic programming features in each of these behaviours, it also makes sense to suppose that some general potential to do things, to acquire new skills, is partly under genetic influence. For example, the actual shape of humans suits the design of a bike: it is difficult to imagine a snake riding a bike. Of course, that is not surprising, because bikes were invented for humans and not snakes. Nevertheless, it goes to show that genes always feature in our potential to do things.

The human/snake example is based on the rather gross case of genetically determined body shape, and how that suits the learning of certain skills. However, there could be 'hidden' genetic factors which influence our learning to ride a bike. Suppose two children of the same age begin learning to ride bikes. One has mastered the skill within twenty-four hours and the other is still struggling after a month. Bearing in mind Piaget's ideas, we might wonder whether the child who acquired the skill rapidly was able to make a parallel between bike riding and some other skill or skills which he had, and apply these to the bike-riding situation. For example, perhaps the child was already an accomplished tightrope walker, and was able to apply his balancing knowledge to bike riding with success. In other words, perhaps a process of assimilation accelerated acquisition of the bike-riding skill. Apart from this, however, we may still wonder whether some people have a general ability to pick things up quickly, whether or not assimilation is brought into play – a general ability that has a genetic basis.

A visit to any classroom can leave us in no doubt that some children simply learn to do things more rapidly than others. It might be because the fast learners have a serious attitude towards study, because they concentrate harder, because they do extra work out of school hours which benefits the process of assimilation. None of these factors needs have anything to do with a general genetic potential to learn to do things. Nevertheless, a belief which prevails in our society is that some children are simply more able than others, whatever their experiences. In other words, some children are endowed with more of this mysterious genetically determined general ability. Of such children, we may say, 'She's bright ... she's clever ... she's *intelligent*.' We may think of these children as being the ones who will attend university, and perhaps have a career as a senior civil servant. In contrast, we may think of the 'less gifted' children as being the ones who will leave school early and take a lower-status job.

Is this prevailing attitude warranted? Are some people really genetically gifted with high intelligence? Perhaps the most difficult question of all: how do we go about investigating whether individual differences in intelligence are determined by our genes?

Intelligence: Heredity Versus Environment

The first requirement is some means of measurement of intelligence. For this, educationists and psychologists use as their tool the IQ test. 'IQ' stands for 'intelligence quotient', and simply means 'intelligence score'. The first IQ tests were devised jointly by Alfred Binet and Theo Simon at the beginning of the Twentieth Century in France. It was at this time that there was a massive expansion in education, and the educational establishment desired a means of categorizing children in order to find out who would benefit from certain types of education. The parallel in modern-day schools is streaming, though it is unlikely that IQ tests are involved in the process.

The rationale for the IQ test seems simple and sensible on the face of things: the educationists were not so much interested with how good the children were at art, creative writing, maths, etc. to begin with, but how good they were likely to be after having the benefit of an education. If they were likely to be excellent, then education served a useful purpose, whereas if they were likely to be no better than when they started, then education would be useless. The educationists, to their great credit, recognized that simply interviewing the child, or presenting some 'home-made' tests of ability, could be biased. The main pitfall with the interview is that some extravert children would appear confident and relaxed, perhaps giving the impression that they were intelligent, while some introverted children might be intimidated by the experience and appear mute and dull. Extraversion-introversion is almost certainly not related to intelligence. The trouble with home-made tests is that a given child may or may not matriculate, depending upon the nature of the particular test. What was required was a *standardized* test. This is where Binet and Simon entered the scene.

They devised a paper and pencil test which presents a series of problems that rely minimally on practical knowledge or experience. The belief was that if practical knowledge and experience are of no help in solving the problems, then the child must call upon her 'genetic general intelligence' for the solution. Here is an example of the kind of problem you might find in an IQ test:

Write the next number in the sequence:

2   6   18   54   162   ?

The answer is of course 486. To solve this problem, you have to identify a simple formula which can account for the increased value of each subsequent figure, and then apply that formula to infer the missing final value. In this case, the formula is 'multiply each successive figure by 3'.

A second belief was that speed is important, with the idea that intelligent people can do the same mental things more rapidly than dull people. For this reason, the tests were timed. A third belief was that more of one's intelligence potential can be realized with increasing age, so in calculating IQ score, age of the child is taken into consideration. The idea was that if a boy had IQ 100 at age 7, then he might still have IQ 100 at 15, even though at the older age he managed to solve many more of the problems in the time available. The test designer achieves this simply in the following way: let IQ 100 be the average score. Thus, if on average 7-year-olds solve ten out of thirty problems in the allotted time, then we will say that any 7-year-old who gets ten right has IQ 100. If on average 15-year-olds solve twenty out of thirty problems correctly, then we will say that any 15-year-old who gets twenty right has IQ 100. You can see from this that the number of problems an individual gets right is expected to increase with age, but IQ can remain constant. Consequently, if the number of problems solved correctly does not increase with age, then IQ would decrease. Also you can see how mental age can be calculated. In the example given above, if the 15-year-old solves only ten problems correctly, then we might say that he has a mental age of 7 years. In the early days, IQ score was linked to mental age and contrasted with chronological age in the following formula:

$$\frac{\text{Mental age}}{\text{Chronological age}} \times 100 = IQ$$

If we select, say, 500 people from the population at random, and then gave them all an IQ test, we would find that the pattern of the 500 scores conformed to a 'normal distribution'. The average score would be 100. Sixty-seven per cent of scores would be between 85 and 115, and 96 per cent of scores would be between 70 and 130. In other words, most people have IQ 100, or somewhere near that figure. Only a small minority of people have extremely high or extremely low scores. This normal distribution fits many natural phenomena, such as height or weight of people. For example, most adult males are about 175 centimetres tall. Few are above 200 centimetres, and few are below 150 centimetres. Height is under substantial genetic influence, and, like many genetic traits, we can see how the pattern of heights in the population conforms to a normal distribution. To argue that intelligence is a genetic trait, like height, it is useful, but not conclusive, to show that IQ scores conform to such a distribution. As a result, devisers of intelligence tests have been at pains to make sure that the pattern of population IQ scores is normally distributed. This has been achieved by adding or removing specific IQ problems, according to how they influence the population distribution of scores the test yields. IQ tests are still in use today, and the construction of these owes a great deal to Binet and Simon's original attempts.

So far everything may seem fine, but there is a very serious flaw in the reasoning behind all this. Namely, it is wrong to assume automatically that IQ tests probe a general genetic intelligence. Although children may never have experienced the particular problems presented in the test, it is possible that some had the benefit of experiences of a more general nature they could call upon in solving the problems. For example, if one is well practised in manipulating numbers and using formulaes, then presumably one would have a head start in solving the problem presented above, compared with someone who does not have the benefit of such experience. In other words, the process of assimilation could be brought into play to help solve the problem, showing that experience of a general nature could aid performance on the IQ test. A second point, which is related, is that as one's experiences become more enriched and varied, so perhaps this would be reflected in higher IQ. If this turned out to be true, then it is patently wrong to think that IQ could serve as a useful tool for predicting how a child is going to progress through education.

We can see how general experience *might* affect IQ, and therefore that IQ *might* change with age. However, it could also be the case that although it is possible in principle for experience to affect IQ, in practice it does not. In this case, IQ might indeed be the measure of general genetic intelligence which some (e.g. Jensen, 1980) claim it to be. How can we find out?

We can find out by comparing the IQs of identical twins. Identical twins, known technically as monozygotic twins, develop from the union of a single sperm with a single egg. Shortly after conception, the fertilized egg splits to form two separate individuals who are genetically identical. These individuals are different from fraternal twins, known technically as dizygotic twins. In this case, the mother has two eggs, both of which get fertilized by different sperms. Genetically, these twins are just like ordinary brothers and sisters, having 50 per cent genetic constitution in common, and they are only special in that they share the mother's womb. Because identical twins have the same genetic constitution, any differences in their IQ can be attributed to experiences – environmental factors. Conversely, if IQs were identical, this could either be because genetic constitution is identical, or it could be because the twins have had the same experiences. Therefore, the really big question concerns how similar is the IQ of identical twins who are brought up in different families.

On the other side of the coin is the case of a pair of previously unrelated children adopted into the same family. We can think of these children as having 0 per cent genetic constitution in common, yet sharing a very similar environment, which could have an important influence on IQ. For example, a house rule could be that all children in the family have to do homework for an hour each day after school. It is possible that such a regimen could improve educational and IQ performance. Note, however, that we can never say that any two people have an identical environment, or identical experiences. The best we can do is say that members of the same family are likely to have similar experiences. The point is that if it emerged that children who had been adopted into a family from birth had completely different IQs from each other in their teens, it would not necessarily show that experiences are irrelevant to IQ.

Before we take a look at some figures, we need a tool for comparing the similarity between IQ scores. The tool we use is the correlation coefficient. This is a statistical test performed on pairs of scores, which yields a figure that indicates how related the pairs of scores are. For example, suppose one member of a pair of identical twins has an IQ of 125, and the other has a score of 121. Suppose in another pair, one has an IQ of 87 and the other has IQ 95. How could we justify the claim that members of twin pairs have similar IQs? We don't need a justification, but instead simply apply the correlation test to the data. The correlation score can range from –1 to +1, where +1 indicates a perfect relationship between pairs of scores. This is what we would find if each twin had the same IQ as his identical twin brother. We would find a correlation of 0 if IQs of twin pairs were unrelated, and we would find a correlation of –1 if there was a negative relationship. This could result if it was always the case that when one twin had a high IQ, his brother had a low IQ. In practice, correlations usually appear as a fraction, falling somewhere between the extremes of –1 and +1.

Identical twins reared apart from an early age are rare, but during the course of this century, many researchers have found samples of such children. In an analysis of data combined from all these studies, Plomin and DeFries (1980) found that the correlation between pairs of IQ scores from identical twins reared apart is .75. Similarly, the most recent and largest ever study (Bouchard, Lykken, McGue, Segal and Tellegen, 1990) has yielded a correlation figure of .70. In the latter, there were 56 pairs of monozygotic twins from all over the world separated within the first two years, who typically were not reunited until adulthood. These correlation figures are very similar to each other and both are very high, showing a strong relationship between the IQs of members of each pair of twins. In plain language, a member of an identical twin pair identified as bright by the IQ test was very likely to have a co-twin who was also identified as bright according to the same test, even if that co-twin was brought up in a different family. Similarly, a member of an identical twin pair identified as dull was likely to have a co-twin also identified as such, again, even if they were brought up in different families. This shows that the IQ of identical twins is strongly related, even when they live apart: shared genes rather than shared environment seems to be responsible for this.

The correlation for fraternal twins reared together is .60. As mentioned previously, these individuals have a 50 per cent shared genetic constitution. The remarkable thing is that the correlation for identical twins reared apart is higher than that for fraternal twins reared together, sharing the same environment.

Studies investigating the IQ of biologically unrelated teenagers, who had been adopted into the same family at an early age, find no relationship (e.g. Scarr and Weinberg, 1983). In other words, the IQs of pairs of unrelated children brought up in the same family show no resemblance to each other, with the correlation around zero. This seems to suggest that shared environment is unimportant to IQ.

On the face of it, these findings seem to provide overwhelming testimony to the importance of genetic inheritance for IQ, and the virtual irrelevance of environment. Supporters of the heredity position have used these figures to argue that approximately 80 per cent of intelligence is inherited via our genes.

In view of the correlation figures cited above, it is clear that performance on IQ tests is influenced by genetic constitution. This point is no longer in dispute. However, many feel that advocates of the heredity position could be over-stating the case for a genetic contribution in claiming that 80 per cent of IQ is determined by genetic factors. Let us take a look at some of the reasons for this feeling.

We can be confident that whatever difference we find in the IQ of identical twins is due to environmental influence, or differences in experience, if you like: it cannot be due to differences in genetic constitution because that does not vary across identical twins. Looking at the correlation between IQs of identical twins reared in different families is not very meaningful without knowing in what way the families were different. It may be that in many cases the families were very similar, in which case it might not be accurate to say that co-twins were reared in a different environment. In fact, many twin pairs classified as 'reared apart' had been adopted into different households belonging to the same family. For example, one member of a twin pair may have been adopted by an aunt in a neighbouring street. In this case, although the twins do not live in the same house, presumably they have a very similar life style and education. Even in the case of twins adopted into unrelated families, in many cases the class status and education is comparable. Given all this, what we need to know is whether IQ is different in co-twins who are reared in radically different environments. If so, this would show that particular experiences do have a bearing on IQ.

In a classic study, Robert Woodworth (1941) studied nineteen pairs of identical twins, some of whom were reared in similar environments, and some of whom were reared in completely different ones. He found that when separated identical twins were reared in similar environments, IQs were very nearly the same. For twins reared in different environments, another picture emerged. In the case of one twin pair, the difference in IQ was twenty-four points – a very substantial figure indeed. The twin with the higher IQ was reared in a prosperous family, went to college and then became a schoolteacher. The twin with the lower IQ was reared by a poor family, and attended school for only two years. Since that study, several subsequent researchers have found the same. Namely, identical twins reared apart who enjoy a similar life style have very similar IQs. Those who have completely different life styles have big discrepancies between their IQ scores. Differences in IQ of monozygotic twins reared apart are also reported in the latest study (Bouchard *et al.*, 1990), but they are the rare exception.

What do these findings tell us? They tell us that environmental factors can have a large influence on IQ. They also tell us that there is an important genetic factor involved in IQ, given that identical twins reared apart but in similar environments have very similar IQs. To appreciate the importance of the genetic contribution, this fact has to be considered in relation to the lack of correlation between the IQs of unrelated children adopted into the same family. In this case, similarity of environment has been insufficient to bring about similar IQ scores. What we see in the case of high correlations between identical twins reared in similar environments, whether or not they are in the very same family, is shared genetic constitution and similarity in environment acting together to contribute to IQ.

So how much intelligence, reflected in IQ, is transmitted to us through our genes? Nobody really knows the answer to this question. Indeed, some see it as a silly question, for the simple reason that intelligence must be a product of heredity and environment in combination. IQ is impossible without both acting together. As a result, it comes down to opinions. The authors of the most recent and largest study argue persuasively that the genetic component to IQ is in the order of 70 per cent (Bouchard *et al.*, 1990). However, they do not necessarily suppose that there is a direct link between certain gene combinations and providing the correct answer to IQ questions. Rather, they suggest that the similarity in IQ between mono-zygotic twins could stem from a more general similarity of personality between the two individuals – such as temperament, inquisitiveness, aggression and so on. For example, a child whose genetically determined temperament is not well suited to the social dynamics of the school situation may experience a discomfort that exists as an impediment to getting on with learning and developing academically. As a consequence of this individual's unpleasant experience in school, he may perform badly on the IQ test and other scholarly measures. In this case, the poor performance would be due to the individual's unfortunate experiences, and had his temperament been otherwise, he could have flourished in an academic setting. Yet we can suppose that if he had an identical twin brother, who therefore shared the genetic temperament, he would likewise perform badly on an IQ test. In sum, Bouchard *et al.* argue that nature (genetic constitution) could exert its influence via nurture (experiences).

Another reason why identical twins (who are reared together) are likely to share experiences is because they may be treated as being the same person by others who find it difficult to distinguish between them. In contrast, fraternal twins are only as alike as ordinary brothers and sisters. In this case, it is unlikely that members of twin pairs would be treated as the same individual. We can see, then, that not only do identical twin pairs share more genetic constitution than fraternal pairs, but they are more likely to have the same experiences.

The best way to proceed is to look at environmental influences on IQ. Apart from anything else, this course of action makes the most practical sense. There is nothing we can do about an individual's genetic constitution, but there is an awful lot we can do to change the environment. In other words, what kind of experiences might be of benefit, or to the detriment of, an individual's IQ?

Environmental Factors and IQ

The question we pose is straightforward: does an enriched environment give rise to higher IQ in children? The question is a simple one, but things can become tricky when we try to define 'enriched' in relation to the environment. Let us begin with a basic issue. Common sense says that the environment should be such that children are well provided for in terms of diet and nutrition. Bearing this idea in mind, perhaps it comes as no surprise that schoolteachers often feel that their children underperform in academic activities due to an intake of too much 'junk food' and not enough decent wholesome food. Is this feeling completely unfounded, or is there hard evidence to support it?

One schoolteacher, Gwylim Roberts, teamed up with my colleague David Benton (1988) to find out. They gave an 8-month course of tablets to thirty Welsh 12-year-olds. The tablets contained a wide range of vitamins and minerals. Another thirty similar children received an inert tablet that was indistinguishable from the vitamin tablet. Children were ignorant as to whether the tablets they were taking were vitamins or the inert substance. Subsequently, all sixty children attempted an IQ test and the results were startling: the IQ of those who received vitamin supplementation increased by approximately nine points on average, whereas the IQ of those taking the inert tablet hardly changed.

When the findings of this study were published, the news swept across the nation like a whirlwind, and stocks of vitamins in pharmacies were rapidly depleted! Since then, however, the finding has been called into question. Crombie, Todman, McNeill, Florey, Menzies and Kennedy (1990) tried to replicate the Benton and Roberts (1988) study with a group of Scottish schoolchildren, but found no improvement in IQ score following a course of vitamin supplementation. However, another investigation was successful in replicating Benton and Roberts' finding on a group of 15-year-olds in the USA (Schoenthaler, Amos, Doraz, Kelly and Wakefield, 1991).

Benton (1991) explains discrepancies in the results of studies as follows. He proposes that providing the child's diet is adequate in terms of vitamin content, additional vitamins would be redundant, and therefore of no benefit to performance in an IQ test. In contrast, if the child's diet is vitamin deficient, this could prevent her brain operating at its full potential, just as a car running on low-grade fuel lacks high performance. To investigate this possibility, Benton and Buts (1990) supplemented the diets of several groups of children in Belgium. In this study, the researchers monitored the daily nutrition of the children over and above that which they received through the vitamin tablets. The findings were exactly as Benton predicted, in that the unfortunate children who had an impoverished diet benefited considerably from vitamin supplementation, reflected in higher IQ score. In contrast, those who already had a good healthy diet showed no improvement in IQ following vitamin supplementation. Apparently, the good diet of these children enabled them to function at full potential, so in their case vitamin supplementation was redundant.

The lesson to be learned, it seems, is that a healthy diet is not only to the advantage of physical development, but also to mental functioning. Vitamin supplementation can improve mental functioning in some cases, but if the child already eats enough healthy food, this will be unnecessary. So it is clear that an environment which provides adequate nourishment is one that is conducive to good mental performance.

What about the social and psychological environment – to what extent can this affect IQ? The first step we need to take is to identify factors which we might suppose would facilitate cognitive development. Such an undertaking was carried out by Elardo, Bradley and Caldwell (1975). They compiled a list of items which they judged contribute to an enriched environment, which included such things as: when speaking to the child, the mother's voice conveys positive feeling; mother structures child's play periods; mother reads stories at least three times weekly; family provides learning equipment appropriate to age of child; child gets out of house at least four times a week; mother shouts at child relatively infrequently; mother spontaneously vocalizes to child relatively frequently.

Elardo *et al.* visited seventy-seven children from lower-class homes, when the children were aged 6 months, and again when they were aged 24 months. The investigators had compiled a check list to establish whether the family environment conformed to their definition of 'enriched'. Having done this, the investigators visited the children two more times, once when they were age 3, and again when they were 4½. This time, the visit was to administer IQ tests.

Elardo *et al.* correlated the score assigned to the family after administering the check list, with the IQ of the child. The correlations ranged from .44 (family visit at 6 months, IQ tested at 4½ years) to .70 (family visit at 24 months, IQ tested at 3 years). In all cases, the correlations were substantial, showing a strong relationship between family environment and the IQ of the child.

These figures give the distinct impression that an ideal environment can yield a higher IQ. However, this conclusion could be too simple. It is possible that the children who had high IQs did so because they had 'intelligent' genes, passed onto them by intelligent parents. In other words, the role of the environment in the high IQ could have been illusory. This could have come about if more intelligent parents, because they are more intelligent, arrange the environment in such a way that happens to conform with Elardo *et al.*'s vision of what is ideal. For example, the more intelligent parents could be the ones who structure the child's play periods, read stories to the child and so on. Yet it might be the intelligent genes transmitted from parent to child that is responsible for the high IQ, and not the way the intelligent parent arranges the environment.

What we need to know is whether the findings reported by Elardo *et al.* could be repeated in the case of children who are adopted into a biologically unrelated family. Such a study was conducted by Plomin, Loehlin and DeFries (1985), who found much the same as Elardo *et al*. It must be said that the correlation between family environment and IQ was not as high, but nevertheless a relationship between the two was clearly evident. Given this, it seems appropriate to conclude that family environment can have an important bearing on IQ.

Another important factor in the family environment, which we have not considered yet, is the number of children in the home. Zajonc (1983) reports that the more children there are in the family, the lower the average IQ of the children. Also, within families, the average IQ of the first born is higher than that of the second born, which in turn is higher than that of the third born and so on down the birth-order list. These effects are small, but nevertheless we can be confident that they are present. Note that this is a trend derived from averages, so there could be many exceptions to this pattern in individual families. Zajonc explains the pattern by suggesting that as the parental attention becomes divided between more children, so each individual child gets the benefit of a smaller portion of adult intellectually stimulating interaction.

We can be left in no doubt that environmental factors have an important influence on IQ. Also, there can be no doubt that the genetic material transmitted to us from our parents makes a contribution. Genetic and environmental factors combine in determining IQ: both are essential, and IQ is impossible one without the other. To illustrate how the two factors might combine, a child who is mentally retarded, due to genetic error, may never be able to attain a high IQ, no matter how stimulating the environment. That is not to say that the child's IQ could not be improved. On the contrary, no doubt appropriate treatment could prove to be very beneficial to IQ. However, the point is that perhaps the mentally retarded child may never attain a high IQ. In contrast to all this, the child who has the potential for very high IQ may never demonstrate this potential if he lives in a severely impoverished environment.

Debates about how much of IQ is due to genes and how much to the environment seem rather futile for the simple reason that it is difficult to envisage how we could ever arrive at a definitive answer. Perhaps the more useful approach is to accept that both are important, but given that we cannot or would not want to do anything about the genetic side of things, we should channel our energy into determining what might be the most intellectually beneficial environment.

Further Reading

Never has the heredity versus environment debate generated so much heat, which now seems to have become of historical interest. Perhaps the best response to the hereditarian position is captured in Leo Kamin's book:

KAMIN, L. J. (1974) *The Science and Politics of IQ*, Hillsdale, N.J., Erlbaum.

Chapter 5

The Development of Perception

There are various ways in which we perceive: touch, hearing, taste, smell and vision. In this chapter we shall focus primarily on vision, simply because most research has been carried out on this sense. It is amazing that we are able to see. If we reflect for a moment, it seems astonishing that in our heads we should have a lens covering a light chamber that has a light-sensitive surface at its rear (called the retina). It is further remarkable that this light-sensitive surface is able to transduce the light energy into neuronal signals that can be interpreted by the brain. Perhaps most remarkable of all, however, is that the brain can make sense of this information, in such a way that we experience seeing things in the world. This 'making sense of ...' is what we call perception.

The really impressive thing is that the brain performs a phenomenal number of computations on the input from the eye which enables us to see items stably located in space. Consider these examples. We look at a chair from one viewpoint and then move to another. From the new viewpoint, the pattern of light falling on the retina is very different from that of the original viewpoint. Yet this experience does not throw us into a terrible confusion about chairs changing in shape as we move around the room. We have no difficulty in recognizing that the shape of the chair remains constant (shape constancy), which shows that our brains are equipped to take our movement into account, and work out that it is this movement that gives rise to the different image emanating from the chair, and not a curious metamorphosis that the chair has gone through.

Moreover, on our travel from one point to the other, although images move across the retina as we move, we do not experience this as an earthquake, with the environment suddenly becoming unstable. Our brains take into account body movement, and work out the implications for this in terms of the images moving across our retinas. The brain can do this to work out whether the movement of the retinal image is just due to our movement, or whether it is instead, or also, to do with the movement of the object itself. This is a process we take for granted so much that it is sometimes difficult to comprehend how amazing it is. Only when the brain makes a mistake are we alerted to some of the processes which automatically take place. One such error occurs when travelling by train. We stop at a station next to another train which has a destination in the opposite direction. After a while, we find that we move off, leaving the stationary train behind. Then we find our brain has made an error, that we are stationary, and that really it was the other train that moved away.

Another perceptual facility is size constancy. As we move away from a chair, it projects a smaller image onto our retinas. Again, this poses no problem. Our brains do not tell us that the chair is getting smaller, but instead takes into account that an effect of greater distance is smaller retinal image (size constancy). A related issue is the perception of depth. If we are blindfolded, and then taken to an unknown vantage point, on removal of the blindfold we will find that we have a fair idea of the distances of various objects from us. We might not be able to express this accurately in units of measurement, such as metres or kilometres, but it is very likely that we would judge accurately which object is nearer or more distant than other comparison objects.

Do we have to learn to do these wonderful feats of perception, or are they something our genes equip us to do? One of the very first psychologists, William James, stated at the beginning of the Twentieth Century that the newborn's world is a 'blooming, buzzing confusion'. Apparently, James took the view that perceiving is something the infant has to learn to do. In recent years, psychologists have set out to investigate whether this is indeed the case, and their attempts are fascinating not just because of the conclusions they have arrived at, but for some of the ingenious methodology that has been devised as a means for coming up with answers.

Perception of Depth

Let us begin by taking a look at the perception of depth. One of the first, yet still highly pertinent, studies on this was conducted by Gibson and Walk (1960). The now famous apparatus they constructed is known as the 'visual cliff'. The design of this apparatus was inspired by a visit to the Grand Canyon, when Eleanor Gibson wondered whether her baby would get dangerously close to the precipice, or, like adults, would show a healthy respect for the great height and keep well away from the edge. An experiment which utilizes the Grand Canyon seems a little ungainly, not to mention risky! Gibson and Walk set out to recreate a miniature, perfectly safe, precipice in their laboratory, and examine whether babies display fear when near the edge.

The visual cliff apparatus was essentially a very large box, the top of which was clear perspex (Figure 5.1). Under the perspex was a black and white chequered surface. The surface under one half of the perspex, known as the shallow side, was pressed against the underneath of the perspex. The surface under the other half, known as the deep side, was a substantial way below the surface. Dividing the deep and shallow sides was a plank, forming a kind of bridge across the apparatus. On the deep side of this bridge there appeared to be a nasty drop. On the shallow side, there was no such drop. Of course, this is the impression we adults have, but what about babies? Would they be reluctant to venture onto the deep side, suggesting that they could perceive depth?

Gibson and Walk put a baby onto the bridge, and asked the mother to call to her baby from the shallow side and then from the deep side. The youngest babies

Figure 5.1:   The visual cliff

tested were about 9 months, for the simple reason that babies under this age are unable to crawl. The findings were that babies were perfectly willing to crawl to the mother across the shallow side, but exhibited a very strong reluctance to go onto the deep side. This neatly demonstrates that 9-month-olds perceive depth: we can make the simple inference that the infants' reluctance to go onto the deep side was because they had some kind of awareness of the danger of a precipice. This could only have resulted from being able to perceive that the deep side was deep.

How did the infants perceive depth? One clue to the distance (or depth) of things that we use all the time without realizing it is 'binocular parallax'. This rather technical-sounding phrase simply means that as an item gets closer to our face, so the discrepancy in the image of the object between our two retinas increases. You can carry out a little demonstration to show that this is so. Look at an item very near to you, say 10 cm from your face, then switch from closing your left eye to closing your right eye, repeatedly. You get the illusion of the item shifting around as you do this. Now focus on a distant item, say a kilometre away if possible, and do the same. This time, you find that the item does not shift around quite so much. This is because the difference between the location of your two eyes in your face is relatively unimportant where great distances are concerned, but important where small ones are concerned. When the object is close to your face, there is a considerable difference in the view from each eye.

Does the perception of depth make use of binocular parallax from a very early age, possibly from birth? The answer to this question may or may not be 'yes', but what we do know for sure is that the babies in Gibson and Walk's study were not reliant upon binocular parallax for perceiving the depth of the visual cliff. We know this because babies continued to show unease about the deep side even when they wore an eye patch, making it only possible to see through the remaining uncovered eye. In this case, binocular parallax could not have provided a clue to depth.

Although we can rule out one clue to depth that the babies might have used, we cannot be certain how they achieved depth perception instead, and it boils down to opinion and argument. Gibson and Walk put forward the plausible suggestion that the babies perceived depth on the basis of 'motion parallax'. This is something we experience most often when travelling. As the train speeds along, close things, like signals, speed past the window. Distant things, such as hills, move past the window slowly. Indeed, very distant things, such as the moon, seem to travel along with us! The relative speed at which items move past our area of vision as we travel along, gives us a clue to relative distance of the items.

In the case of the visual cliff, perhaps the babies could make use of the information that as they moved their heads, the bridge they were crawling on moved about much more in their visual area than did the chequered material on the deep side of the cliff. This gives the clue that the deep side is further away than the bridge. In contrast, there would be no such discrepancy between the apparent movement of the bridge and the chequered material on the shallow side.

Assuming Gibson and Walk are correct, and infants perceived depth on the basis of motion parallax, can we conclude that the ability to utilize motion parallax information in perception is with us from birth? Gibson and Walk's study suggests it is with us from an early age, but it cannot rule out the possibility that by 9 months of age, when the babies were tested on the visual cliff, they had learned about the link between motion parallax and depth. Younger babies could not serve in the experiment, for the simple reason that they were not mobile. However, some precocious animals, such as goats, lambs and baby chickens can walk within twenty-four hours of birth or hatching. These creatures were tested on the visual cliff, and the findings were clear. The animals ventured onto the shallow side, but not onto the deep side. This strongly suggests that for these creatures, depth perception is innate. If it is innate for these animals, then perhaps it is also innate for humans. That seems a plausible suggestion, but we cannot be entirely sure it is true.

A very imaginative experiment suggesting infants are capable of depth perception at only 3 months of age has been conducted by Bower (1965). Bower placed a 30 cm cube before the infants, one metre away. At the beginning of the session, the babies had been supplied with a pacifier, which was wired to a sensor that detected sucking. If they sucked on the pacifier when the cube was present, they were rewarded by an adult popping up and saying 'peekaboo'. The peekaboo experience gave the babies pleasure, and so they repeated sucking in order to repeat the pleasurable experience. However, sucking only brought about a peek-aboo when the cube was present. As a result of this, babies learned that it was use-less sucking when the cube was absent, and so did not bother to suck then.

Having done all this, Bower then presented a variety of cubes of different sizes and distances, and noted which combination elicited the most sucking. He found that a cube the same size as the original, but more distant and therefore giving rise to a much smaller retinal image, produced considerable sucking by the infants. Indeed, the sucking was at least as great as that elicited from a larger cube at greater distance that produced the same size of retinal image as the original. In contrast, a cube of different size from the original, situated at a distance that resulted in a different retinal size also, elicited relatively little sucking from the babies.

In this experiment, the babies' sucking served as an indication of recognition of the original cube. Since babies sucked a great deal when the original cube was moved into the distance, it suggests that the babies recognized this as being the original cube presented to them during the peekaboo game. This demonstrates that young babies have some understanding of depth, since they seem to appreciate that an object which moves into the distance produces a smaller image in the eye. This shows that they know something about the features of depth or distance, at an age younger than demonstrated by Gibson and Walk. The earlier in development we can demonstrate an ability, the more likely it is innate, yet we cannot rule out the possibility of learning in these studies.

Recent research shows that size constancy is indeed innate – newborns are genetically equipped with an understanding about the relationship between distance and apparent size of objects. This was demonstrated by Slater, Mattock and Brown (1990), who tested 2-day-old babies. It is a well known fact that new-borns prefer to look at novel things, and show less interest in familiar objects. Slater *et al.* began their study by repeatedly showing babies a cube with a distinc-tive pattern on it at a fixed distance. Over the course of this familiarization period, we can suppose that the babies' interest in the cube would wane. Slater *et al.* then introduced a second cube similar to the first in all respects except for its size, and over several trials varied the distances of the two cubes. If newborns have size constancy, they would exhibit preference for looking at the new differently sized cube, no matter what distance it was presented from. In other words, they would prefer to look at the new cube even if its distance was such that the size of the image it projected onto the baby's retina was the same as that of the first cube during the familiarization trials.

The findings were that newborns did prefer to look more at the new cube, no matter how near or distant either cube was, and therefore no matter what the reti-nal size of each. In other words, babies recognized the new object as new, and the old object as old, despite apparent changes in size. This seems to demonstrate unequivocally that size constancy, and therefore an aspect of depth perception, is innate.

Regarding innate behaviour, when interpreting findings and trying to think of new ideas for experiments, it is often useful to think of the survival value of such behaviour. The perception of depth obviously has some kind of general survival value. For example, if the baby can perceive a precipice, then she is better equipped to avoid a nasty fall than if she were unable to perceive a great depth beyond the precipice. Also, if the infant can perceive a source of food in space, then, providing she is mobile, she is unlikely to go hungry. However, in addition to these general benefits, there is a much more specific requirement to perceive depth from the moment the infant is born. Namely, objects fall or fly through space, and in some unfortunate cases, collide with the baby. There are everyday examples of such events, for example where the mother is preparing to bottle-feed the baby, but then the bottle slips from her hand and drops onto the baby's face.

In view of this, perhaps from birth, or at least from a very early age, we might find infants show some kind of defensive reaction to an object that is heading towards them on a collision course. Such reaction, if it minimized harm, would be of great benefit to the infant's health and safety. Bower, Broughton and Moore (1970) constructed an apparatus which made an object project towards the infant's face, but for obvious reasons stopped short just prior to collision. The reaction of infants as young as 2 weeks was typically defensive. Their eyes widened, they pulled their heads back and raised their hands in front of their faces. This finding clearly suggests that the infants could perceive depth, and were equipped to take appropriate defensive action on perceiving an object on a collision course.

This is evidence in support of the suggestion that depth perception, or at least an aspect of it, is innate. Some parents may feel that 2-week-old infants have had the opportunity to learn a defensive reaction to imminent collision. However, the baby's defensive reaction seems so universal and so well defined, with such little learning opportunity, that it is most likely that perception of depth, and the accompanying defensive reaction when threatened with a rapidly approaching object, is a behaviour pattern that is written into our genes.

As mentioned previously, there are many aspects to a perception of depth (binocular parallax, motion parallax, etc.). How did infants perceive depth in Bower *et al.*'s study? One of the visual features of a rapidly approaching object is that a very small retinal image quickly becomes a very large one. Consider a rapidly approaching train. At first, the train is just a dot in the distance, then, as it gets closer and closer, eventually the image of the train occupies the whole of one's visual space. In this case, the expansion of the image of the train tells us not that the train is getting larger, but that it is getting nearer. Was it the expansion of the image of the approaching object that provoked the defensive reaction in Bower *et al.*'s infants?

Ball and Tronick (1971) set out to assess this possibility, testing infants under the age of 2 weeks. They supported babies in front of a screen, onto which a pattern was projected. This pattern could be expanded at the experimenters' desire. Ball and Tronick found that a rapid expansion of the pattern produced a defensive reaction in the infants, similar to that reported by Bower *et al*. To adults, the expansion of the pattern created the illusion of an approaching object on a collision course. Another form of expanding pattern used in the study created the illusion of an approaching object, but one that was not on a collision course. When presented to the babies, this pattern did not cause a defensive reaction. This suggests, then, that one aspect of our perception of depth at least is innate. At birth, the rapid expansion of an image has meaning for us. That meaning is that a distant object is rapidly approaching.

Other Perceptual Abilities

It must be the case that a substantial amount of perception is dependent on past experience and learning. This is true in so far as there is a vague dividing line between what is perception and what is general knowledge about the world. As I look out of the window, I *see* a hedge. Yet to a trained botanist, this is no mere hedge. The botanist can *see* a collection of different shrubs. There is a holly, a beech tree, a privet, brambles, ferns, etc. In some sense, my botanically uneducated eye does not see all these things, even though all the information is available to discriminate one kind of shrub from another. Therefore, it must be that the botanist and I differ in our experiences and our learning in a way that influences how we perceive things. Of this there can be no doubt. However, it could be that all of us have an innate tendency to see things in a certain way, a tendency for our brains to organize what we see.

It is possible that there is a link between innate perceptual organization and early social behaviour. Parents typically note that as they look into the cot of their 6-week-old, the baby smiles on seeing the parent's face looming over her. This gives a great sense of joy to the parent, who is then encouraged to devote attention to the baby. Not surprisingly, parents interpret the baby's smile as a sign of happiness at the recognition of the parent's face. However, the smile could be much more mechanical than parents think, and may be a result of innate recognition of certain patterns.

Bower (1982) reports that even a crude mask will elicit a smile from a 6-week-old. Further research, to find out what aspect of the mask produced the baby's smile, revealed that it was just the two dots that formed the eyes. This is demonstrated by the fact that if we show the baby a card with two dots on it, separated according to the proportion of eyes in an adult face, the baby will smile. Moreover, Bower reports that young babies are even more likely to smile at a card with six dots on it than at one with two.

The best interpretation of this finding is that the baby is programmed, through its genes, to smile at dots! What possibly could be the value of such behaviour? The behaviour could in fact be of great use to the baby. The dots which the baby is most likely to be confronted with are those in the face of parents or caregivers: the eyes. If the baby smiles at eyes, then it is likely that she will be rewarded with attention and love from the adult, rewards which are of obvious benefit to the baby's survival and development.

All this seems rather mechanistic, and certainly a little far-fetched to anyone who has a 6-week-old baby. Surely the baby has some recognition of her parents' faces? A study conducted by Carpenter (1975) showed that indeed babies of a mere 2 weeks do recognize their parents' faces. Carpenter propped up the babies in front of a screen which had a face-size window in the middle. Various people appeared in the window, sometimes the baby's mother, and sometimes a female stranger. Carpenter found that these young babies looked at the mother's face much more than at a stranger's, demonstrating that the babies had a preference for their mother. This indicates not only that their mother was attractive to them, but also that they were able to recognize her. In other words, they were able to discriminate between faces in the first 2 weeks following birth.

It could be that an innate attraction to dots results in young babies being particularly attentive to faces, given that faces are a prominent source of dots in the baby's environment. This attraction could then serve as a basis for facial recognition. It may be that once attracted to the eyes, the baby is then in a position to attend to specific features of the face. The point is that an innate preference for eyes could accelerate learning to distinguish between patterns of a special kind: the human face.

The case of dots shows how there might be a specific innate organization of visual perception. One feature of an innate organization may enable the newborn to appreciate that items joined together in a certain way constitute a specific object, no matter how the collection of items is oriented in space. This was shown to be the case by Slater, Mattock, Brown and Bremner (1991). They exposed 2-day-old babies to a pair of straight lines joined end-to-end at an angle of 45 degrees, and presented this stimulus rotated through a variety of orientations. Subsequently, they presented the stimulus in the company of another pair of lines joined together in a similar way, but this time at the obtuse angle of 135 degrees.

Slater *et al.* found that the babies spent much more time looking at the new pair of lines, irrespective of how either stimulus was oriented in space. This suggests that the babies could distinguish between the two stimuli according to whether they were familiar or novel, indicating that they could conceptualize line pairs as forming a single object no matter how it was positioned in space. In other words, the babies must have had an innate understanding of the stable properties of objects, in the sense of appreciating underlying stability despite changes in position of the object.

Another aspect of perceptual organization that could be present from birth is the rule of 'good continuation'. This means that if we see one object partly covering another, we assume that the contours of the partly hidden object that are out of view continue in much the same way as those in view. For example, if we see a painting hanging on the wall, we may automatically assume that the pattern of the wallpaper continues behind the painting just as it does all around the painting. Of course, it could be that this assumption is wrong, and that in fact the painting is strategically placed to hide a hole in the wall. Nevertheless, unless we happen to be a property surveyor, it is highly unlikely that we would be suspicious in this way. Our default assumption seems to be that the pattern is a continuous one, carrying on behind the painting.

In an ingenious experiment similar to that on the perception of distance of cubes reported above, Bower (1967) investigated whether 6-week-old babies make similar assumptions. If they do, this would be strong evidence in favour of the suggestion that good continuation is innate, though it would not prove that such is the case given that the infant would have had 6 weeks' learning opportunity. Babies were supported in a sitting position, and periodically what seemed to be a triangle with a bar across it appeared in front of them. At the beginning of the session, the babies had been supplied with a pacifier, and were rewarded with a 'peekaboo' if and only if the triangle with the bar across it was present.

After babies had learned to suck only when the bar-triangle was present, Bower then presented a variety of figures similar but not identical to the original. He wanted to know which figure elicited the most sucking (and therefore recognition) from the babies. The one that elicited the most sucking would be the one that the babies perceived as most similar to the original. The findings were clear: infants sucked most in the presence of the complete triangle. Bower interpreted this to mean that babies believed this figure to be most similar to the original, indicating that they assumed that there was a complete triangle in the original figure, which was partly hidden by a bar.

If you were asked to find out whether 6-week-old babies make the assumption of good continuation, you would be forgiven for thinking that this was an impossible problem. Yet Bower's ingenuity shows us how this kind of problem can be addressed. His findings suggest that the assumption of good continuation is likely to be an innate one. Additionally, they suggest that infants perceived the triangle as being complete *behind* the bar. In other words, it seems that young babies have the potential for understanding that if one object partly covers another, then the partly covered object is more distant. This might be another clue to depth babies use which could be innate.

The bar-triangle figure has figure-ground properties. That is, as we focus on the bar, so the triangle becomes background to that figure. Another way of saying this is that the bar-triangle figure does not appear as just a pattern, but as one object in front of another. Bower's experiment suggests figure-ground perception is innate, for the reasons given in the preceding paragraph. There is evidence suggesting the same coming from studies on people who had been blind from birth, but then had vision repaired as adults. These are cases of people who had eye cataract problems, but who did not have an operation to remedy the problem until they were adult because the surgical technology had not been available sooner.

Shortly after coming round from the operation, these people were able to perceive figure-ground, showing that this feature of perception must be innate. In other words, the patients did not just see a coloured pattern of light after the operation, but were able in some sense to see objects in a background of other things. However, in other respects their visual perception was very poor. For example, although these people knew what squares were, through their long experience of getting to know the world through touch, they had great difficulty in identifying a square put before them. Some developed ungainly strategies for identifying squares, by carefully counting the corners. It seems that these patients, unlike people with normal vision, were unable to take in objects at a glance, but had to study their features carefully in order to say what they were.

It is very difficult to draw conclusions from findings such as these, regarding learning involved in perceptual development. It might be that babies learning to perceive also experience an initial period of having to scrutinize objects in order to recognize them. Alternatively, it might be that babies have no such problem, and that adults with restored vision have special difficulties arising through lack of use of the parts of the brain involved in visual perception. If we left a car standing for twenty years it would be a very optimistic person who would expect to get in and drive away without problems. The lack of use and attention the car suffered would cause deterioration. So we could expect the same with parts of the brain not used for such a long time. This lack of use must have been at least partly responsible for the difficulty repaired-vision patients experience.

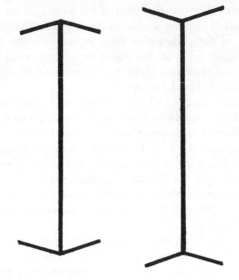

Figure 5.2: The Muller-Lyer illusion

Susceptibility to visual illusions may be revealing about the learning involved in perception. Consider the Muller-Lyer illusion (Figure 5.2). The impression we get is that the line with the inward-pointing arrowheads is much longer than the line with the outward-pointing ones. In fact, measurement demonstrates that they are the same length. Susceptibility to this illusion can be demonstrated quite simply. Suppose the line with the outward pointing heads is a fixed length because the arrowheads cannot be moved. Adjacent to this vertical line is another one running parallel which in fact is much longer, though the bottoms of the two lines are in alignment. At the bottom of this line is an inward pointing arrowhead in fixed position. Now the subject is supplied with another inward pointing arrowhead which she is carefully to position at a point higher up on the line such that she is satisfied that the part of the vertical line between the two arrowheads is the same as that between the adjacent line with outward pointing heads. What we usually find is that people make the line between the inward pointing heads shorter than it ought to be because the illusion makes them think this line is longer than it really is. The difference between the length of this line and that of the adjacent line with outward pointing arrowheads can then serve as a measure of illusion strength.

Why are we susceptible to the Muller-Lyer illusion? According to Richard Gregory (1966), it is because the arrowheads, by their very shape, give perspective clues to depth (Figure 5.3). The outward-pointing heads make the line between appear to project towards us, as in the corner of a building. Because we perceive the line as being nearer, we wrongly compensate regarding its size, which makes us think it is smaller than it really is. The opposite effect occurs for the inward-pointing arrowheads.

According to Gregory, our susceptibility to the Muller-Lyer illusion is dependent on our exposure to straight edges and corners, which are in abundance in the

Figure 5.3:   Muller-Lyer lines superimposed on shapes that are common in our 'carpentered environment'

'carpentered' environment of the industrialized world, as he calls it. Gregory reasoned that in some cultures, in which straight edges and corners are uncommon, we may find that people are not so susceptible to the Muller-Lyer illusion. Gregory reports studies in which the illusion has been presented to hunter-gatherer tribes, whose environments contain few straight lines or corners. The findings suggest that the people of these tribes may well be less susceptible to the Muller-Lyer illusion than people brought up in a Western culture. This research serves as strong testimony to the role of learning in some aspects of perceptual organization.

Conclusion

The findings reported in this chapter serve as definitive evidence to the effect that William James was wrong. James suggested that the world of the newborn is a blooming buzzing confusion. Thanks to some excellent research, we now know that is untrue, and that in fact young babies can perform an astonishing range of perceptual feats. The newborn is capable of figure-ground perception, and perception of depth by other means, such as by expansion of the image of an object. The newborn appears to have the rudiments for a perception of faces, in the attraction that eyes hold for them. Young babies seem capable of size constancy, recognizing that an object is the same size, even though its retinal image changes with distance. They also seem to recognize an object as the same one, despite changes in orientation. In sum, the baby is equipped with a considerable range of basic perceptual abilities, which provides her with a potential to make sense of what she can see from a very early age.

However, it hardly need be said that perception is only possible with an environment to be perceived. Features of this environment, and one's particular experiences of it, could have an important bearing on some aspects of perception. There can be no doubt that much of the detail that we are able to perceive is dependent on our knowledge base, and therefore on our learning. Gregory's argument about the carpentered environment illustrates this point neatly. We can see, then, that being able to perceive as we do is influenced in a substantial way by both genetic and environmental factors.

Further Reading

Either of Bower's books will provide interesting reading. The first is pitched at a lower level. The second book is still highly readable, but is much heavier in detail.

BOWER, T.G.R. (1977) *A Primer of Infant Development*, San Francisco, W.H. Freeman and Company.

BOWER, T.G.R. (1982) *Development in Infancy*, 2nd ed., San Francisco, W.H. Freeman and Company.

Chapter 6

Language Development

Language is something we use to communicate. Many living things communicate with each other. For example, bees communicate the location of rich sources of pollen to other inhabitants of their hive with an elaborate 'dance'. Is this dance something we should call language? I think not, and prefer to reserve the term 'language' for the system of communication used by humans. Human language is similar to bee dancing in that both are tools of communication, but in other respects they are very different.

None of us can remember much about our first attempts to acquire our mother tongue. However, many of us have the experience of trying to learn a second language, and that gives us insight into the complexity of the grammar of language. It is sometimes said that the easiest way to acquire a second language is to pick up an extensive vocabulary of it. That may be a big help, but there can be no doubt that there is much more to language than simply knowing lots of words. Inside our heads, whether or not we realize it, there is a store of rules that governs the way in which we combine words, particularly with regard to the categories of words we choose to use in order to speak in sentences. Consider the two simple statements:

The dog chased the cat.

The cat chased the dog.

The words used in both are identical, yet each statement has a completely different meaning. To an alien visiting earth for the first time, it would not be at all obvious why one arrangement of a specific set of words had one meaning, whereas another arrangement of the same words meant something else. This simple example shows that sentence meaning amounts to more than the sum of the component words used in it. Meaning also depends on word order, which is governed by what we call grammar, a set of syntactic rules stored in our brain.

There is nothing inevitable about the particular rules we happen to use. It might have been that 'The dog chased the cat' referred to a scene in which it was the dog being pursued by the cat. In learning a second language, we find that some orderings of words turn out to be right, and others turn out to be wrong. It is not always obvious to us to begin with which will be the correct ordering and which incorrect. To know that, we have to get to grips with the rules of grammar of the language.

Bees, like humans, have rules of communication stored inside their brains. The rules are used to govern the way in which a communicating bee dances, and are used by the observing bees to interpret the dance in terms of navigation to a source of food. In the case of bees, the rules of communication are on the surface, and can be transcribed from the movements in the dance. The dance is little more than rules of communication. In contrast, human language involves both rules and *words* which are to be manipulated by those rules. Like bees, we use rules of language, but unlike bees we use these in conjunction with words to produce an infinite variety of sentences. This allows us to say virtually anything about anything. That is not true of bees, who have no equivalent to 'words'. Their more rigid system allows them only to communicate the whereabouts of food. The flexibility provided by the combination of grammatical rules and vocabulary affords a communication system that is the most powerful on earth.

Most 5-year-olds are highly competent users of language. If babies and young children can acquire language easily, then perhaps the rules of language are simple. That could not be further from the truth. To illustrate this point, once again consider the case of learning a foreign language. In most cases, this involves not just considerable exposure to the language, and practice at using it, but also tuition, even to degree level to gain what we might call a high level of competence. Even then, there is a big difference in the fluency of the person speaking a second language and one speaking his mother tongue. In educational circles learning a second language is considered intellectually demanding, just like learning high-level algebra. Bearing in mind this comparison, it seems remarkable that a child below the age of 5 picks up language with no effort on her part, and in the absence of formal tuition. Indeed, it would be difficult to prevent the child from acquiring language. Yet the idea of a young child learning complex algebra is unimaginable!

Another example provides further testimony to the difficulty involved in getting to grips with language other than one's mother tongue. This is the case of hieroglyphics. Hieroglyphics are the systems of writing involving stylized drawing found on tombs in such places as ancient Egypt, developed 5,000 to 2,000 years ago. These vaguely resemble the symbols found in travel brochures indicating the amenities of hotels and such places. Linguists, people highly educated in languages, spend decades trying to decipher hieroglyphics to understand how the language works and thus learn about the culture portrayed in them. Despite the considerable attention of highly trained experts, some hieroglyphics remain uninterpreted, demonstrating how elusive unfamiliar codes and grammar can be.

For these reasons, the child's acquisition of language presents us with an intriguing puzzle. The newborn lacks the scholarly intellect of the professional linguist or the university student studying a second language – indeed, she knows next to nothing about the world. In the face of this, it is miraculous that the young child is rapidly able to master her mother tongue, apparently with the greatest of ease, and with minimum effort.

Perhaps the young child does not need to acquire language at all; perhaps the rules for language are written into our genes, just as they are with bees. It cannot be the case that specific features of English, French, Chinese, etc. are written into the child's genes. If an English newborn were adopted into a Chinese family, there is no doubt that the child would acquire Chinese, equally well as a native Chinese child. Yet if the specific features of language were written into our genes, then we would find the English child reared in a Chinese family speaking English. This shows that in some sense language acquisition is dependent upon experience and the environment. To help unlock the mystery of language acquisition, let us begin by examining the way in which it proceeds.

A Description of Language Development

During the first month following birth, the baby uses its voice for little other than crying. Between about 1 and 8 months, the baby develops an increasing repertoire of vocalizations, including laughing and cooing. Until 8 months, the baby makes little other than vowel sounds, and a developing variety of pitch is noticeable during this period. Then, at about 8 months, the baby's vocalizations go through a sudden and radical alteration. One day the baby will begin babbling, and will continue doing so periodically from that moment on. The babbling is actually a combination of vowels with consonants, and sounds remarkably like speech, but without meaning.

There comes a point, perhaps two months after the first babbling, when the parents feel that some of the babbling is the baby's first words. Unlike the onset of babbling, it is hard to identify when it is appropriate to say that a babbling sound the baby makes is a word. To qualify as a word, the baby has to make a sound, or sequence of sounds reliably used in relation to a thing. The first words are typically names of things, used to point something out or to catch the adult's attention, for example, 'pussie' as the cat enters the room.

The expansion of vocabulary is slow to begin with. Although the baby may use one or two words at 12 months, by 18 months it is likely that she only has a repertoire of ten words. After this, she will undergo a rapid increase in vocabulary to approximately fifty words. Then by 24 months, the baby is likely to have a vocabulary of around 300 words. In most cases, these early words are nouns – the names of objects around them. Following this, vocabulary expansion is of astronomical magnitude, giving the average 6-year-old a repertoire of 14,000 words. The figures I present are averages, and there are many individual children who do not conform closely to this pattern. That does not necessarily mean there is anything amiss.

It is one thing for babies to use single words to refer to objects around them. It is quite something else for the child to use words in combination, that engender the kind of meaning you might find in a sentence. Yet babies succeed in conveying sentence-like meaning via combinations of single words and gestures prior to the multi-word stage. For example, the baby might say 'rattle', whilst at the same time grasping out in the general direction of the rattle. As parents we cannot help but interpret this as 'pass me the rattle'. These single-word gesture combinations, which embody sentence-like meaning, are known as 'holophrases'. Holophrases are characteristic of the baby in the second year of life. After this, the baby begins to use combinations of two, and then three and four words, making communication of the intended meaning not so highly dependent on gesture.

When the young child begins to use words in combination, we find that she has a very characteristic pattern of speech. For example, she might say 'Big doggie drink water', to mean 'The big dog drinks water', or 'The big dog is drinking water'. This style of early language is known as 'telegraphic speech' for obvious reasons. The child's telegraphic speech is highly ungrammatical in some respects. Many grammatical words are absent, such as 'the' and 'is'. Also, words are not adapted to form grammatically correct sentences. For example, the child says 'drink' instead of 'drinks'. However, in other respects, the young child does adhere to grammar, particularly with respect to word order. It is highly unlikely that the child would use a word order of the kind 'Drink water big doggie'. This shows that although young children have a lot to learn about the way in which words must be modified, according to grammatical tense and so on, they already possess the rudiments of a grammar of word ordering.

By the age of 3 years, the child's speech is less telegraphic. The child begins to acquire some of the finer points of grammar, reflected in the use of grammatical words. She also begins to alter words in order to indicate past tense. For example, whereas the younger child may have said 'Walk Mummy shop', the older child may form the correct sentence, 'I walked with Mummy to the shop'. Unlike the younger child, the older one has learned that a different form of the verb *to walk* is used for the past tense. Young children sometimes use irregular verbs correctly: 'I *ran* with Mummy to the shop'.

Beyond this point, however, the child's grammar seems to take a curious backward turn. It is common to find a 5-year-old who had a year previously said *ran* now saying *runned*. This phenomenon is known as 'over-regularization', where the child treats all verbs as regular, adding *ed* to the end in order to form the past tense. It seems that whereas the younger child had learned the past forms of verbs individually, the older child has discovered the *ed* rule of verbs and has applied that rule to form the past tense right across the board. The trouble is, as we all know, some verbs are irregular in this respect, with the result that the child says *runned* instead of *ran*. We have to wait a couple more years to find the child once again using irregular verbs correctly. Although over-regularization is a kind of error, it also shows that the child is acquiring the principles or rules of the grammar.

It takes many years for the child to acquire most of the subtleties of grammar, apart from failure to use irregular verbs correctly. The acquisition process can extend well into the school years. For example, it seems that not until age 8 or 9 do children have a good comprehension of passive sentences, such as 'John was hit by Mary'. Prior to this age, children hearing this sentence often have difficulty identifying whether it was John or Mary who did the hitting. Despite the continuing development of grammar at this older age, there can be no doubt that the biggest leaps in acquisition of grammar occur before the child is 5 years old.

The acquisition of grammar is only one aspect of language development. The child also has to learn the meaning of words, and a great deal of attention has been devoted to young children's developing use of nouns. Researchers have studied this in the hope that it might give insight into the relationship between cognitive development and language development. Nouns usually refer to a class of objects. Take the word *fish* as an example. This could be used to refer to cod, trout, pike, carp and so on. What is the essence of *fish*, if you like the rule that permits us to use this word in relation to certain creatures? Perhaps it would be: 'a creature that can swim and spends most of its time in water'. This definition will not do, since it would make dolphins fish, whereas in fact they are mammals. They breath air and do not lay eggs. Obviously, the definition of *fish* has to be more precise to prevent it from being over-inclusive. Perhaps we could add to the definition 'creature with scales, lays eggs, has gills'. However, this then presents a problem of under-inclusiveness. Loaches are fish, yet they do not have scales. Also, guppies are fish, yet they are live-bearers that give birth to baby fish rather than eggs. This example shows that when we use words correctly, we exhibit some understanding of the category of things included by that word, and by implication, the category of things excluded.

What we find in the case of children aged about 2 years is that they seem to err on the side of over-inclusiveness in their use of nouns. This phenomenon is known as 'overextension'. For example, in playing a ball game with the child, we may find that the child picks up the word *ball*, and uses it correctly in the context of the game. We may find subsequently that the child wrongly uses 'ball' to refer to the moon, eggs, round cakes and a miscellany of other rounded or spherical objects. In other situations, overextension can lead to amusing and embarrassing situations. The baby calls her father 'Daddy', but overextends and calls all men 'Daddy'. Suspicious expressions sometimes appear on faces of visitors to the household when the child calls the milkman 'Daddy'!

We could argue that overextension is at the same time illuminating about cognitive development and suggestive of it not being determined by language development. Perhaps it is illuminating about cognitive development in that it suggests young children understand their environment in terms of broad classes of things, and only later in development come to distinguish between subclasses of items. For example, maybe the young child is inclined to pick up the word ball in relation to any round or spherical object because she thinks of her environment in terms of broad categories such as 'round', 'square', 'living', 'big' and so on. This kind of cognition may then be reflected in the child's use of nouns, particularly in the error of overextension.

However, another side of the coin is that since young children clearly have a strong urge to communicate, combined with limited vocabulary for communicating about things, perhaps they use the best words at their disposal which gives rise to the impression that they overextend word categories. So, for example, the young child may well be aware that although the moon is like a ball in that it is circular, it is different in important ways: it is not possible to play 'piggy in the middle' with the moon, or to put it away in a toy cupboard. The child could recognize this, yet call the moon 'ball' for no other reason than that she does not know the word 'moon'. In that case, the phenomenon of overextension would not be revealing about a tendency to lump together things in broad categories, but instead would be a symptom of trying to make the best communicative use of a limited vocabulary. Therefore, all we can say is that as yet we do not know what the cognitive developmental implications are as regards the phenomenon of overextension.

Theories of Language Acquisition

So far we have been looking at the way the child's language development proceeds, which amounts to a description of what happens in language development. Now we come to the more tricky subject of how the child acquires language. Thirty years ago, the two main protagonists involved in this debate were B.F. Skinner and Noam Chomsky. Skinner took an extreme environmentalist position, while Chomsky took an extreme nativist position. Skinner's account had prevailed for some time, when Chomsky wrote an exposition which shattered Skinner's stronghold. Let us first take a brief look at Skinner's view of language development.

Skinner's view of language development is just one aspect of his general account of learning. It is based on the simple principle that behaviours which are rewarded are more likely to be produced in the future, whereas behaviour not rewarded, or behaviour which is followed by punishment, is less likely to be produced in the future. In ordinary parlance, 'reward' usually means money, sweets, or some other goody. Skinner means something much more general than this when he talks of reward. He means anything which happens to be gratifying to the individual.

Most of Skinner's research into learning was done with pigeons and rats, and in the light of his research, there can be little doubt that very nearly every action these animals make can be understood in terms of reward and punishment: behaviour which has pleasant consequences is likely to be repeated in the future, whereas behaviour which has unpleasant consequences is likely to be extinguished. Circus performers have impressed audiences for centuries with their enchanting control over animals, a control which arises from the careful administration of reward and punishment. Skinner himself has frequently demonstrated astonishing feats of control over animal behaviour. He trained pigeons to play the piano and to play games of table tennis. Skinner assumed that his principles of reward and punishment are universal principles of behaviour, and therefore could account for such things as human language development.

Skinner's view is not that parents know all about the principles of reward and punishment, and apply these to train the child to speak. Rather, the parent's excited reaction to the child's attempt at speech is rewarding to the child, so the parent unwittingly trains the child in the skill of language. Skinner's idea is that in a way, language development owes a great deal to serendipity.

Let us consider Skinner's view of language acquisition in a little more detail. When the baby makes a sound that is similar to a word, the proud parent exhibits joy, which is rewarding to the baby. The baby makes a similar sound shortly after, with the same reaction from the parent. Eventually, however, the word-like sound from the baby no longer excites the parent quite so much, and so her reaction diminishes. Then the baby happens to make another sound that is not just babble, but actually resembles a known word, such as *doggie*. Again the parent becomes excited, with rewarding consequences for the baby. Again, however, the sound the baby makes begins to lose its impact on the parent. When the baby makes that sound in the presence of a dog, then the parent's excitement is rekindled. When the baby says 'doggie' in the absence of the dog, it provokes less of a reaction in the parent, so the baby learns to say 'doggie' only in the presence of a dog. At this point, the parent may announce to friends and relations that her child knows the word for 'dog'.

In this way, the adult's rewarding reaction to the baby's babbling is such that it has the effect of shaping that babbling into speech. According to Skinner, that is all there is to language development. We might ask why animals do not speak, in that case. The answer is quite simple, according to Skinner: only humans, and perhaps parrots, have the appropriate vocal physiology to talk. In other words, animals would be perfectly capable of talking if they had the same throat and mouth as us.

On a superficial level, Skinner's account is highly appealing, but the results of studies on parental reaction to child speech show that it is wrong. The really big question is, does parental reward enable children to acquire the rules of grammar? Plainly, the answer is that the nature of parental reaction does not permit that. Brown and Hanlon (1970) observed parental reward and punishment following child speech, in the form of approval and disapproval, and found that there was negligible reaction to bad grammar. When children said such things as 'feets' and 'they sings', their parents did not disapprove, just as their parents did not approve when their children used correct grammar. In contrast, when children made factual errors in their speech, such as calling the moon a ball, then the parents offered a correction. In a nutshell, parents reacted to the meaning of what their children said, and overlooked the good or bad grammar their children used to express that meaning. Yet children's grammar continues to develop. For this reason, it becomes very hard to believe that the rewarding and punishing effects of parental reaction has much to do with their children's development of grammar.

In relation to all this, Chomsky comments that if Skinner's account were true, we would expect children to grow up speaking ungrammatically, but telling the truth – saying things which are factually accurate. Chomsky makes the comment that what we actually find is the opposite!

A second nail in Skinner's coffin comes from a study by Katherine Nelson (1985). She identified some parents who rewarded their children's good pronunciation and punished bad pronunciation, and found that these children had smaller vocabularies, compared with those who did not have such corrective or directive parents. This suggests that parental reward and punishment concerning certain aspects of language development could have indirect detrimental effects on other aspects of language development, namely vocabulary development.

Skinner's account is an extreme environmental one, in that it seeks to explain language development just by specifying things in the environment (parental reward and punishment). Skinner's particular environmental account, focusing on reward and punishment, appears to be unsatisfactory, but perhaps language development can be explained with reference to other environmental features. The most obvious feature in the environment likely to affect language development is the language of other people, particularly the parents. Given that the aural environment is suffuse with speech, why not suppose that the child simply imitates her parents, and acquires language via that process? In this way, the child's language is just a mirror of whatever happens to prevail in her linguistic environment. Presumably this is largely how parrots acquire their repertoire of words.

There can be no doubt that the child's imitation is an important factor in her language development. After all, children do speak the same language as their parents, rather than some other language. Moreover, they have the same accent as the parents, and many of the verbal mannerisms. Children can often be heard parroting words or sentences they hear, apparently for no other reason than the sheer pleasure of repetition for its own sake. Also, children who have a tendency to imitate others seem to acquire language more rapidly than those less likely to imitate (Bates *et al.*, 1982). The imitation in question is of a general nature (actions and gestures), but it is plausible to suggest that imitation specifically of the language of others accelerated the child's own language development. There are other interpretations of the link between imitation and accelerated language development. One is that those who imitate more are also more alert and attentive, and tend to develop any new skill more rapidly. In other words, instead of imitation causing rapid language development, both could be symptoms of a sagacious intellect.

Although imitation obviously does feature in language development, a very severe blow to environmental accounts has been dealt by Noam Chomsky (e.g. 1975): the child hears relatively few utterances; these are often grammatically imperfect; yet it is only a short period of time between the birth of the child, and the child using grammar. Apart from all this, language acquisition is universal amongst normal children, so it seems that no matter what the environment, language will be acquired. Indeed, it is difficult to imagine how we could prevent language development. This led Chomsky to conclude that language, or at least the important bits of language, have a big innate component.

Chomsky's Theory of Innate Language Development

What Chomsky needed to do was explain how it could be that even though different people speak different languages, depending on the culture in which they grew up, language is largely innate. To solve this problem, he suggested that there are two levels to language, the *surface structure* and the *deep structure*. The surface structure is the specific grammatical features of individual languages. The deep structure is the innate language, stored inside our brains, passed onto us through our genes. As such, this has a universal grammar, possessed by all humans. The universal grammar works on the level of grammatical subject and object, according to Chomsky. His claim is that subject and object relations in all human languages are the same, a claim which nobody has ever disputed to my knowledge.

Chomsky argues that babies are equipped with a 'language acquisition device', which identifies the specific features of the grammar of a language, and translates these into the innate deep structure. According to Chomsky, the idea of an innate deep structure, based on grammatical subject and object, casts a whole new light on the mystery of babies being able to master such a complex ability as language. The reason babies find it so easy to acquire language, according to this view, is that the rudiments of the language already exist inside their brains.

Chomsky further suggests that there is an innate grammatical mechanism which can translate one grammatical form into another. For example, we can change a sentence from active voice to passive:

'John hit Roger.' → 'Roger was hit by John.'

Chomsky suggests that these relations between subject (John) and object (Roger) are stored in the deep structure, and they can be translated into various surface structure forms by a mechanism that Chomsky called 'transformational grammar'.

Chomsky's theory is philosophical rather than psychological. In other words, Chomsky is not engaged in a programme of research studying children acquiring language, but instead reasons about how language acquisition is likely to take place. It is difficult to envisage how anyone could identify evidence which would show grammar has an innate component, but Goldin-Meadow and Mylander (1990) have sought to do just that. They studied a group of unfortunate children aged approximately 3 years who were born deaf, and received no language tuition of any kind – whether oral or gestural. These researchers wanted to know whether the children would display any of the rudiments of language in the gestural system they developed spontaneously.

We can say with some confidence to begin with that the very fact that the children were so willing to attempt communication through gestures shows that they were born with an inclination to communicate. However, as we have already discussed, mere communication does not necessarily count as language. What we look for is evidence of grammar. Was there any grammatical pattern to the gestures used by the children?

Anyone not acquainted with sign language may view this as a peculiar question, but it is not. Deaf people without speech who use a formal gestural code to communicate combine gestural units as 'words' according to rules of grammar to form 'sentences', and for this reason we can say that such languages are every bit as deserving of that label as are spoken languages. What about Goldin-Meadow and Mylander's (1990) children? Did their gesture combinations conform to any word order rule? It was certainly the case that the children used gestures to name things, and therefore, their gestures qualified as words. Also, they used gestures in combination, and these did appear in certain orders rather than others.

A common-sense explanation for this is that perhaps the children's parents provided the initiative, by generating gestures for their children to imitate in the first place, and in terms of using gestures in certain combinations. However, Goldin-Meadow and Mylander (1990) rule this out, and report that it was the children who pioneered the gestures and the gesture combinations, and the parents followed suit. Goldin-Meadow and Mylander conclude that their findings show that children are born with an appetite for communication, and that they know via their genes that communication is formed from patterns of units of meaning.

Goldin-Meadow and Mylander's (1990) study provides evidence in support of Chomsky's view that language has an innate basis. Despite this, it falls short of demonstrating that we have an innate deep structure based on subject-verb-object relations, or demonstrating that we are genetically equipped with a language acquisition device. The point is that language is something that develops in the child over a period of time, and learning must be involved since the child speaks the particular tongue of her parents. Is it the case, as Chomsky claims, that the learning involved is controlled by genetic factors?

The account Chomsky presents is frequently very technical, and often esoteric. That said, it is not necessary to grasp all the details of his idea about innate features of language development in order to assess whether such strong emphasis on innate factors is warranted. In claiming that language acquisition is largely determined by innate factors, Chomsky implies that language acquisition benefits little from whatever might go on in the environment: the environment is largely irrelevant in this respect. Putting it that way, perhaps it is useful to take a second look at what goes on in the environment. We might find that there is little in the environment that could be beneficial to language acquisition, which is what we would expect from the point of view of Chomsky's theory. Alternatively, perhaps we will find that there are ways in which the environment could be highly profitable for the process of language acquisition. If so, that might be sufficient to persuade us that it is the environment that is most important in language acquisition, rather than innate factors.

A Second Look at the Environment

The business about reward and punishment determining language acquisition is unacceptable, but let us take another look at the influence parents might have. Chomsky argued that the language babies are exposed to is often degenerate, in other words, grammatically poor. He uses this argument to convince us that parental speech is of little help to the child's language acquisition. In fact, this seems to be far from the truth, as Catherine Snow has pointed out (e.g. Snow and Ferguson, 1977). When speaking to babies and young children, adults usually speak shorter and simpler sentences. These typically have simpler grammar, and are more likely to be grammatically correct, compared with speech to other adults. Adult talk to babies and young children is generally slower, with longer pauses at the end of each sentence. The talk is nearly always about concrete things which are present, and therefore which the child can see. Also, the pattern of adult speech seems to be well tailored to the child's linguistic level. As the child speaks longer and more complex sentences, so the adult talks to the child in a more mature manner. It seems that the adult usually pitches her speech at a slightly more advanced level than the child's. This distinctive style of adult speech to children is known as 'motherese', not because it is used exclusively by mothers, but because mothers are usually caregivers of babies and young children, and therefore the ones who use this style most.

As I said before, without studying what goes on in homes, Chomsky presumed that babies are subjected to 'degenerate' language. However, researchers who have visited homes and observed parental speech have found that is not so. On the contrary, motherese seems to be an ideal form of speech for introducing the baby to language. This raises the possibility that the measures taken by parents regarding the linguistic environment of the home, whether or not they know it, might be instrumental in the child's language development. So although Skinner's account about reward and punishment is obviously not viable, other features of the environment could be crucial for language acquisition.

In an excellent book, Jerome Bruner (1983) has detailed a theoretical framework which suggests how the home environment might contribute not just to language development, but to culture acquisition. Bruner views language development as a part of the overall culture transmission from parents to children. He calls this a 'language acquisition support system' (LASS) to contrast it with Chomsky's 'language acquisition device' (LAD).

Bruner proposes that we should think of the psychological environment in the home as a supportive edifice of 'scaffolding'. The scaffolding supports the child initially, and is then removed piece by piece as the child develops and becomes more able to stand alone. People often use the phrase 'stand alone' in an emotional context, but here I use it in a cognitive sense: as the child gets a cognitive grasp of the environment, particularly the prevailing language, the parent withdraws the scaffolding which has been supporting the child's intellect, thereby allowing him to become more cognitively independent. An example of this in motherese is that parents speak in longer and more complex sentences to their child as the child's language develops and becomes more sophisticated. As the child develops, parents gradually withdraw the linguistic support they provide.

Bruner also lays emphasis on the fact that the child must be strongly motivated to acquire the rules of grammar, since that provides the key to communication, and therefore provides a means to fulfil his desires. If the child wishes to eat, play, use the potty, and so on, it is much easier to communicate these things if he can express his meaning in a way that can be understood by the parents. The most efficient way to do that is by using grammar.

In this respect, Bruner's analysis helps us to view language development in a completely different light, compared with Chomsky's approach. The impression we get from Chomsky's view of language development is that of a computer having a program loaded into it, detached from the environment and completely in isolation. This is nothing like what goes on in language acquisition. Language is acquired in an environment in which the child's well-being is greatly aided by having a channel of communication – namely, language.

Conclusion

Although children may be born with the knowledge that communication takes place via patterned units of meaning, as yet no one has shown that most aspects of language acquisition are dependent upon a specific innate process or mechanism. Indeed, it may never be possible to show this, and it may always remain that we have to juggle with ideas to help determine the contributions of heredity and environment.

What I would like to suggest is that looking at motherese, and coupling what we know about that with Bruner's theory of scaffolding, it is plausible to suppose that grammar acquisition is much the same as other aspects of culture acquisition. In other words, there is no need to think that there might be an innate language acquisition device. In that case, why did Chomsky's theory ever seem so appealing?

Perhaps its appeal came from a peculiarity in the development of the two disciplines of linguistics and psychology. Prior to Chomsky, the dominant account of learning was Skinner's theory about reward and punishment. Because that could not explain language acquisition adequately, it gave Chomsky's theory a niche to provide an explanation on innate grounds. That is, perhaps Chomsky's strength lay largely in Skinner's weakness. Now that we have a better environmental account, perhaps there is no longer reason to think that innate factors feature quite so prominently in language acquisition.

What I have suggested may be a little glib, giving the impression that we have now solved the mystery of language acquisition. That is not true, and a considerable amount of research is needed in order to arrive at a more complete picture. However, perhaps the progress which has been made in recent years suggests that the best way to proceed, in unlocking the puzzle of language acquisition, is in terms of research examining environmental influences.

Further Reading

In my opinion, the most enjoyable, well written account of language acquisition can be found in Bruner's book.

BRUNER, J.S. (1983) *Child's Talk: Learning to Use Language*, Oxford, Oxford University Press.

A very good basic account of the nativist position can be found in the following text, which is notable for its amusing prose.

AITCHISON, J. (1989) *The Articulate Mammal*, 3rd ed., London, Unwin Hyman.

Chapter 7

The Development of
Verbal Communication

Without reflection, we may think that language and communication are the same thing. That is not true. There are many ways of communicating without using verbal language. One way is with gestures. Deaf people use a system of gestures which qualifies as language. However, this is not the only way of communicating with gestures, and we all frequently convey meaning with gestures which do not qualify as language. For example, we may put a thumb up to signify approval, or show two fingers if we wish to be rude. These gestures do not form part of a language because, unlike sign language, they do not have any rules of grammar to govern the organization of units of meaning. To put it simply, you could not string together these informal gestures to make a sentence, whereas you could do that with the gestures of true sign language.

Nevertheless, it is possible to convey meaning very effectively with informal gestures. A thumb up or two fingers could leave the recipient in no doubt about what it is you wish to communicate to him. It is possible to communicate even more information more efficiently with verbal language, but it does not necessarily follow that one who is skilled at using the rules of grammar to form sentences, and has an extensive vocabulary, will automatically be skilled at communicating the appropriate meaning to a listener.

Consider the case of people with autism. They are well known for having great difficulty with communication. In cases of profound autism, there may be little or no communication. In less severe cases, the person with autism could have considerable mastery over language, yet have great difficulty with conveying meaning in speech. Uta Frith (1989) cites the case of a teenage boy who, on a request from his mother to go out and get some cloves, because she was short of them, promptly went to a dress shop and purchased a variety of women's clothes!

According to Frith, failures of communication in people with autism are rife because such people find it very difficult to infer others' intentions, due to a lack of theory of mind. Presumably, a normal teenage boy would recognize that it was not appropriate for him to go out buying his mother clothes (unless the mother was disabled) and therefore would recognize that she must have intended something different. Perhaps the normal helpful teenager would have requested clarification, or reflected a little, and discovered that his mother really wanted a flavouring for food which has a name that closely resembles 'clothes'.

The communication difficulty people with autism experience raises the possibility that normal young children will have great difficulty with communication, prior to their theory of mind being well developed. The point here is that verbal communication is as much reliant upon having some kind of theory or ideas about people's intentions, what is going on inside their heads as they speak, as it is to do with knowing how to string together words in a grammatical way.

This ability, to make inferences about others' intentions, is important both in speaking and in listening. I have already illustrated how problems might arise for a listener who is ineffective at assessing others' minds, with the case of the teenager with autism. Assessing minds is at least as important when speaking. Anyone who has had a telephone conversation with a 5-year-old will appreciate the point. The young child often talks on the phone as though he presumes that his listener shares a visual experience with him. The child might say, 'I got this for my birthday. It opens there and things come out, and goes along and there's a light here....' If we could see the toy the child was talking about, no doubt it would become clear what opens, what things come out and so on. The trouble is, the young child seems to talk on the phone as though we can see what he can see. Again, this appears to be a symptom of young children failing to take into account the minds of their listeners.

Jean Piaget noted the curious form of child speech, and characteristically viewed it as a symptom of egocentrism, perhaps the most obvious symptom. Piaget's use of 'egocentrism' means 'failure to take into account views of the world other than one's own'. The case of the young child speaking on the phone serves as a good example of what Piaget had in mind, with the child apparently failing to take into account the fact that the listener cannot see what he can see.

Piaget divided egocentric speech into three categories, as follows:

(i) *Repetition.* Young children sometimes repeat sentences or phrases immediately after someone else has spoken them, so the child's voice acts as an echo. There is no apparent reason why the child repeats the utterance, and it seems to be a case of repetition for its own sake. The meaning of the utterance seems to be irrelevant, and indeed often is of no importance so far as the child is concerned.

(ii) *Individual monologue.* Piaget observed children who thought they were alone engaged in some activity (in fact they were being observed by Piaget). He noticed that younger ones sometimes made a running commentary on what they were doing, as though thinking aloud. In fact, this is an experience familiar to all of us: sometimes adults talk aloud when tackling a taxing problem. Piaget's point seemed to be that this phenomenon was particularly common in the case of young children.

(iii) *Collective monologue.* Piaget suggests that the child may intend to communicate information to others in the group, but the egocentric nature of his speech prevents anyone else being able to grasp the meaning. Piaget portrays the idea of a group of children all talking, but none understanding what anybody else says. It is not possible to grasp the meaning because the child does not elaborate it sufficiently to allow

Figure 7.1: The communication game devised by Krauss and Glucksberg

that, in much the same way that the child speaking on the telephone fails in the example given above. Piaget claimed that approximately 30 to 40 per cent of 5-year-olds' speech is in the category of collective monologue.

Since Piaget's writings, a considerable amount of research has been undertaken in order to make a systematic examination of young children's communication abilities. This research set out to investigate whether it really is appropriate to suppose, as Piaget did, that when young children speak they take no account of the communicative requirements of their listeners, in a characteristically egocentric manner.

Krauss and Glucksberg (1969) paved the way with their pioneering research. They designed a game which requires a great deal of explicit communication. The game involves two players, one of whom takes the role of speaker, while the other acts as listener (Figure 7.1). The two players sit at opposite sides of a table which is divided in the middle by a wooden screen. The two players are opposite each other, but cannot see each other because of the screen. The speaker is supplied with a dispenser, which issues forth six blocks, one at a time. Each block has an abstract line design on it. The listener, meanwhile, has an identical set of six blocks, not in a dispenser, but spread out before her. The aim of the game is for the speaker to describe each block as it comes from the dispenser in such a way that the listener can select a matching one from her set.

Children aged between 5 and 10 years participated in the experiment. They had no difficulty understanding the instructions, and were perfectly happy to play the game. The findings were that at first all children in the role of speaker, irrespective of age, had difficulty describing the designs in a way that allowed their listener to choose the matching block from her set. However, on successive attempts, a substantial difference in the abilities of children above and below the age of about 6 years became evident. Older children were very successful with practice, frequently giving descriptions that enabled listeners to choose the correct block. In contrast, the young children continued with idiosyncratic descriptions, which meant little to their listeners. For example, on looking at one design, a 5-year-old said, 'Daddy's shirt.' On seeing the next, the child said, 'Another one of Daddy's shirts.' Although this child could imagine some kind of resemblance between the designs and her father's shirts, the descriptions were completely use-less as an aid to the listener's selection. Krauss and Glucksberg's findings offered support for Piaget's suggestion that young children are poor at communication because they are insensitive to the communicative needs of their listeners; appar-ently, Krauss and Glucksberg had identified a case of egocentric communication.

Since that early work, many researchers have set out to investigate whether young children are totally insensitive to their listeners, or whether they sometimes alter their speech according to the requirements of the listener. This research generated a substantial number of findings, suggesting that young children do modify their speech according to the needs of the listener, giving the impression that their communication was not plagued with egocentrism. What follows is a couple of examples of that research.

Shatz and Gelman (1973) allowed 4-year-olds to play with a novel toy, and then asked them to explain how it worked either to an adult, or to a 2-year-old. The 4-year-olds communicated in a very different way when addressing the 2-year-old rather than the adult. When speaking to 2-year-olds, they used shorter and simpler sentences. Also, they took more care to make sure the 2-year-old was looking at the appropriate part of the toy when they were giving the explanation.

Another study found much the same. Menig-Peterson (1975) staged an acci-dent, witnessed by 3- and 4-year-old children. An adult who was serving drinks of orange to the children clumsily spilt one of the cups and made a mess. The exper-imenter then involved the children in a cleaning-up operation. The following week, an adult interviewed each of the children, and asked them about the events of the accident. This adult was either the one who had spilt the drink, and therefore had witnessed it also, or a person who had not witnessed the scene. Menig-Peterson noticed that these young children provided the adult who had not witnessed the accident with detailed descriptions. In contrast, they were not nearly so explicit when relating the event to the adult who was at the scene of the accident.

Far from being insensitive to the requirements of their listeners, these findings show that young children are capable of tailoring their speech to the needs of their listeners. When speaking to younger children, 4-year-olds seemed to recognize that care was needed to speak in a simple way, otherwise the 2-year-old would not understand. Also, they seemed to realize that more detailed information was in order when relating an event to someone who knew nothing about that event. These findings seem to fly in the face of the claim that young children are egocentric in their communication.

At this point we seem to have a contradiction. On the one hand, Piaget's observations, coupled with the findings of Krauss and Glucksberg, suggest that young children are negligent when it comes to communicating effectively, as though they fail to adapt their language to the requirements of the listener. On the other hand, more recent findings show that young children can tailor their speech to the needs of the listener. How can we reconcile these two conflicting sets of findings?

A study by Sonnenschein (1986) seems to provide the answer. The children she tested formed two age groups, 6-year-olds and 9-year-olds. She showed the children a set of ten drawings of toys, which included a spinning-top, a wagon train and a sledge, and asked them to describe one of them so that another child would know which one she meant. The 'other child' was either the speaker child's best friend, or an unfamiliar child. Sonnenschein assumed that people tend to communicate with more explicit detail when speaking to an unfamiliar person, rather than when speaking to a close friend. She wanted to know if this kind of sensitivity to the listener would be evident in children's descriptions of the pictures.

In one respect, Sonnenschein's findings were consistent with those from the earlier studies carried out by Shatz and Gelman (1973) and Menig-Peterson (1975): children in both age groups gave more information about the picture they were thinking about when the listener was an unfamiliar person rather than their best friend. In another respect, the findings were consistent with those of Piaget and of Krauss and Glucksberg: there was an important difference in the quality of the information provided by the two age groups. The information given by 9-year-olds was specific to the picture they were thinking about and none other, whereas the information given by 6-year-olds very often could have referred to any of the pictures. For example, 6-year-olds might have said 'it's something you play with', 'you can get it from the shop', etc. This information could have applied to any of the items in the pictures. In contrast, 9-year-olds might have said 'it's got wheels', 'it's red', etc. thus providing specific information which enabled the listener to single out the particular card she was thinking about.

From these findings, the following preliminary conclusion seems to be in order. Young children appear to understand that they should alter their speech to satisfy the specific needs of different listeners. Sometimes this leads to effective communication, as in the case of 4-year-old speech to 2-year-olds. However, it seems that up to the age of about 6 years, children might find it difficult to understand the relationship between the information in the message and the understanding of the listener. In particular, they seem not to grasp that in order to help the listener comprehend, the information in the message has to be specific to the item they are thinking about, and only to that item.

Recent research I have been involved in has probed young children's understanding of the communicative value of messages using another procedure (Mitchell, Munno and Russell, 1991). We read stories to children depicting events in which it was made explicit that a speaker protagonist had given an inaccurate description to a listener. In one scene, for example, a customer (the listener) was in a supermarket looking for the manager. She asked a shop assistant (the speaker) who he was, and the shop assistant commented (the message) that he was the man standing over there holding the pen. Children had been told earlier that in fact it was a pencil the manager was holding. In this case, the description was inaccurate (pen instead of pencil) but it was only mildly discrepant, and we could suppose that the listener would know who the manager was after hearing this. Under two other conditions, the description was grossly discrepant (man holding a sack of potatoes) or perfectly accurate.

Five-year-olds frequently judged that the listener knew who the manager was after hearing a mildly discrepant description, and curiously they judged likewise after hearing a grossly discrepant one. Nine-year-olds, in contrast, judged that the listener knew who the manager was less frequently when the description was grossly discrepant. This finding is what we might have predicted from Sonnenschein's (1986) research, that young children lack understanding of the relationship between the communicative value of the message and the listener's understanding. However, another of our findings suggests that Sonnenschein's view of things may require modification. Although 5-year-olds frequently judged that the listener knew following a discrepant message, they judged that the listener knew even more frequently when the message was perfectly accurate. This shows that although they do not presume that a discrepant message would necessarily pose an impediment to listener comprehension, they recognize that it would be more likely to pose an obstacle than a perfectly correct message. Therefore, they obviously have some conception of the relationship between communicative value of the message and listener understanding.

Regarding young children's difficulty with communication, Elizabeth Robinson (e.g. Robinson and Whittaker, 1987), one of the most eminent researchers in this area, urges us to think of them as failing to recognize the clue-like characteristics of verbal messages. The speaker wishes to communicate something to a listener about an idea in her head, or about something in the world, and she uses verbal messages to provide the listener with clues about it. That is, the message is *merely* a clue, which may or may not furnish the listener with adequate understanding, depending on how good a clue the message is. According to Robinson, young children have difficulty understanding this.

Robinson shows how young children's non-understanding about the clue-like characteristics of messages is manifest in a variety of ways. First, children below approximately 6 years judge ambiguous messages to be good and informative. She showed children three men, two of whom were wearing hats, and told the children that she was thinking about one of the men, and he was wearing a hat. Children then had to judge whether she had told them enough, in order to pick out the correct man. Those below around 6 years selected one of the men wearing hats, and judged that she had told enough (i.e. that her message was good). Those above this age said they did not know which man she meant, and that she had not told enough because she did not say which of the two men wearing hats she was thinking about. This is a highly reliable phenomenon, and it is very likely that you will find that any young children you know will judge an ambiguous message to be adequate for communication.

You might feel that the young children judged Robinson's ambiguous message adequate not because of failure to recognize the communicative inadequacy of ambiguous messages, but because they thought it would be inappropriate to call into question an adult's ability to communicate effectively. This alternative explanation can be rejected, however, since young children judged ambiguous messages to be adequate even when they were inadvertently generated by the child herself or by a puppet.

Robinson also engaged children in a communication game, similar to that devised by Krauss and Glucksberg. In this game the two players had identical sets of play people, and experimenter and child took turns at describing one of the play people so that the listener could choose the identical play person in his or her own set. As in Krauss and Glucksberg's game, the players had to rely on verbal communication because a wooden screen prevented each player from seeing which play person the other had chosen. Occasionally, on removal of the screen, it turned out that the two players had selected different play people because the message had been ambiguous. Sometimes it was the experimenter who gave an ambiguous message (on purpose, though the child did not know that), and sometimes it was the child. On these occasions, Robinson asked the children whose fault it was that they had chosen different play people. Children below around 6 years judged it was the listener's fault on the grounds that she had chosen the wrong one. Children above that age judged it was the speaker's fault for failing to be more precise with her message. It never made any difference whether the speaker was the adult experimenter or the child. Again, this finding seems to show that young children do not understand how an ambiguous message can lead to communication failure. The finding is consistent with the idea that young children have difficulty viewing messages as merely clues to meaning.

Clearly young children do understand that messages have to be relevant to the thing they purport to communicate about. If the experimenter says she has selected the man, when in fact she has selected the horse, young children will judge that the message is inadequate. This is similar to our (Mitchell, Munno and Russell, 1991) finding that young children correctly judge that accurate messages are more likely to result in successful communication than discrepant ones. Therefore, their difficulty in the case of ambiguous messages is in judging when a relevant message is sufficiently precise to allow selection of an item in a set with 100 per cent certainty. Perhaps judgments that ambiguous messages are adequate is part of a more general tendency in young children to overestimate their own comprehension or knowledge of things.

In more recent research, conducted in collaboration with myself (Mitchell and Robinson, 1990, 1992; Robinson and Mitchell, 1990), Robinson has investigated the features of children's overestimation of their own knowledge. We showed children a set of five pictures of unfamiliar cartoon characters, and then asked them if they could pick out 'Murkor', an invented name which obviously was unfamiliar to the children. Children of around 6 years and below needed no further encouragement to choose one of the pictures. After that, we asked them if they knew that their chosen picture was Murkor. These young children were more likely to say that they did know, compared with older ones.

This finding came as no surprise to teachers, who had many experiences of their young children saying that they knew when in fact they did not. The next task was to find out why the children said they knew. Presumably, we adults would say 'don't know' on the grounds that we had no prior experience of Murkor, and therefore could not know which one he was. Apparently, young children based their judgment on a different criterion. We asked children if they knew who Murkor was in the absence of the set of pictures. This time, they frequently judged that they did not know. This led us to conclude that the children realized that they had no prior experience of Murkor, but judged that they knew when the set of cartoon characters was present according to the criterion that they could choose one of the pictures. We suggested that children felt that providing they could choose a picture, all was well, and judged that they knew on that basis.

In the case of ambiguous messages, being able to choose an item may exert a similar influence on young children's judgments. Providing the message is relevant to items in the set, they will find that they can choose one of them, and derive confidence from that fact. As a consequence, they may feel that all is well with the message, and that they have chosen correctly. In contrast, we adults might feel that it is necessary to scrutinize the message for unfamiliar words, like 'Murkor', or for ambiguities, and feel uncertain about our comprehension if we detect any such problems. Putting it another way, we adults treat the message as a clue to correct meaning, and in so doing we make a distinction between what the speaker means and what she says.

If we do not distinguish what the speaker means from what she says, then this would be an impediment to successful communication: instead of analyzing the message, children may feel that they understand just because they can do something, such as select an item from a set. This possibility has prompted researchers to investigate more directly whether young children draw the say-mean distinction. Beal and Flavell (1984) attempted just this with a task in which children tried to detect problems with messages which were either ambiguous or unambiguous. Six- and 7-year-olds listened to a tape recording of a nursery-age child, called Sheri. Child listeners were told that Sheri frequently made mistakes, and did not say things clearly, and that the children's job was to spot when they could not understand exactly what Sheri meant. The children looked at a selection of paintings, supposedly done by Sheri. Sheri's tape-recorded voice then gave a 'clue' to inform the child which of the pictures she (Sheri) had selected. She said, 'I've picked the one made with paint.' This was ambiguous, because all the pictures were made with paint. Many of the children tested were old enough to recognize that Sheri had not said enough, and that they could not tell which picture she meant.

However, in another similar attempt at the game, the experimenter pointed to the picture Sheri had chosen, as the tape recorder played her message. This time, children heard an ambiguous message, but knew Sheri's intended meaning thanks to the experimenter's help. Under this condition, children often said that Sheri had told them enough to identify the picture she meant. Beal and Flavell suggested that when children knew Sheri's intended meaning, because they were unable to draw the say-mean distinction, they fixated on this, and as a result were unable to analyze Sheri's message for problems.

My research in collaboration with James Russell (Mitchell and Russell, 1989, 1991) suggests young children sometimes do make the say-mean distinction, but find it very difficult to know when there is a difference between what is said and what is meant. In our study, children listened to stories about a girl called Mary who asked John to fetch her reading book. She gave a description of the book, including a comment that it had a picture of a dog on the cover. We then told the children either that Mary had a really good memory for things, or that she had a really bad memory for things. In the story, John subsequently went to look for the book, and found one that conformed to Mary's description in every detail, except that it had a picture of a cat on the front, rather than a dog. We then asked children if this was the book Mary had intended. Even 5-year-olds judged just as much as older children that this book with the cat on the cover was the one that Mary intended. They seemed to understand that what Mary had said (book with dog on the cover) was not what she intended (book with cat on the cover), and as such it seems that they were making the say-mean distinction.

However, in another respect, these young children differed greatly from older ones. When the story reported that Mary had a very good memory for things, 9-year-olds usually judged that the book John found with a cat on the cover was not the one Mary intended. When the story reported that Mary had a bad memory, they judged that it was the one Mary intended. These older children seemed to understand that if Mary's memory is bad, then she is likely to get the details of the reading book wrong, and so the one John found with the cat on the cover is really the one she intended. Five-year-olds, in contrast, were not influenced by information about Mary's memory. So although they often seemed to understand that what Mary meant was not what she had said, they appeared not to understand the connection between Mary having a bad memory and Mary giving wrong details about the reading book. In other words, they seemed to be unclear about precisely when there was a difference between what Mary had said and what she had meant.

This study demonstrates that young children have considerable difficulty in understanding the implications of bad memory in the speaker in relation to the accuracy of the speaker's description, but suggests that they can be aware of the communicative intent of the speaker over and above the meaning of her message. With a new procedure, we have now shown that even 3-year-olds are capable of this distinction (Robinson and Mitchell, 1992). We acted out a scene with two play people, one representing a girl called Jane, and the other representing her Mum. The story was set in Jane's living room. Mum was tidying the contents of two drawers, one with a red front and the other with a blue front. Mum placed one bag of material (bag A) into the red drawer, and another bag of different material (bag B) into the blue drawer. Mum then went away into another room. In Mum's absence, Jane got the bags out and played with them. The trouble was that she got them mixed up and swapped them as a consequence. So she put B into the red drawer and A into the blue one.

Later, Mum was doing some sewing when she discovered that she needed a little more material to finish the job. In fact, no material was in view, and children had to engage in make-believe. We stressed that it was very important Mum got the right kind of material. She called through to Jane, and asked her to get her the bag in the red drawer. We then asked observing children which bag Mum really wanted, the one in the red drawer or the one in the blue drawer. Now we know that Mum really wanted the bag in the blue drawer because we know that the bag she thought was in the red drawer was really in the blue one. The 3-year-olds we tested exhibited an astonishing amount of insight into the scenario, and a good many of them judged correctly that Mum really wanted the bag in the blue drawer.

A competing explanation for the finding is that the children did not really follow the story at all, and sometimes said 'blue' simply because they had not listened to Mum's message properly. In other words, they may have given the right answer for the wrong reason. Fortunately, we were able to rule out this explanation by having another condition in which after playing with the bags, Jane replaced them in the drawers Mum had put them in originally. Under this condition, children had no difficulty in judging correctly that Mum really wanted the bag in the red drawer, as she had said. Therefore, the confusion explanation will not do, because it would have predicted that sometimes children would have judged 'blue' even when Jane had restored the bags as Mum had left them.

This study demonstrates unequivocally that even 3-year-olds can grasp the distinction between meaning conveyed by a message and the real intention of the speaker over and above that. Consequently, we can say without hesitation that although young children experience difficulty with some aspects of communication, as documented in the studies reported above, these difficulties are not due to a complete inability to distinguish message meaning from intended meaning.

Regarding young children's problems with communication, research reported here shows that they require much more besides grammar and vocabulary. What they also grasp during the early school years is the basic skills of communication, part of which involves conceptualizing messages as clues to meaning. This understanding underpins the child's formation of good messages, or in Piaget's terminology, non-egocentric speech. It also allows the child to analyze messages she hears in order to assess whether she can be confident in her comprehension of what the speaker intended.

It seems appropriate to think there is a link between communication and theory of mind. Good communication requires an understanding of the way verbal messages affect the contents of the listener's mind (Mitchell *et al.*, 1991). Also, accurate judgments about one's own comprehension involve a good awareness of one's own mind. However, Piaget's view was that the poor communication of young children is a symptom of egocentrism. There is some similarity between the claim that young children are egocentric and the claim that they lack a mature theory of mind. Therefore, is it appropriate to say that young children's poor communication amounts to egocentrism?

Probably not, because the term 'egocentrism' as used by Piaget carries with it the implication that poor communication abilities in young children are just one manifestation of a more general stage of egocentrism that children pass through. In other words, the implication is not that poor communication is due to a lack of certain experiences specific to communication, but rather that, irrespective of the child's experiences, his speech will be egocentric if he is in the stage of egocentrism. Was Piaget right in this respect?

Other work by Robinson (Robinson and Robinson, 1981) suggests Piaget was wrong. Robinson assessed children's ability to detect the problem with ambiguous messages, and then observed the children communicating with their mothers at home. Mothers usually know what their children mean, no matter how poor the communication. This is evident from the fact that even though the child's teacher and classmates may not understand what he says, the mother nearly always does. Despite this, in some households, Robinson found that mothers refused to hazard a guess at what their children meant when the communication was poor. These mothers told their children that they had not spoken clearly enough, and that it was impossible to understand what they meant. Robinson discovered that children who had this kind of mother were much better at communicating in a non-egocentric manner, and also were better at judging ambiguous messages to be inadequate. This strongly suggests that it is children's specific communication experiences that is responsible for their poor communication abilities, rather than a general stage of egocentrism, contrary to Piaget's claim.

Conclusion

The findings from research on children's communication can seem rather confusing on the face of things. Some findings suggest young children lack a certain skill or understanding, whereas others suggest the opposite. Let us see if we can come up with some clear conclusions. For a start, I think we can say with confidence that it is inappropriate to attribute young children's communication problems to egocentrism. First, the idea of a stage of egocentrism has now been discredited, and second, Robinson's findings suggest poor child communication is related with home experience rather than with a general cognitive stage.

Having said that, it is apparent that young children are poor at communication compared with older ones. Even though they adapt their speech to the requirements of the listener, this could be due to a general strategy they have learned to deploy, rather than to a good understanding of the relationship between the communicative value of the message and listener comprehension. Sonnenschein's (1986) research suggests as much. However, it could be that it is not so much that young children are completely lacking in understanding of the relationship between message adequacy and listener comprehension. My research (Mitchell *et al.*, 1991) suggests that while 5-year-olds are lacking in some respects, at least they have an incipient conception of this relationship.

Finally, turning to young children's understanding of the distinction between what is said and what is meant, we now know that even 3-year-olds understand speaker intent over and above the meaning conveyed by the words of the message (Robinson and Mitchell, 1992). Nonetheless, it seems children continue beyond this age to develop in their understanding about the relationship between what is said and what is meant, given the findings of Beal and Flavell (1984) and Mitchell and Russell (1989). So although it may look as though there is contradiction in the findings on the face of things, in fact there is not. The apparent contradiction is eradicated simply by accepting that development is not an all or nothing phenomenon, and that instead it takes place gradually: 3-year-olds grasp the rudiments of the say-mean distinction, but only after another few years do they acquire the concept in a more elaborate form.

Further Reading

The book I recommend is not a broader review of the literature than the one I present here, but rather is a different kind of text. It is a detailed study of communication in nursery school children, written in a way that makes it understandable to a reader with no background knowledge of the subject.

TIZARD, B. and HUGHES, M. (1984) *Young Children Learning: Talking and Thinking at Home and at School*, London, Fontana.

Chapter 8

Children's Drawings

Drawings serve as one of the most basic forms of human communication. Thousands of years ago, our ancestors depicted scenes on the walls of caves. These scenes communicate to us events that took place, which enables the viewer to gather something about these events without experiencing them directly. This is one of the defining features of communication: to convey something without the need for direct experience of it.

Then, in Egypt, between 5,000 and 2,000 years ago, people used sequences of small stylized drawings we know as hieroglyphics. They are drawings of things, but ones which are so abstracted that it is necessary to know something about the convention of drawing the Egyptians used in order to interpret each drawing. The Egyptians also put the drawings in sequences, which adhere to rules of organization, thus qualifying hieroglyphics as the first written language. Perhaps we could view this as pictorial art at its most lucid and communicative (providing we can read the inscriptions). The Egyptians also painted single scenes, using less abstracted images.

In more recent times, people still paint in order to communicate. Under royal edict, painters have depicted the glory of victorious armies and navies. Victorians had a passion for portrayals of an idealized rustic life. These paintings seem to communicate the beauty and simplicity of rural life, but conveniently overlook the squalor and tedium. The brilliant work of van Gogh communicates the three-dimensional solidity of things through gradations of colour rather than relying so much on gradations of light and dark, unlike previous painters. Lucian Freud communicates something about the stark ugliness of the human figure in his nude paintings. In all these examples, and in very different ways, painters do not just copy what is to be seen in the world, as a camera does, but instead they communicate something about the world, or about the way the world can be portrayed.

For thousands of years humans have communicated to each other through the medium of pictorial art. Perhaps there is a natural inclination to communicate through art, and if so, we should find that children are predisposed to communicate through their drawings.

One feature of children's drawings relevant to this issue is the phenomenon of 'intellectual realism', first described by the Frenchman G.H. Luquet in the 1920s. If you ask a 6-year-old child to draw a picture of a car, you might find that she draws a fairly neat view from the side, but seems compelled to show the four wheels in the drawing. As a consequence, two of the wheels may appear on the roof of the vehicle! Young children very often draw in this curious way even when asked to draw the car exactly as they see it from the side (i.e. with only two wheels in view). Young children's drawings thus seem to be influenced by what they know is there, rather than what they can see, and hence the term intellectual realism.

Piaget (Piaget and Inhelder, 1969) saw a link between intellectual realism in drawings, and children's tendency to choose their own view on the three mountains task. He argued that both arose from a failure to recognize the possibility of multiple perspectives. Therefore, although he did not say it in so many words, Piaget seemed to take the view that intellectual realism in drawings arises from a more general egocentrism in the young child.

Another way of looking at intellectual realism, however, is to view it as the product of a basic human desire to communicate through drawings, first seen in the cavemen. The child knows that the car has four wheels. If she drew only two, therefore, the drawing would fail to adequately communicate an important aspect of the form of the car. Indeed, perhaps the child feels that if the drawing only shows two wheels, then the vehicle could be mistaken for a motorbike, and so the drawing would be inadequate as an attempt at communication of what the vehicle is.

Looking at it this way, intellectual realism seems just the opposite of what Piaget claimed it to be; a desire to communicate 'what is there', rather than what can be seen at any one time, seems unlike an egocentric tendency. Consider the three mountains task in contrast. The egocentric child is said to be dominated by what he can see from his particular vantage point, and is unaware that the scene may have a different appearance when viewed from another side. Piaget's argument with respect to this matter was that as the child's egocentrism peels away, he comes to understand that appearances can be illusory, and that there is an underlying objective and universal reality. In this respect, it seems odd to claim that intellectual realism arises from egocentrism, if intellectual realism arises from a desire to communicate what is there really – that which underlies the specific appearance from any particular viewpoint. It seems odd in two ways. First, it is odd that the young child who is supposed to be egocentric, seems to have a concern about the way things really are objectively, rather than being dominated by surface appearances. Second, it seems odd that the young child might be concerned to communicate something. A concern to communicate something in itself seems like a non-egocentric tendency.

In recent years, researchers have put effort into a systematic study of intellectual realism, particularly with regard to the possibility that it arises from the child's desire to communicate accurately the way things are. We shall now take a look at some of this research.

The basic phenomenon of intellectual realism was demonstrated experimentally by Bremner and Moore (1984). They asked children aged between 5 and 7 years to draw a cup placed on the table in front of them. The cup had a handle which was not in view from where the child was sitting. Some children were first allowed to stand up and have a good look at the cup. They were able to see the handle round the back. The other children did not see the handle, and could therefore have mistaken it for a sugar bowl. Despite being asked to draw the cup exactly as they saw it, those who had seen the handle were very likely to include it in the drawing, thus displaying intellectual realism. In contrast, those who did not have the knowledge of the handle were less likely to include it in the drawing.

It seems that intellectual realism takes a specific form. Freeman and Janikoun (1972) asked children to draw a picture of a cup exactly as they saw it. The handle was out of view, whilst in view was the image of a flower on the side of the cup. Children below about age 7 omitted the flower and included the handle. Children above that age did the opposite, omitting the handle, but including the flower. This suggests that the young children were not concerned to include all information in the drawing, but only that relevant to its identity as a cup. A flower is irrelevant to identity: different cups have different patterns. The handle, in contrast, is highly relevant to whether or not an item of pottery is a cup. So far as the child is concerned, cups are things that have handles. Therefore, intellectual realism has a great deal to do with including the identifying features of the kind of thing being drawn, but little to do with individual features of that thing.

Just as young children include the handle to identify the object as a cup, so they draw other opaque things as though transparent in order to capture hidden detail in them. Crook (1984) pushed a rod though a ball and asked children to draw it as they saw it. What was in view was the ball, with the two ends of the rod protruding at opposite sides. Five-year-olds typically drew a circle, then a line right across it to represent the stick. These drawings identified the thing as a ball with a stick all the way through it. Under another condition, Crook poked a short stick into each of the two holes of the ball. This produced the same appearance, except children knew that it was not a single stick all the way through. When asked to draw this, 5-year-olds were much more likely just to draw two lines at either side of the circle, rather than a line right through. It seems that by not drawing a continuous line all the way through the ball, children were concerned to depict the rod through the ball as discontinuous.

Intellectual realism also occurs when we ask children to draw two objects exactly as they appear, with one of them behind the other, and therefore partly hidden. For example, if we ask children to draw two apples in such an arrangement, young ones characteristically draw them side by side, and separated by space. Light and MacIntosh (1980) demonstrated that this tendency arises from an apparent desire in the children to depict the relationship between the items as it really is. They asked 6- and 7-year-olds to draw a glass beaker with a small model house situated behind it. Often, children drew the two things side by side, showing that the two items were separated by space. Under another condition, the house was inside the beaker, yet from the child's viewpoint, it looked just as it did when it was behind the beaker. This time, children always drew the house within the outline of the beaker. This strongly suggests that the children were motivated to capture the relationship in space between the two items. Apparently, when the house was behind the beaker, children drew them side by side to show that the two items were separate from each other.

Children's depiction of relationships between things was further demonstrated by Light and Humphreys (1981). They put a red and a green pig, one following the other, on the table in front of 5- and 6-year-olds. The children had to draw four pictures of the pigs, one from each side of the table. From two sides of the table, one pig was partly hidden by the other, and from another two sides, they were both in full view, side by side. The findings were that these young children always drew the pigs side by side, whichever part of the table they did their drawing from. As such, children always showed that there was a space between the two pigs. Moreover, the children often captured the relationship accurately, with the green pig following the red one.

Children's desire to portray relationships between objects accurately seems sufficiently powerful to override a desire to depict the correct identity of objects. This was cleverly demonstrated by Davis (1983). She put two cups in front of 4-to-7-year-old children, one with the handle in view and one with the handle out of view. Children were much more likely correctly to exclude the handle out of view when drawing the cups, compared with a condition where they were asked to draw just one cup with the handle out of view. It seems that children excluded the handle on one cup when drawing the pair because this was the best way of depicting the relationship between them. Apparently, it was more important to the children to depict this relationship than it was to identify the cup with its handle out of view as a cup.

Is a desire to portray relationships between objects, or the identities of objects for that matter, motivated by a desire to draw the world as it is, or is it primarily a desire to communicate something accurately to whoever might see the drawing? There is a subtle but important difference between these two possibilities. The desire to communicate implies a desire to present information in such a way that it is to the benefit of the recipient of that information. In contrast, the desire to portray things as they are may or may not be to the benefit of whoever sees the drawing. A study by Light and Simmons (1983) illustrates how this distinction can be realized. The experimenter put a red and a blue ball side by side on the table in front of the child. The child sat at any one of the four sides of the table, and had to draw the balls in such a way that the next child, waiting outside, would be able to tell from the drawing where he had been sitting. The view from two sides of the table was of one ball behind the other. Would children with this view draw one ball behind the other, in such a way as to communicate to the next child which side of table he had been sitting? In other words, would the drawing be for the benefit of someone else? Alternatively, would the child persevere drawing the balls side by side, presumably based on a desire to show the balls as they really are, separated by space? In this case, the drawing would not benefit the next child in helping to determine the artist's vantage point.

The findings were clear: unlike older children, those aged 6 years drew the balls side by side. They continued to do this even after having seen the consequences of their first attempt at drawing, when the next child went to the wrong side of the table after looking at the drawing. Despite having seen that the side by side drawing communicated the wrong location to the next child, 6-year-olds continued with similar inappropriate drawings on a subsequent attempt.

The case of intellectual realism seems to be one where the child is dominated by what he knows is out there in the world, and appears to have little to do with a desire to communicate something for the benefit of someone who might see the drawing. Perhaps the phenomenon of intellectual realism is a reflection of the child's striving to understand how the world is really, revealing that particular viewpoints are less important to the child. In a nutshell, although intellectual realism in drawings is a kind of error, perhaps we should look at it as a case of objectivity getting the better of subjectivity in the child's cognition. In one respect, this is consistent with Piaget's view of human cognition. He asserted that the best adapted cognition is the one that is based on objectivity. In another respect, it calls into question Piaget's ideas about egocentrism. If intellectual realism represents striving for objectivity, then it cannot at the same time be a manifestation of egocentrism: that is a dominance by surface appearances, and a failure to understand that there is an underlying objective reality. Also, there can be no doubt that a kind of intellectual realism prevails in a good many adult would-be artists. One of the commonest experiences in entering art school is the instruction to draw what you see, not what you know. The latter is a characteristic of the uninitiated. Intellectual realism in adulthood is of a different degree, compared with that in childhood, but perhaps like children, there are vestiges in our drawings of what we know is out there in the world at the expense of what we see. For these reasons, it seems improbable that childhood intellectual realism has anything to do with a childhood stage of egocentrism.

Size of Drawing as an Indication of Significance of the Topic

For thousands of years artists have exaggerated the size of the principal subject in paintings. In ancient Egyptian art we find that Pharaohs take on huge proportions compared with their underlings. This characteristic is repeated in court paintings of the middle ages, where kings are of giant proportions, compared with others in the scene. This is not just a perspective phenomenon; often, the principal subject is no nearer to the viewer than other characters. Only in the relatively recent times of the Renaissance period has the fashion for exaggeration of the size of important people diminished.

From our own experiences, we often express incredulity on finding that a world leader is only of small stature. I often feel surprised to see news film of President Gorbachev, revealing him as the smallest person in the group of statesmen. It almost seems a contradiction that he should be the smallest but most important. If this is a common experience, then it comes as no surprise that over the centuries, the most important figures in paintings are depicted as much larger than less important ones.

If this is something basic to humans, that we overestimate the size of important things or people, perhaps such a tendency will be evident in children's drawings. In an early study to investigate this, conducted by Solley and Haigh (1957), children were asked to draw a picture of Santa Claus both before and after Christmas. As Christmas approached, children's drawings of Santa became larger, but once Christmas had passed, their drawings became smaller. Presumably, as Christmas approached, Santa became more important to children, occupying their thoughts a greater proportion of the time. This could well account for the increased size in their drawings. However, another interpretation (Freeman, 1980) is that as Christmas approaches, children's greater exposure to images of Santa makes them aware of potential for more detail in their Santa drawings. As a consequence, perhaps they draw a larger outline in order to accommodate this extra detail. However, Fox (cited by Thomas and Silk, 1990) found that children do draw more important figures larger than less important ones, even though there is no extra detail in the more important figure. Therefore, it seems that, like our artistic ancestors, children may well have a tendency to portray important people as being relatively large. This could reflect a tendency to think of important things or people as being relatively large.

Whether children view a person as pleasant or unpleasant also influences their size of figure drawing. Thomas, Chaigne and Fox (1989) asked children to draw a picture of a person. They also asked them to draw a picture of a 'nasty' person, and found that children reliably drew this figure smaller compared with when the experimenter gave no specifications about the person to be drawn. Further, Fox and Thomas (1989) found that children who said they were scared of witches drew smaller pictures of witches compared with those who said they were not scared. To account for these findings, Thomas and Silk (1990) suggest that children may draw small figures of threatening or unpleasant figures as a kind of defensive re-action. The idea is that if the subject of the drawing is unpleasant, then this might have less of an emotional impact on the child if she draws only a small figure: the smaller the figure, the less there is of it to threaten the child.

Both importance and how pleasant something is concern emotion, and the size of drawings of things or people with such properties could be classified as an emotional response to these things. Therefore, we can see that children may express their emotions and feelings about the world through their drawings. As such, children's drawings could be revealing about their emotional states, possibly even their psychological adjustment. This is certainly a view held by psycho-analysts, but the trouble is that it is difficult to find a system of interpreting drawings that is unproblematic.

Children's Drawings in Cases of Incest

In cases of suspected incest, the clinician given the task of assessing the child is faced with a difficult problem. We need to establish the details of the child's complaint so that we can decide whether action is essential to protect the child from the possibility of further abuse. The decision has to be considered very care-fully, since apart from attempting to protect the child's future well-being, there could be drastic consequences for the future of the child's family, and the future of the alleged perpetrator of the abuse.

Asking children to make drawings has a potential to help such a serious decision-making process. First, medical examinations and lengthy interrogations could protract the child's trauma, which could be alleviated by an emotional release through the act of drawing. The resulting drawing itself could be informa-tive about exactly what has gone on. Secondly, it may be easier, for younger chil-dren at least, to communicate through the medium of pictures rather than words, given that the child may find it difficult to formulate a sequence of events accu-rately in words. This could be the case if the child simply does not have the requi-site vocabulary for describing events which are beyond the domain of normal childhood experiences, especially if the child is not sufficiently verbally competent to give a detailed description of any event, let alone one giving rise to profound trauma such as incest.

Goodwin (1982) asked nineteen children aged between 5 and 16, who were alleged victims of abuse, to draw various pictures, which included a picture of the alleged perpetrator, and their family, doing something. These nineteen cases were ones of difficult diagnosis, and so were referred for psychiatric consultation to aid with the assessment. All the children were girls, and the alleged perpetrator was the father or the stepfather.

Ten of the nineteen children were teenagers, and in seven of these cases, abuse was eventually adjudged to have taken place. Asking the adolescents to produce drawings proved to be useless. Either they refused to draw, or they produced factual drawings which were irrelevant so far as the alleged incest was concerned, irrespective of whether the father was ultimately convicted. In sharp contrast, drawings made by children aged between 5 and 12 years appeared to be highly revealing.

This was particularly in evidence when children were asked to draw a picture of the alleged perpetrator. Although the children could demonstrate their artistic skill in various drawings, when it came to drawing the alleged perpetrator, they seemed to experience great difficulty, with frequent crossings out. Of the seven children who were finally adjudged to have been abused, six included an obvious penis in their drawing of the perpetrator. Of the two finally adjudged not to have been abused, neither included a penis in the drawing. The inclusion of a penis was not prompted by the clinician who simply asked the children to do a drawing of the father.

In at least three cases the drawings seemed to be informative about the situation in highly specific ways. In one of these the father had homosexual tendencies, which were contributing to his estrangement from the family. The child's drawing showed him in women's clothes, but with a penis prominently on display. In a second case, the father had administered severe beatings to the child during abuse sessions, and the child drew him with a large penis that had a baseball bat resting against it. In a third case, the father turned out to suffer from schizophrenia, and the child drew him with a penis in view and with various heads, which seemed to represent his 'voices'.

It is very unusual for a 'normal' child to include a penis in a drawing of her father, and the abused children's drawings seem to indicate clearly that there is some problem in this respect. We could not take such drawings as definitive evidence that there has been abuse, but it might be useful as a complement to other evidence from medical examination and interviewing the child and family. As the cases detailed above show, specific aspects of the drawings could prove to be informative about the nature of the child's trauma. This is useful in helping us to understand the nature of the child's problem and in deciding how the perpetrator should be dealt with. For example, if the father was operating under the instruction of delusional voices rather than criminal intent, then he may be considered better dealt with through psychiatric rather than purely legal channels.

As Goodwin points out, drawing could have therapeutic value to child victims of abuse. Through a drawing, the child finds a medium of communication, and could get benefit from the experience of being understood. This could well be the reason why abuse victims seem to get a sense of relief from doing drawings which are connected with the emotionally sensitive topic of the perpetrator. Also, drawing is a characteristic of childhood, just like pretence in play. As such, asking the child to draw may help her to identify herself as a child, and so distance herself from her premature venture into the adult domain of sexual activity.

It seems highly unlikely that incest could be confirmed purely or even largely on the basis of a child's drawings. Similarly it is highly unlikely that an alleged perpetrator could be convicted on the basis of the child's drawings as evidence. However, the drawings could help furnish some of the details of the child's trauma and perhaps serve in a therapeutic way. These are values which may be specific to child abuse, as opposed to cases of adolescent incest. Adolescents, in contrast to children, show a reluctance to express their experiences of abuse through drawings, and as a consequence are less in a position to benefit therapeutically through doing drawings.

Further Reading

I strongly recommend the following book, which provides an up-to-date and well written account of this interesting subject:

THOMAS, G.V. and SILK, A.M.J. (1990) *An Introduction to the Psychology of Children's Drawings*, London, Harvester Wheatsheaf.

Chapter 9

The Development of Love and Attachment in Infancy

The origins of bonds of love can be found in infancy. It is very difficult to identify precisely what love is. We can describe physiological changes people experience when they are in the presence of someone with whom they are infatuated. We can try to describe emotional feelings of security we enjoy when in the company of a loved family member. However, it is difficult to pinpoint what it is that forms the bond of attachment that occurs between human beings which we call love.

Throughout life we may occasionally meet people who seem incapable of love. This could be true of those unfortunate people with autism. However, there is another category of person, often depicted in works of fiction. These are people who seem devoid of any moral scruples, people who are ruthless and act only for their own gain. In sum, people who love nobody other than, perhaps, themselves.

It is likely that there are fewer such people in the world than we imagine. When somebody takes action that is counter to our interests, because we are offended and affronted we may be tempted to think the perpetrator is a person who acts only in their own interest. Yet we might find that this individual has the capacity to be highly altruistic in other contexts. Thus, we have a tendency to overgeneralize about people's personality traits after witnessing isolated acts. A common example is that of resenting admonition from someone who holds an office of higher status than ourselves, and then rationalizing the affair by assuming that rather than us really being in the wrong, the superior is a nasty individual who is incapable of sympathy regarding our difficult plight.

These instances apart, it would appear there are people who behave in a ruthless way in all contexts, with no regard for loyalties, who apparently betray 'friends' without a second thought. Indeed, such people may have no conception of loyalty, and in such cases friendships could only be one-sided. Anyone who betrays the trust of another individual without any bad feeling of conscience cannot be said to have genuine friendship bonds. Unfortunately, those betrayed may have assumed there had been friendship with trust.

These loveless people are known as affectionless psychopaths. Thanks to Alfred Hitchcock, the term psychopath conjures images of a murderer who experiences delusions and hallucinations about dead people telling him to carry out heinous deeds. The truth of the matter is that affectionless psychopaths do not experience such hallucinations unless they have the misfortune to have a schizophrenic disorder also.

According to John Bowlby (1965), affectionless psychopathy can arise from either a failure to form a bond with the mother during infancy, or it could arise if a bond has been formed, but then is broken in the event of mother and child being separated. Bowlby was careful to stress that the mother need not be the biological mother, and in fact could be anyone who played the role of mother. The individual need not even be a woman. Bowlby's claim was that due to 'maternal' deprivation, the resulting affectionless psychopathy could manifest itself in delinquent behaviour in later years, due to the individual's lack of moral concern for others.

This is a contentious claim, and has prompted some vigorous debate. Later, we shall look in some detail at Bowlby's claim about maternal deprivation, and its consequences for a disordered personality. First, let us look at what we know about the forming of a bond between caregiver and baby in normal development.

One of the major figures in this area is Mary Ainsworth (e.g. 1973), and much of what follows is based on her research. There comes a time when we can say that the infant has formed a bond of attachment with the caregiver, usually the biological mother. We could call this a bond of love, which certainly is not present until around the age of 9 months.

Nonetheless, prior to that age, the infant does have a preference for the caregiver. For example, at 2 to 3 months, the baby will smile and 'coo' more at the mother than at other people. Indeed, the baby will show such preference for the caregiver, even if fed all her life by another individual who otherwise does not provide as much attention as the caregiver. Also at this age, the baby may seem equally attached to a secondary caregiver who gives lots of attention, but who spends a relatively small amount of time with the baby: for example, the father.

If it is not feeding which is the primary factor responsible for this preference, then what is? It is most likely that physical bodily contact is the important ingredient, as in picking up, carrying and cuddling the baby. This suggestion comes from a study by Anisfeld, Casper, Nozyce and Cunningham (1990), who noted the extent to which mothers made bodily contact with their babies through carrying them. They found that babies who had been picked up and carried a great deal in very early infancy were much more securely attached to their mothers at 13 months of age. The authors of the study concluded that early bodily contact between mother and baby promotes the development of a bond of love between them.

Although the baby shows preference for the caregiver at this young age, a substantial change takes place at about 9 months. This can be demonstrated by the onset of 'separation anxiety'. This is how the test is performed. The mother takes the baby into an unfamiliar room, where he is allowed to play with some toys which are provided. Then a stranger enters, and shortly afterwards the mother leaves the room. Some time later, the stranger leaves, and then returns after a short absence. Finally, the mother returns. This scenario is used to provoke a response from the baby, a response which should be revealing about the baby's sense of security and comfort he gets from the presence of his mother. In sum, his response should be revealing about the extent to which he is attached to his mother.

Before approximately 9 to 10 months of age, the baby may appear rather indifferent to the mother's departure. Beyond this age, we see a very different reaction. When the mother gets up to leave the room, we see the baby walking, if he is able, or perhaps crawling after her. When she goes through the door, the baby cries, and generally appears distressed. In the mother's absence, the baby is likely to remain immobilized, and perhaps will continue crying. On the mother's return, he will appear relieved, and might initiate cuddling with her.

The baby's reactions to the mother's departure are more pronounced when he finds himself left alone with a stranger, compared with when left in an empty room. Thus, the baby experiences 'stranger anxiety'. This is a fear of strangers which is manifest around 9 to 10 months of age, coinciding with separation anxiety.

Another demonstration of the 10-to-12-month-old's attachment is social referencing. When the baby is confronted with a stranger or a new toy, he is likely to turn to the parent apparently in order to read her emotional expression to find out whether the person or thing is safe. If the parent's expression shows fear, then the baby is likely to stay close to her. If the expression is of joy, the baby is likely to venture near to the person or thing. This reference to the facial expression is specific to the main caregivers (e.g. the mother and father), and babies do not seek information or reassurance from other people's faces in this situation (Zarbatany and Lamb, 1985). Although many infants spend more time with their mother than with their father, typically the father's facial expression will have just as much influence over the baby's behaviour as the mother's (Hirshberg, 1990; Hirshberg and Svejda, 1990).

These findings suggest that the 10-to-12-month-old baby uses the parents as a safe base from which to explore the world. The attached person also becomes a source of comfort when the baby is stressed or distressed. In sum, the caregiver's love provides the baby with a platform from which he can project himself into the world.

On the face of things, the relatively late onset of separation anxiety is a rather curious phenomenon. We have already seen in the chapter on perceptual development that babies as young as 6 weeks recognize the mother, given that they spend more time looking at their mother's face than looking at an unfamiliar woman's face. Also, as reported earlier in this chapter, babies of 2 to 3 months smile and 'coo' more at their mother than at other people. What is responsible, then, for the sudden change at about 9 to 10 months?

In the chapter on Piaget's theory, we examined the claim that babies do not have the concept of object permanence, in other words, that they do not distinguish between self and not self. The implication is that as far as the young baby is concerned, once an object is out of sight, quite literally it is out of mind: the baby has no conception of the existence of things which cannot be perceived directly. As you will have discovered in the earlier chapter, this claim is somewhat controversial, but nevertheless has been put forward to explain the sudden onset of separation anxiety at the age of about 9 to 10 months.

Piaget's claim was that the concept of object permanence in the complete sense is not acquired until about 18 to 24 months of age. However, he also suggested that object concept undergoes changes prior to this, and interestingly an important change seems to take place between about 8 and 12 months of age. This coincides neatly with the onset of separation anxiety. As you might recall, Piaget's test was to put two cloths (A and B) side by side, and place a rattle under one of them (A). A typical 8-month-old will have no difficulty in whisking away the cloth and grabbing the rattle. This is repeated three times, with the baby successfully retrieving the rattle on each occasion. Then, on the fourth hiding, in full view of the baby as usual, we put the rattle under cloth B. The baby will search under A, and then lose interest in the game having failed to find the rattle there. In contrast, a typical 12-month-old will search directly at B and recover the rattle.

The 8-month-old's failure to retrieve the rattle from B could be symptomatic of a lack of awareness of the existence of objects once they have gone out of sight. This could explain why babies of that age do not exhibit separation anxiety. They might not be able to conceive that the mother has moved to a different place, perhaps even quite some distance from the baby. In contrast, an older baby will be capable of this, and will become anxious at the mother's absence as a consequence.

Lester (1974) conducted an intriguing study to examine the relationship between the concept of object permanence and separation anxiety. Babies aged either 8 or 12 months were allowed to play in an unfamiliar room in the company of their mother. Then the mother left. More of the older babies froze on the mother's departure, losing interest in the toys, which can be taken as a sign of separation anxiety. However, independent of age, there was a very close relationship between passing the A-B object permanence test and manifest separation anxiety.

This finding tells us that separation anxiety, and perhaps by implication the first genuine bond of attachment, arises when the baby comes to recognize that other people are separate from himself. It seems that the baby develops a strong emotional attachment to the caregiver when he realizes that she is an autonomous individual who continues to exist in another part of the world once out of sight. In other words, bonds of love are formed when the baby recognizes that other people are other people.

Attachment bonds, once developed, take various forms, and researchers have found it useful to place these forms into three broad categories. 'Secure attachment' is evident in approximately 50 to 67 per cent of baby-caregiver relationships in industrialized countries. When the mother returns to the room, following a short absence, the baby will often provide an overt display of delight at her return. The baby will smile, laugh, wave, and crawl towards her. If the mother picks him up, he will smile, kiss, hug and sink into her body. He will never act aggressively, pushing away, biting, hitting or squirming.

'Unsocial attachment' is evident in about 20 per cent of caregiver-baby relationships. Compared with the securely attached baby, the unsocially attached baby is less likely to give the mother a warm greeting when she returns, yet is more likely to cry when she departs. When the mother picks up the baby, he rarely smiles, laughs, kisses or hugs, yet he is likely to protest when put down. The unsocially attached baby also seems susceptible to temper tantrums, throwing toys and hitting the mother. In the strange situation, when left alone with a stranger, these babies are less likely to display overt anxiety, yet clearly are anxious since measures of heart rate show increases consistent with an anxiety experience. When the mother returns, the baby might avoid her, or move towards her but move away again without making any physical contact.

In approximately 20 per cent of cases, the baby is 'anxiously attached' to the mother. Like the unsocially attached baby, he reacts coolly when the mother picks him up, and may cry, bite, hit and squirm. However, these babies are unlike the unsocially attached ones in another respect. They seem actively to seek the mother's comfort and attention, yet reject it when it is offered. They sometimes go to the mother, as though to initiate picking up, but when picked up react in a hostile way by biting, kicking and so on. These babies seem to crave for comfort from the mother, yet paradoxically are unable to receive it.

Ainsworth's studies serve to show how strongly the baby becomes attached to his caregiver, and the distress he experiences when separated only for a short period of time. Just knowing this might be enough to persuade us that a prolonged separation from the caregiver could be severely damaging to the baby's mental health. Bowlby (1965) suggests that prolonged separation from the caregiver, or the lack of opportunity to form a bond of attachment to any single individual, will cause a personality disorder which might be manifest later on as affectionless psychopathy, or at the very least as delinquency.

Two of Bowlby's concerns focused on the lack of opportunity for children to form a bond of attachment when reared in an orphanage, and the disturbance to a bond, for example if the baby had to be separated from his mother for a stay in hospital. Bowlby points out that when deprived of maternal care, the baby's development is nearly always retarded, physically, intellectually and socially. Additionally, symptoms of physical and mental illness may appear. In particular, Bowlby tells us that a separated baby differs from a normal one according to the following criteria:

- failure to smile at a face;
- failure to respond to a 'coo';
- poor appetite, no matter how desirable the food;
- failure to gain weight, irrespective of how nourishing the food is;
- sleeping badly;
- lower IQ.

Bowlby argues that the forming of a bond of attachment is programmed into the baby for sound biological reasons. Babies who stay close to an adult are likely to benefit from an umbrella of protection against an environment which can be very harsh both in climate and predators. Therefore, babies who have a trait to attach themselves to a caregiver stand a good chance of reaching maturity, and passing on their genes into the next generation, genes for the attachment trait. In that case, failure to form a bond in infancy, or the disruption of a bond, would be counter to the baby's natural tendency, and as a result might have dire social, psychological and physical consequences.

Another way in which it makes biological sense that the baby should attach himself to a caregiver is that the reward of love to the caring adult is likely to encourage her to return love and take the baby under her wing. I use the feathered metaphor here for good reason. The sociobiologist Konrad Lorenz has demonstrated a primitive form of attachment in geese. He observed that shortly after hatching, the chicks would follow the mother wherever she went. This has obvious implications for the survival of the chicks, so he wondered whether this tendency was innate. The chicks could not have a perfect image of their mother programmed into their brains from birth, so Lorenz wondered instead if they are programmed to attach themselves to the first conspicuous moving thing they see. This would almost certainly be the mother.

To find out, Lorenz isolated some eggs and hatched them in his own presence. The result was that the chicks attached themselves to him, and followed him around. The chicks ignored their biological mother, and any other goose for that matter.

If, however, chicks were deprived of an opportunity to attach themselves to anything during the first thirty hours after hatching, then they never formed an attachment bond after that, even when presented with the opportunity to do so. These chicks grew up to be socially isolated from other geese, and often seemed incompetent at mating.

Taking a lesson from sociobiology, Bowlby supposed that the attachment between mother and child might be of a similar kind to that between chick and mother goose. In both cases, attachment has the same biological survival value. Bowlby believed that if the baby is prevented from forming an attachment bond, or if a bond is disrupted, then the individual would suffer problems relating to social attachment in later years, and would show a lack of empathy and sympathy for others.

For the baby goose, attachment occurs up to thirty hours after hatching. Bowlby believed the timetable for humans might be different, and viewed the period between 6 and 9 months as crucial. This is roughly the period when the baby first shows signs of separation anxiety. He observed that babies separated around this age would undergo radical changes in behaviour. In the initial period of separation, the baby is likely to scream, shout and run or crawl about wildly, and get no comfort from the attention of a sympathetic adult. Following this comes a period of despair, when the baby seems to become immobilized by a lethargy of depression. If the baby sees traces of his mother during this period, he might become enraged. Bowlby suggested that he is unable to deal with reminders of earlier more secure days. If the mother should return after a protracted separation of several months, the baby might seem uninterested in her presence, and subsequently be unable to form an attachment with anybody.

Bowlby believes that the period between 6 to 9 months and 4 years is the most important as regards the baby's immediate and future emotional adjustment. Beyond the age of 4, the baby seems able to accept the mother's temporary departure, perhaps for a few days or even weeks, without experiencing excessive trauma. By this age, the child can accept substitute attachment figures, such as the grandparents.

If the baby is separated for 3 months or more, or has no opportunity to form any attachment, Bowlby suspected that there could be permanent emotional damage. To investigate the possibility of lasting damage, Bowlby conducted a study on forty-four people convicted of stealing, to find out whether their anti-social behaviour could be traced back to maternal deprivation. He compared the thieves with forty-four emotionally disturbed people who did not commit anti-social acts such as stealing. Of the thieves, fourteen were diagnosed as having affectionless characters, and seventeen had suffered complete and prolonged separation of 6 months or more during their first year of life. Nearly all the affectionless characters turned out to have a history of maternal deprivation. In contrast, the emotionally disturbed people who had not committed anti-social acts were fortunate enough to have had intact relationships with their caregivers during early development.

This, coupled with a variety of case studies, led Bowlby to conclude that maternal deprivation has the following detrimental consequences for later personality. The individual has only superficial relationships with no capacity to make friends. He is psychologically inaccessible to others, and displays little emotional response or concern. He frequently engages in pointless deceit, evasion and stealing, and has an inability to feel guilt.

There can be little doubt that the prolonged separation from a caregiver during infancy can be profoundly damaging to physical and mental development, and that the damage could well be of a permanent nature. However, two details of Bowlby's claim have generated controversy, and we shall give some consideration to these. In particular, Bowlby stressed that to ensure mental well-being, the baby must form an attachment with a single person, usually though not necessarily the mother. Second, he suggested that a consequence of maternal deprivation is likely to be the development of a delinquent personality.

As regards attachment to a single person, this idea has implications for parental practices, particularly for the wisdom of the concept of the working mother. In modern society, many more mothers go out to work compared with a few decades ago. Could this give rise to 'partial deprivation', as Bowlby called it, resulting in damage to the child's emotional adjustment? If so, perhaps we should recommend that mothers do not go out to work. Obviously we would not want to jeopardize the baby's health, but such a recommendation could have serious consequences for the mother's and the family's well-being. First, the family budget may pressurize the woman to work. Second, the woman's psychological adjustment could be enhanced by the independence, interest and general fulfilment that work has to offer. In sum, we need to know whether the mother can be confident in the knowledge that when she leaves her baby with somebody, perhaps another family member, the baby's emotional development will not be compromised.

If we could establish that babies are capable of forming multiple bonds, bonds with two or more people, this would show that separation from the mother, at least for relatively short periods, need not have detrimental consequences – that is, providing the baby is in the company of someone else with whom he shares a bond of affection.

Several studies have employed the strange situation to examine whether babies display separation anxiety in relation to each of several caregivers. One study (Fox, 1977) investigated separation anxiety in children reared in an Israeli kibbutz. The kibbutz system is based on an ideal of men and women having equitable rights, avoidance of materialism and avoidance of possessiveness. Although babies sleep in the same quarters as their parents, they are cared for by groups of adults dedicated to babycare, thus freeing the parents of the restrictions of parenthood. These babies displayed separation anxiety when left alone by both their parents or by their daytime caregiver, showing that they had formed multiple bonds.

Schaffer and Emerson (1964) discovered that even in conventional families there can be multiple bonds. They found that the more bonds the baby formed, the greater the strength of the bond with the main caregiver. This was not always the mother, and in a minority of cases, the strongest bond was with the father.

Leiderman and Leiderman (1974) investigated whether multiple bonding had adverse effects associated with it, which is what Bowlby would have claimed. They studied childrearing pactices in east African farming communities, and identified some homes in which there was a single mother figure, and others in which there were multiple caregivers, with none more prominent than others in this role. Babies with multiple caregivers did seem a little less emotionally secure compared with those who had a single prominent caregiver, as demonstrated by greater stranger anxiety. However, this can be weighed against the finding that babies with multiple caregivers seemed more cognitively advanced than those with a single prominent caregiver, given that they were better at searching for a hidden object.

It might even be possible for babies to form affection bonds simultaneously with each of several other children in a peer group. Freud and Dann (1951) studied six children who had lived in pre-World War Two Germany, and were separated from their families prior to 1 year of age due to Nazi persecution. Eventually, they were taken into Freud and Dann's institution in England, between age 3 and 4 years. The children appeared to be highly attached to each other, but cared little for anyone or anything else. When one of the children was separated from the group, he became very distressed, even for short periods. He would constantly be asking for the other children, and, meanwhile, the rest of the children would seem worried about the missing one. These children had no adult to attach themselves to, but as a consolation seemed able to profit from the love of each other. Their care for each other was quite unlike the normal sibling relationship.

Together, these studies show several things. First, Bowlby's claim that the baby must form a bond with a single person is not only unfounded, but appears to be wrong. Second, those with multiple attachments may be different from babies with just a single bond in some respects, but this difference does not necessarily amount to disadvantage. As a result, leaving the baby with someone who shares a warm relationship with him need not have detrimental effects on emotional well-being.

Perhaps Bowlby's main concern was with the possibility that institutions might be damaging to the baby's emotional development. The potential for multiple bonding shows that in principle this need not be the case. To find out whether in practice institutionalized care is always detrimental, Kagan, Kearsley and Zelazo (1978) studied children between the age of 3½ months and 29 months of age who attended a day-care centre. Compared with similar babies who were reared at home, the day-care infants displayed no ill effects from their day-care experience. It has to be said that the day-care centre had an excellent reputation for the competence and compassion of its staff, and it is conceivable that had the care not been of such a high standard, the children could have suffered. However, presumably the children of incompetent parents would suffer in a similar way. In sum, the potential for multiple attachment need not result in damage to the baby's mental health if the baby is cared for by someone other than the primary caregiver.

This is true at least in the sense of separation from the mother on a daily basis. Given this, Bowlby's concern about partial deprivation seems unfounded.

The other contentious point concerned Bowlby's emphasis on a strong link between maternal deprivation and later delinquency. Although many of Bowlby's thieves had experienced separation from their mother for a prolonged period during their first year, we cannot necessarily conclude from this finding that individuals who are unfortunate enough to have experienced separation in infancy will develop delinquent tendencies; only some of those individuals might become delinquents.

Findings obtained by Goldfarb (1943) serve to illustrate this point. He studied babies separated from their mothers before the age of 9 months. Some of the babies went directly into a foster home, where presumably there was the opportunity for a bond of attachment to be formed between the baby and the foster parents. The remaining babies were put into an institution for three years, before being found a place in a foster home. The institution benefited from the highest standards of physical hygiene, but was lacking in its provision for emotional bonds to develop between staff and babies. Indeed, babies had little opportunity to form a bond with anyone, given that they individually inhabited single cubicles. This was done in the interest of preventing the spread of any diseases, but unwittingly was against the interest of social attachment. The babies only had contact for short periods each day, when nurses would dress or feed them.

The study was a longitudinal one, meaning that the children were studied periodically throughout development. Compared with those who went directly into a foster home, the children in the institution, who were completely deprived of any social bonds, performed worse on assessments of intelligence and ability to make friends. Evidently, early deprivation of attachment bonds had the expected damaging effect in some respects. However, only one of the children who had been institutionalized truanted, stole and committed other anti-social acts. As such, although separation can have a devastating effect on the child's emotional development, contrary to Bowlby's claim it seems far from inevitable that the child will grow up into a delinquent.

A study by Rutter (1972) yielded similar findings. In a broad survey of teenagers, Rutter found that many who had suffered a prolonged separation from their mother during infancy seemed well adjusted. Those who were maladjusted had experienced a particular kind of family breakup, namely, due to divorce or psychiatric illness in the family. Such experiences in themselves could be disturbing to the young child, over and above the separation. Therefore, perhaps the particular circumstance of separation is the factor which gives rise to permanent emotional damage, and not so much the mere fact of separation. Obviously separation is traumatic for a young child, but perhaps there is scope for emotional repair when normal family life resumes in many cases.

In contrast with all this, Rutter found that teenagers who had no opportunity to form an attachment bond during infancy typically were disturbed. He suggested that we should make a distinction between individuals who experience separation and those who never form a bond in the first place. He proposed that perhaps only the latter group of people suffer from the syndrome described by Bowlby.

Altogether, it seems that Bowlby correctly recognized the importance of affection bond formation during infancy, and what can go wrong with later development if a baby is deprived of bond formation. However, he overlooked the importance of multiple bonding in normal development, and perhaps over-estimated the adverse effects of separation. Having said that, for obvious reasons it would be preferable if separation did not occur. The point is that if separation does occur, the child's emotional adjustment forever afterwards is not necessarily doomed.

Further Reading

BOWLBY, J. (1965) *Child Care and the Growth of Love*, 2nd ed., Harmondsworth, Penguin.
This provides a complete account of Bowlby's findings and arguments.

RUTTER, M. (1972) *Maternal Deprivation Reassessed*, Harmondsworth, Penguin.
This provides a view which contrasts with Bowlby's, suggesting that interruption of the relationship between mother and baby need not result in permanent emotional damage.

FOGEL, A. (1991) *Infancy: Infant, Family and Society*, New York, West Publishing Company.
This book provides a general comprehensive overview of the psychology of infancy.

Chapter 10

The Development of Personality and Gender Identity

Psychologists use the term 'personality' to refer to the features of our psyche which make each and every one of us psychologically unique. One of the first personality theorists was Sigmund Freud. Freud is the best known figure ever to emerge from psychology, and his theory of personality development has had a major impact on society and the way we think. Among other things, Freud is responsible for our concern about the meaning of dreams, and the embarrassment we experience concerning what slips of the tongue reveal about our unconscious thoughts. He drew attention to the irrational side of human behaviour, which had been largely neglected by other psychologists, particularly developmental psychologists. Freud is responsible for the common use of the terms 'ego' and 'defence mechanisms'. As regards society, Freud is responsible for the fact that sex in humans is no longer the taboo topic it was in the Victorian era. Public attention to sex perhaps reached its height in the 1960s. Just as we might say that Queen Victoria died in 1960 (a remark once made by Spike Milligan), so we might say that Freud was born then, at least in terms of the popular impact or repercussions of his theory.

Above all, Freud was an original thinker, who leapt free of the intellectual tramlines which constrained the work of most of his contemporaries. As Miller (1989) points out, he is on a par with the handful of other very great thinkers of the modern world, such as Albert Einstein and Karl Marx.

It might come as a surprise, in that case, to find that Freudian theory has fallen out of favour with modern mainstream developmental psychology. In this sense, Freud's theory differs from Piaget's. Piaget did much of his writing over fifty years ago, but in many ways his theory remains a very modern one. A substantial amount of research in developmental psychology that is being carried out at this very moment is inspired either directly or indirectly by Piaget's psychology. In contrast, Freudian theory seems highly dated for the reason that it inspires hardly any modern research. This is because modern mainstream developmental psychology is a discipline which seeks to follow scientific procedures. Freudian theory is not scientific, so it is difficult to imagine how further research relevant to it could be conducted.

Nevertheless, this book would be incomplete without consideration of the developmental psychology of one of the greatest psychologists of all time. As a compromise between old and modern psychology, we shall first look at some of the detail of Freud's theory, and then examine implications for the development of gender identity. Recent studies have been carried out on this topic, which have distant roots in Freudian theory, or at the least seem to have benefited from his ideas in certain respects.

Freud was born in Moravia in 1856, and was to be the eldest of eight children. He moved to Vienna in 1860, where he remained until the age of 81. He developed cancer of the jaw, and as a sick man had to flee to London due to Nazi persecution of Jews. He died in London in 1939. Freud's early interest was in medical research, particularly neurology and nervous disorders. However, his economic predicament soon forced him into private practice. It was being confronted with patients who suffered neurotic or 'hysterical' disorders, with no apparent physical basis, which first persuaded Freud that the human psyche is akin to an airtight vessel in which steam pressure builds. Without any other means of release of the steam, abnormalities emerge in the form of obsessions, neurosis and paralysis. In other words, Freud's theory is concerned with a kind of hydraulics of psychological and emotional energy.

The buildup of nervous energy comes mainly from two instinctual drives, Eros and Thanatos. Eros is the sex drive, based not on the narrow sense of copulation, but on the broader sense of survival, reproduction and the general welfare of one's genes. Freud referred to the nervous energy of Eros as the 'libido'. Thanatos is the opposing death drive which is responsible for aggression and the destructive capacity of humans, which Freud supposed gripped the world during the horror of the Great War.

Through a process of what Freud called 'catharsis' nervous energy can be rechannelled, which might make a potentially dangerous need harmless. For example, suppose Thanatos causes a buildup of violent impulses. Rather than commit murder or some other heinous deed, the individual might engage in vigorous physical sport, such as rugby or boxing. In this way, the nervous energy is dissipated in a socially acceptable pursuit, if not an entirely innocuous one. Freud used the term 'sublimation' for this substitution.

Freud utilized four main tools in his investigations into personality, which were free association, hypnosis, dream analysis and introspection. Free association is where the patient lies on the proverbial couch and says the first thing that enters her head, and continues verbalizing her thoughts as they come into consciousness, no matter how repulsive or obscene. Hypnosis is the same, except the patient first goes through a hypnotic induction procedure. Freud came to believe that hypnosis offered no advantage over free association, and so eventually he dispensed with hypnosis altogether. Dream analysis is self-evident, but relied upon Freud's assumptions about the symbolic significance of events in dreams. Introspection is the inward inspection of one's own psyche. Freud believed that these tools were the best means of discovering the unconscious mind, which is required in order to understand an individual's personality. He believed that personality is based on the unconscious thoughts and feelings he presumed we all have.

Armed with these tools of psychoanalysis, Freud simultaneously sought to treat patients referred to him with neurotic disorders, and to construct a theory of personality development. Although the people he treated were suffering from some kind of nervous disorder, Freud was not just concerned with development of an abnormal personality. He believed that by looking at what happens when personality goes wrong, we can gain insight into normal personality. This parallels an argument which might be made about the study of brain-damaged patients. For example, if we find that damage to the posterior part of the brain causes blindness, which it probably would, we might conclude that the part of the brain in question is responsible for visual perception in people with intact brains. So the same holds for personality: things that can go wrong in personality development are revealing about how 'normal' personality should develop.

In all cases but one, the patients Freud wrote about were adults. We shall take a look at the exceptional case of the child later. Given this fact, we can see that Freud made assumptions about events in childhood on the basis of what his patients could remember about these.

Freud claimed that personality consists of three components, the id, ego and superego. The id is the spoilt child of the personality. It is the part of personality which demands instant gratification, whatever the cost. It thus operates according to the pleasure principle which might delve into the realm of fantasy as a substitute for real gratification. For example, if the baby wants the mother's breast instantly, it might fantasize about the breast as a substitute for the real thing. The id is most evident in infancy, but remains throughout life as a component of personality. It might become prominent if our normal constraints are relaxed by the intoxicating effect of alcohol or some other drug. At such times, we may lose control and satisfy our base needs even at the expense of others' well-being, and with no regard for law and order. We might consider that Mr Hyde was Dr Jekyll's id.

The ego is the second component of personality, and operates on the reality principle. The ego is the rational side of personality, whose task is to satisfy needs in ways that are acceptable to the external world. The ego serves to distinguish fantasy from reality. However, sometimes reality, or id, can pose a threat to the ego. The ego has to be protected from the base aspects of one's own psyche. Defence mechanisms function for this purpose. Here are four of the defence mechanisms Freud described. 'Repression' is the denial to oneself, and, for that matter, anyone else, that there is any problem or that anything is amiss. An example is the forgetting of one's childhood sexuality. 'Reaction formation' is acting in a way opposite to one's feelings. For example, if one feels lustful, one may behave as though sex is the last thing on one's mind, and appear shocked if the subject is raised. 'Projection' is the attribution to others of one's own base feelings. 'Regression' is the return to an earlier form of behaviour when under threat. For example, if severely reprimanded, an adult may adopt a child-like behaviour pattern.

'Superego' is the term Freud used for what we commonly think of as our conscience. It serves as a model for correct moral behaviour, which is an ideal passed on to us from our parents. It is not especially rational, since the ideals could be far beyond the capabilities of the average mortal. For this reason, a conflict is generated with the ego, since it places demands on behaviour which simply cannot be met. Of course, the conflict with the id is even greater, since this exists as a collection of our basest instincts.

Like Piaget, Freud was a stage theorist, and we are now equipped to take a look at his stages of psychosexual development. The stages are called 'psycho-sexual' because Freud believed that each stage of personality development is dominated by the prominence of its own particular erogenous zone. The child's personality during each stage will revolve around the significant erogenous zone.

The 'oral stage' is from birth to about 1 year of age. As the name indicates, the erogenous zone is the mouth. Again like Piaget, Freud believed that the baby is unable to distinguish between self and environment. This is because the baby's psychology is based purely on id, the ego not yet having emerged. The ego operates on the reality principle, so, prior to its emergence, the young baby has no conception of the reality of the external world as distinct from self.

The baby does not just receive nutrition from the breast, but also derives gratification from the very act of sucking. As a consequence, the baby loves the breast. However he does not yet love the mother, since he has no notion of the mother as a separate individual to be loved. His lack of understanding of the mother's existence is an instance of not understanding reality in general.

If the baby has the benefit of motherly comfort and love during this stage, he will grow up to be trusting and optimistic. In contrast, if the mother frustrates the baby by frequently depriving him of the breast when he demands it, he may grow up to be suspicious and pessimistic. If frequently frustrated, the baby may become obsessed with achieving the gratification of which he feels deprived. As a result, he will perpetually seek oral gratification to compensate. In contrast, if the baby is allowed to over-indulge on the breast he will develop a dependence on oral gratification of which he is unable to rid himself. Either way, the baby will fixate at the oral stage.

The result of fixation is that the baby does not progress fully to the other stages, and grows up to be an oral personality. In some sense, the oral personality never comes to distinguish between self and reality. As a consequence, an oral personality is one who does not recognize other people as individuals, but rather treats them as objects to be used as required. In addition, the oral personality constantly seeks oral gratification, which might be manifest as nail-biting, guzzling with accompanying obesity, smoking or alcohol intake.

Freud recognized that it is during infancy that the infant first becomes attached to the mother. He argued that if the attachment is too strong, perhaps nurtured by an over-protective mother, the baby might develop into an overly-dependent personality who is constantly anxious about possible rejection. In this case, the baby would acquire a passive and pusillanimous character, always leaving the decisions to others.

If the baby manages to negotiate the oral stage successfully, then libidinal energy is rechannelled as he passes into the 'anal stage' which is from 1 to 3 years. The name of this stage comes from Freud's claim that the significant erogenous zone becomes the anus as the child derives gratification from withholding and then releasing faeces, along with the accompanying bowel movements. Because of their association with bowel motion, the child comes to love excrement.

The anal stage coincides with potty training, and the nature of this can have profound consequences for later personality. If the parent lays great emphasis on the child expelling the contents of his bowels, he may overcompensate and come to feel over-possessive about his precious defecation. This may lead the child to get pleasure from fingering his faeces. Possessiveness concerning faeces may subsequently generalize to possessiveness over all things, resulting in the child growing up to be a miser.

If the parent is too strict during potty training, the child could fixate in this stage. The result could be one of two possible personality types which fall at opposite extremes along the same continuum. As a reaction to strict training, the child could grow up to be messy, unreliable and irresponsible. Alternatively, the child could take on the too-strict attitude of the parent, and grow up to be bossy, obstinate, over-orderly and righteous. This latter type conforms to the typical anal personality profile.

It is during the anal stage that the ego makes its emergence. First, reality impinges on the child in the form of the parent demanding that natural involuntary expulsion should be replaced by controlled expulsion at the time deemed appropriate. Second, the child has to come to terms with reality in order to navigate to the toilet and use it in the correct way. For the first time, id does not have direct rule over every action of the child.

Providing the child passes through the anal stage in one piece, he then enters the 'phallic stage', which is from 3 to 5 years of age. The erogenous zone, as the name suggests, becomes the region of the genitals. Freud attributed mature sexual feelings to young children, which he claimed are directed at the parent of the opposite sex. Thus, the boy desires sexual possession of the mother, while the girl desires sexual possession of the father. This poses a dilemma for the child, since the parents appear to be involved in a monogamous sexual relationship with each other, which excludes everyone else. The child's desire, therefore, is not only to have sex with the opposite-sex parent, but to exterminate the same-sex parent.

In the case of boys, Freud called this the Oedipus complex, based on the Greek tragedy of Oedipus, who left his parents at an early age and then returned whereupon he unwittingly murdered his father and married his mother. In the case of girls, he called it the Elektra complex.

Because the boy recognizes that it is wicked to desire his mother and have thoughts of killing his father, he lives in fear of his father discovering his thoughts and then administering punishment. According to Freud, the boy lives in fear of a particular kind of punishment from the father: castration. Hence the boy suffers from castration anxiety. The boy's predicament is further worsened by the rebuff he receives from his mother, following his awkward attempts at love-play. Eventually, the boy comes to terms with the situation by identifying with the father, meaning that he adopts the father's morality and sex-role identity: masculine mannerisms, activities and interests. The boy comes to appreciate that the mother loves the father because of such qualities, and therefore comes to believe that the best way to gain the mother's favour is to mimic the father.

For girls, the story is slightly different. They do not suffer from castration anxiety for obvious reasons. Instead, they suffer from penis envy. Freud claimed that girls believe that they have already been castrated in order to account for the difference between their own physiology and their brothers'. This causes a similar kind of anxiety, however, and makes the girl hate the mother, but eventually identify with her in order to get attention and favour from her father.

During the phallic stage, the superego first becomes a force in personality.

The moral ideals of the parent, as perceived by the child, are assimilated into the child's personality as the appropriate moral code. The superego may place strain on the child, since its values are usually unrealistic. However, it has the benefit of making the child considerate of others, and thus enables her to enter society as a conscientious and caring individual. Thanks to this, the child can move beyond the bounds of the family, and enter school and other institutions as a socialized person.

If the child fixates, perhaps due to being severely punished or threatened for masturbating, he or she might forever long to marry the opposite-sex parent, or an older person as a substitute. He or she might continue to fear castration, or suffer from penis envy, and become a frigid lover as a consequence.

From the age of 6 years until puberty (early adolescence), the child enters a stage of dormant sexuality which Freud called the 'latency stage'. Then the individual enters the 'genital stage', which is the stage of adult sexuality.

Freud developed this fantastic theory mainly from speaking with patients who visited him in connection with some neurosis that was afflicting their personality. However, the celebrated case of 'Little Hans' is one in which Freud treated a child, albeit through correspondence with the child's father. The father, a physician who happened to be an admirer of Freud's thinking, contacted the great man over his son's phobia. It seemed that Hans had acquired a fear of going out in the street because he had become convinced that a horse would bite him. It was a particularly debilitating phobia in those days of horse-drawn transport.

There are no prizes for guessing that Freud diagnosed Hans as suffering from castration anxiety, caused by fear of the father discovering the boy's sexual desire for the mother. He reasoned that horses symbolized the father in Hans' mind, indicated by the following clues: Hans was most anxious about white horses (the father's white skin), with black muzzles (the father's moustache), which wore blinkers (the father's spectacles). Biting, of course, symbolized castration.

Freud's suggested remedy was that the father should take the boy to one side and assure him that he was not going to be castrated! This the father duly did, and, so we are told, Hans successfully identified with the father and developed normally thereafter.

It cannot be disputed that Freud had some interesting, if somewhat eccentric, insights into personality. For example, most of us have detected defence mechanisms of the kind Freud described. Also, his description of certain personality types, such as the anal personality, does provide an accurate depiction of certain people we sometimes encounter. However, in many other respects his theory seems rather absurd. We shall now take a look at some specific weaknesses of his theory.

The data on which Freud built his theory were highly unreliable for several reasons. First, they were based on patients' memories of what happened when they were children. These memories were bound to be subject to distortions and reconstructions. For this reason, it would not be surprising if there were a substantial discrepancy between what an adult remembers to have taken place during childhood, and what actually went on. Second, Freud made his notes after the session had ended, so his own memory of what had been said could have been susceptible to systematic forgetting or restructuring. Third, Freud collected his data during an interactive session, in which his questions, grunts and silences could have influenced the direction in which patients allowed their ramblings to go.

Putting aside the unreliability of Freud's data, there is another problem with his theory, which is that its wording makes it untestable. A testable theory is one which makes predictions that could prove to be wrong. If wrong, then the theory is wrong. If supported, then the theory is not necessarily right, but we might gain confidence to this effect. Because Freud's theory is untestable, we cannot determine, for example, whether events which take place during the anal stage have any connection with later personality. Freud claimed that anal fixation can result in either a messy personality or a too-orderly personality. As a consequence, it is impossible to identify evidence which would falsify Freud's theory: the theory is such that no matter what the evidence, it would be supportive.

Simple intuition tells us that Freud's over-emphasis on child sexuality is far-fetched and misguided. In response to such a criticism, Freud suggested that it only seems far-fetched to the critic who deploys a defence mechanism which denies him access to memories of his own childhood sexuality. Such an accusation might be fine in rhetoric, and indeed is rather amusing, but it has no place in the scientific discipline which psychology seeks to be.

Sex-Role Identity

In looking at links with modern developmental psychology, we could have focused on any of a variety of aspects of Freudian theory, though in all spheres, Freudian influence is weak. I choose to look at sex-role identity because this has an obvious relevance to some of the central tenets of Freudian theory. After all, Freud's view was that sexual matters motivate behaviour and have a substantial bearing on personality development. In that case, it would be interesting to explore the development of an individual's conception of sex-role identity and sex-role behaviour. Are these issues illuminated by Freudian theory, issues which are of central relevance to the theory?

Sex-role identity is the part of our personality which is responsible for our sex-appropriate behaviour. Some behaviours stereotypically defined as male might be drinking beer, playing football, swearing, wearing trousers, smoking cigars or a pipe, flattering women, being decisive, being aggressive. Some stereotypical female sex-appropriate behaviours might be wearing lipstick, sewing, being unassertive, being emotional, wearing dresses, drinking cocktails, flirting with men, being defenceless, being submissive. No doubt this list makes me appear sexist, but I try not to be. The truth of the matter is that although it may be a bad thing, statistically women are more likely to engage in the 'female behaviours' and men are more likely to engage in the 'male behaviours.'

Walter Mischel (1970), one of the major personality theorists of modern times, took the view that sex-role behaviour can be accounted for purely by reference to environmental factors. This is a view contrary to Freud's, who emphasized the importance of stages of development and identification with the same-sex parent following an Oedipus complex. Mischel's claim is that parents present children with sex-appropriate toys and punish, or at least disapprove of, sex-inappropriate behaviour.

Jeanne Block (1983) investigated Mischel's suggestion, and obtained evidence in support. She found that there are indeed systematic differences between boys and girls in the way that they are treated, which would very likely influence whether they grew up to have masculine or feminine personalities. She reports that boys to a greater extent than girls are provided with toys which nurture the mastery of skills, such as balancing objects and making constructions. Boys are encouraged to be more exploratory and independent in their thinking. They are encouraged to change their beliefs in the face of disconfirming evidence, whereas girls are encouraged to make the anomalous information fit in with their belief. This is likely to encourage more divergence and flexibility in the boy's thinking.

Another environmentalist view is that young children have a tendency to imitate adults (Miller and Dollard, 1941). This bears a resemblance to Freud's claim about identification with the same-sex parent, but differs in the justification for the imitation process. Freud proposed internal anxiety as a motivator, whereas Miller and Dollard put forward the view that parents reward children for imitation. The claim is that the child's sex-role behaviour is determined by the external motivator of reward for imitation: the parents reward the child for imitating same-sex behaviour and punish the child for imitating opposite-sex behaviour.

Albert Bandura (1969) has attacked the imitation thesis in its strict sense on the grounds that it is implausible that the child's imitative behaviours could all, individually, arise from specific reward. Sex-role behaviour is a complex set of behaviour patterns in one's behaviour repertoire. Bandura proposed that young children have a capacity to make mental notes of complex sequences of actions carried out by others, and then replay these actions in their own behaviour if they feel it is appropriate. According to Bandura, young children come to identify with same-sex parents, or other adults, meaning that they selectively repeat the behaviour of such people.

However, this depends on the child recognizing his or her sex, and recognizing that it is appropriate to produce a pattern of sex-appropriate behaviour. In this respect, Bandura's view departs from Freud's. Freud's idea was that a motivation to alleviate an internal anxiety forces the child to identify with the same-sex parent. Bandura's view is that the child's sex-role identification depends on the child's appreciation of the propriety of producing sex-appropriate behaviour. Thus, Bandura believes that sex-role identification could change, or even be reversed, if the individual's value of what is appropriate changes. In this instance, we see that Bandura appears to have taken a lesson from Freud, in his utilization of the concept of identification, but that he has modified the concept to make it more down-to-earth.

Freud's idea that sex-role identity occurs at a certain age, thus forming a stage of development, gets some support from a cognitive developmental approach. Pre-eminent amongst the cognitive developmentalists in this field is Lawrence Kohlberg (e.g. 1966). His central claim is that the child's sex-role behaviour depends on what the child understands in general about such things as gender. For example, if a child does not understand that one's gender remains constant, then it would not be surprising if the child did not appreciate the significance of sex-appropriate behaviour. We shall now take a look at stages relevant to sex-role behaviour.

By age 2 to 3 years, the child first gives a reliably correct answer to the question 'Are you a boy or a girl?' However, not until the child is 4 years of age does he realize that gender is stable. Prior to this, the boy may claim that when he grows up he is going to be a mother. No doubt Freud would attach symbolic significance to this regarding phallic fixation, but the more probable explanation is that the child simply has not yet come to conceive of gender as stable.

Curiously, it might be that only by age 5 to 6 years does the child come to conceive of gender constancy. This is different from gender stability in that it is the understanding that despite transformation in the appearance of another person, that person remains the same sex. To make the distinction explicit, although a boy may understand that he will always belong to the male sex, he may not conceive of the underlying stable gender in others despite their changes of appearance. For example, he may judge that a man dressed in woman's clothes has become a woman.

The age in question coincides with the age of acquisition of the concept of conservation, first introduced to us by Piaget. Conservation also requires the child to understand that an underlying feature (e.g. quantity) remains constant despite changes in appearance (e.g. increased height of a column of water poured into a tall thin glass). Marcus and Overton (1978) found a strong relationship between conservation of quantity ability and the concept of gender constancy. Conservation is related with correct performance on other tasks which require the child to distinguish between appearance and reality (see, e.g. Russell and Mitchell, 1985), and Marcus and Overton's finding suggests that gender constancy may depend upon the child being able to draw such a distinction.

Gender constancy is of behavioural significance, as demonstrated by Ruble, Balaban and Cooper (1981). They showed 4-to-6-year-old children a television cartoon which had a 'commercial intermission'. In this was an advertisement showing either two boys or two girls playing with a particular toy. Subsequently, the children watching the commercial were given an opportunity to play with a selection of toys, which included that shown in the commercial. Those who had failed a test of gender constancy were not influenced in their preference for the advertised toy by whether the children in the commercial were boys or girls. In contrast, those who passed a test of gender constancy were more likely to play with the advertised toy if it had been played with by a same-sex child in the commercial. This study demonstrates that children's conception of gender constancy influences what they understand to be sex-appropriate behaviour. The study thus demonstrates the stage-like development in children's sex-appropriate behaviour, which appears to be related with cognitive factors. There is a similarity here with Freud's notion of gender development forming a stage pattern, but there is a difference, of course, in the factors responsible for the stage.

Although these studies point towards stages dependent on cognitive factors, the stages evidently are not in an all or nothing form. O'Brien and Huston (1985) report that 2-to-3-year-olds have a primitive conception of sex-appropriate behaviour. When placed in a room with a variety of toys, children of this age chose toys in a sex-specific manner. Boys tended to choose guns, trucks, fire engines, and toy tools, whereas girls tended to choose dolls, cooking and housework toys.

Moreover, Leonard and Archer (1989) demonstrated that young children may have a better grasp of the concept of gender constancy than previous studies have given them credit for. They report that 3-to-4-year-olds were correctly able to say that a man who wore a dress was only a pretend woman and not a real woman. Interestingly, there seems to be a parallel between this phenomenon and conservation. When the experimenter asks if the quantity is really different following pouring into a tall thin glass, children are more likely to make a correct conserving judgment (Russell and Mitchell, 1985). Therefore, the transition to a stage of gender constancy may not be as hard and fast as earlier studies suggest, or perhaps the transition occurs at an age earlier than had previously been thought.

Despite this, it remains the case that the more developed the child's concept of gender, the more likely he or she is to engage in sex-appropriate behaviour and exhibit sex-appropriate attitudes. This was demonstrated by Martin and Little (1990), who examined not only gender constancy, but other features of gender concept in a group of 3-to-5-year-olds. These other features included gender stability, and the ability to identify and discriminate between people according to their sex. From this study emerged a clear link between cognitive development concerning gender concept and sex-appropriate behaviour.

To return to, and summarize, Freud's contribution to this topic, his suggestion about identification has provided a useful concept for social learning theory. However, Bandura's claim is that identification is not as rigid a process as Freud would have us believe. Second, Freud's proposal that sex-role identity develops in a stage-like manner has certainly received sympathy from cognitive developmentalists. However, there is no evidence that an Oedipus complex is responsible for the stage. Also, the stages may not be as rigid as either Freud or cognitive developmentalists supposed.

Freud presented some unusual, exciting and often shocking ideas. Unfortunately, his theory does not come within the realm of scientific psychology, and those who adhere to it do so by a substantial act of faith. Most modern developmentalists are too sceptical in nature to have the kind of faith required. Nonetheless, perhaps we shall continue to see fragments of Freudian insight in future research in developmental psychology, as we do in the psychology of sex-role development.

Further Reading

MILLER, P.H. (1989) *Theories of Developmental Psychology*, 2nd ed., New York, W.H. Freeman and Co.
Chapter 2, pp. 122–74, provides a good overview of Freudian theory.

Chapter 11

The Development of Madness

Most children develop behaviour problems at some time or other. A common behavioural malady in childhood is an apparent inability to sit still and concentrate on things. This is seldom so problematical that the child's normal activities in home and school are disturbed, though severe cases can have a disruptive effect. In this case, we might describe the child as hyperactive. In contrast to this relatively common behavioural disorder, severe and persistent disturbances of mood and thought are seen in only 1 in 1,000 children on average (Achenbach, 1982). What we are concerned with in this chapter is one particularly debilitating mental illness which forms some of these serious cases: schizophrenia.

Childhood schizophrenia, unlike autism and hyperactivity, is not usually manifest until later in development, typically in adolescence or adulthood. However, some experts maintain that experiences during childhood can result in the development of the madness which we call schizophrenia. Having said that, there is undoubtedly a genetic factor involved in schizophrenia. Rosenthal, Wender, Kety, Welner, and Schulsinger (1971) studied children whose biological parents both had schizophrenia, but who had been adopted into families with no history of mental illness. These children were at greater risk of developing schizophrenia, compared with children who did not have parents with schizophrenia. This shows that children can inherit genes that make them prone to develop this form of mental illness. Nonetheless, it is not necessarily the case that an individual with parents who have schizophrenia will himself develop schizophrenia. It is most likely, therefore, that although the inheritance of certain genes can make us prone to develop the illness, whether or not we do so in fact will depend on our life experiences. The life experiences most relevant could well be those of childhood, as we shall see in the following pages.

The part of the environment held to be most relevant to whether or not we become mad is that formed by family. So we call a family which threatens sanity a schizophrenogenic one. It might be profitable to view the emergence of insanity in the child or adolescent as a deviant form of adaptation to a psychologically unhygienic environment. We shall consider this possibility in some detail, but first we shall attempt to describe and understand what schizophrenia is.

The nineteenth-century German physician Emil Kraeplin was the first to identify the symptoms of what we now call schizophrenia as distinct from other severe disorders of mood, such as manic depression. He identified the symptoms as hallucinations, delusions, and emotional abnormalities. The hallucinations typically take the form of 'voices' telling the individual what to think and do, as though an external entity has taken possession of the mind. Delusions might take the form of beliefs consistent with these hallucinations: that others' thoughts can be implanted into one's mind, that one's thoughts can be read or stolen by others, that one's mind is controlled by external forces. Additionally, delusions might be in the form of an unfounded feeling of being persecuted by others. In sum the patient may also feel that his behaviour is controlled by some external agent, and not the product of his own volition, and that his own psyche has been annihilated in the process.

It was Eugen Bleuler, working in the earlier part of the twentieth century, who coined the term 'schizophrenia', which literally means 'split mind'. Bleuler operated in a Freudian personality framework, and assumed that the disorder developed as a consequence of a disintegration of personality. A popular notion of schizophrenia is that the patient has several distinct personalities, as in Dr Jekyll and Mr Hyde. However, this is more accurately defined as multiple personality syndrome, where each of the individual's personalities is complete and distinct from all the others. Schizophrenia, in contrast, is viewed as a fragmentation of personality into an incoherent mess. As a result, the patient for most of the time is manifestly insane, unlike the individual who has a multiple personality.

During the 1960s, many people began to challenge the validity of schizophrenia as a mental illness. This was brought to public attention a decade later in the film *One Flew Over the Cuckoo's Nest*. The film sought to show that in many cases patients in mental hospitals are not mad but perhaps a little bad or anarchistic with a misplaced sense of humour. They have a disruptive influence on society, but escape the legal net and cannot be locked up in prison. Instead, they are classified as mentally ill, and locked up in a hospital. Coupled with this was a claim being made by a group of psychologists that an effective way to treat the symptoms of schizophrenia is to train the patients to behave in a way that the psychologist deems 'normal' in much the same way that a circus trainer trains an elephant to waltz. The implication is that there is nothing wrong with the mind as such, but that the individual has simply come to behave in an irregular way: the syndrome can be rectified by changing the behaviour.

However, there can be no doubt that there are some unfortunate people who have hallucinations and delusions of the kind described by Kraeplin and Bleuler, and as such there can be no doubt that schizophrenia is a disorder of the mind rather than just a disorder of behaviour. In retrospect, the controversy which arose in the 1960s was caused by psychiatrists being unclear about the symptoms and diagnosis of schizophrenia. Some patients who were admitted to mental hospitals with disorder of mood or behaviour were classified as schizophrenic, when in fact many would not have conformed to the pattern of symptoms described by Kraeplin and Bleuler. In that climate, it was possible for someone bad to be diagnosed as mad. So we can now see that the problem was not to do with the validity of schizophrenia as a form of mental illness, but rather to do with inappropriate diagnosis of schizophrenia.

Insanity can have a sudden onset during adulthood, and two such cases are reported by Ronald Laing (1969), as follows. A man in his fifties had apparently enjoyed good mental health and adjustment until one day he did something rather bizarre. From that moment, he was admitted to a mental hospital for a prolonged period. The man had gone for a picnic with his family at a popular spot beside a river. After a pleasant if uneventful period on this summer's afternoon, the man stripped himself naked and strolled into the river. This act was out of character, since the man was not fond of making scenes and drawing attention to himself in public, but in itself it does not go beyond the realm of reasonably normal human behaviour. However, the man then declared that he would not come out of the water until he had been cleansed of his sins for not loving his wife and children. Eventually, the police had to be called in to remove him bodily from the scene, whereupon he was admitted to a mental hospital for a long stay.

The second case is of a 22-year-old man who visited the seaside, and spent a period of time floating about in a small inflatable boat near the shore. He then allowed himself to drift out to open sea. Two hours later he was found by the coastguard whereupon he resisted being rescued, claiming that he wished to continue his search for God in the ocean. He also was admitted for a long stay in a mental hospital.

Although both cases are of people who had apparently lived normal and well-adjusted lives until the sudden onset of bizarre behaviour, Laing argues that the developmental history of each has the potential to reveal that these people in fact had been coping with serious problems of maladjustment. The problems eventually forced themselves into the open. According to Laing, these people had suffered from insanity for a prolonged period, but they had managed to hide the insanity by pretending to be normal. Laing goes on to suggest that it might be that when these people return from mental hospital, their resurrected sanity is achieved by once again pretending to be normal. In other words, these people may have continued to be insane, even though outwardly that appeared not to be the case. In his book, Laing makes a very ambitious attempt to take the reader on a journey through the personal history of the mad person, particularly the period covering childhood, with the aim of identifying the life experiences which can contribute to the development of schizophrenia. We shall now take a look at Laing's theory.

Laing's theory is a psychoanalytical one, which is based on the reports of his patients rather than experimental methods of investigation. We can suppose that information which is obtained from experimental techniques will be more reliable, but these techniques are not best suited to all requirements. Laing sought to build up a picture of the insane person's mind, which required considerable imagination on his part to 'get into the shoes' of the insane person. This he did by prolonged interview sessions with his patients and members of their family, and by looking at past medical records.

Laing suggests that madness is the final of three distinct phases: good, bad and mad. He reports the case of Julie to illustrate this. During the good phase, the child apparently is normal and healthy. Indeed, the youngster may seem like a model child. Julie's mother stated that Julie was weaned without difficulty, was out of nappies at 15 months, was never any trouble and always did as she was told.

Babies often engage in a game in which they throw their rattle from the cot and then communicate to the parent by whatever means at their disposal that they wish to have the rattle returned. When the parent duly presents the rattle to the baby, she blatantly throws it out of the cot once more. If the parent returns it again, the baby will throw it. So the baby involves the parent in a game of 'fetch the rattle'. In Julie's case, things were different. Julie threw the rattle just like a normal baby, but her mother refused to fetch it. Her mother declared that she wouldn't have any of that nonsense, but instead asked Julie to fetch the rattle when she was old enough to crawl, which she obediently did.

Julie was deprived of control, and instead was controlled by her mother. Her mother perceived Julie's obedience as a sign of goodness. Julie's goodness was also manifest in precocious crawling, weaning, potty use and walking. In sum, Julie was no trouble.

Julie's mother was proud of the fact that Julie was no trouble, but Laing views this as an unhealthy sign. He argues that normal babies are a trouble, and that the absence of demands for gratification and the mother's attention are symptoms of a failure in Julie to present and develop her own personality. She had no personality, and acted as an agent of her mother, under the mother's control. Of course, all babies are under the control of their mother to some extent, but in Julie's case, it seems this went to an extreme.

As she grew older, Julie showed no initiative, and was completely lacking in self-will and determination. She expressed no opinion about the kind of clothes she wanted to wear, and did not engage in any attempt to make friends.

At the age of 15 she entered her 'bad' phase. Her mother encouraged her to go out, even to have boyfriends. She went out, but always alone, and doing nothing other than wandering the streets. She also allowed her room to get into a terribly untidy state and remain that way.

Most adolescents experience emotional difficulties and find it hard to adjust from childhood to adulthood. However, Julie was particularly difficult and, significantly according to Laing, began to make certain accusations about her mother. She claimed that her mother had not wanted her, that her mother had prevented her from being a person, that her mother had smothered her, that her mother had not let her breathe. To casual observers, these accusations seemed totally unfounded, and most considered Julie's mother to be very caring and careful to bring up her children in a respectable way.

Laing's interpretation of Julie's remarks is that Julie faced inner turmoil brought about by the conflict between her own will and that of her mother's. Julie was just an agent of her mother's strong will, but wanted to be liberated and assert her self. So she began to criticize her mother for the control which she exerted over her. Although these accusations were themselves a sign of triumph of Julie's will over her mother's, they apparently gave no respite from the continuing inner turmoil: Julie continued to be bad.

Julie began to call herself Mrs Taylor. She pointed out that this name encapsulated the fact that she was tailor-made, with a personality manufactured by her mother. Laing takes this as one of the first signs of mental illness, or psychosis, in Julie. It may have been perfectly accurate for Julie to describe herself as having no personality of her own, and that she was moulded by her mother. In that case, it seems rational to claim that she has been tailored by her mother. That kind of rational thought process is not psychotic, but the cryptic way in which she expresses herself (i.e. calling herself Mrs Taylor) is psychotic.

Julie's complete transition from bad to mad was yet to come. It seemed to revolve around a specific incident, which occurred when she was aged 17. Julie had a doll that she had kept since she was a young girl, and which she continued to play with and dress. She called this her Julie doll, and used to pretend that the doll was herself in the games she played with it. Julie's mother had begun chiding her for playing with the doll, pointing out that she was now a big girl, and that it was no longer appropriate behaviour. One day Julie discovered the doll had vanished. She accused her mother of stealing it, but her mother denied that she had. Julie became profoundly disturbed by the loss of her doll, and, shortly after its disappearance, she heard a voice telling her that a child wearing her clothes had been beaten to a pulp by her (Julie's) mother. Julie reported this to her family, and proposed to inform the police. Following this episode, she was admitted to a mental hospital where she had remained until the age of 26 when Laing began his investigation.

By this time, Julie's sanity had deteriorated considerably. Partly, this could have been due to the monotonous life of an institution, punctuated by the bizarre activities of some of the other patients. Partly, it could have been due to the medication Julie received, which may have inadvertently exacerbated rather than improved her symptoms. It would seem that this can happen in some cases, confounding the intention of the doctors. Alternatively, perhaps it was simply that her mental illness had continued in its progression, unabated by all the attempts at treatment.

Julie's behaviour and personality appeared to be totally lacking in cohesion and coherence. Segments of her speech were comprehensible, but it was impossible to identify how one segment related to the other. It was not just that the content of Julie's speech was confused, but also that her intonation mannerisms and gestures lacked stability. It was as though several fragments of her personality were competing to be heard, resulting in none making much sense.

Julie often referred to herself as 'she', 'you', or 'her', as though she imagined aspects of herself not to be herself. In this case, according to Laing, she must have failed to distinguish between what was her and what was not her. For example, she claimed that the rain on her face was her tears, and that part of her existed in the wall and in the chair. Similarly, she seemed to have difficulty in recognizing which were and were not her thoughts. If Laing expressed something similar to what had been passing through her mind, Julie accused him of stealing her thoughts, or of having her brain in his head.

Despite all the incoherence, Laing reports that threads connecting Julie's present schizophrenic state with her earlier childhood experiences could be identified in her ramblings. Sometimes she seemed to speak in a voice that possessed all the negative qualities Julie attributed to her mother (Laing, 1969, p. 200):

> This is a wicked child. This child is wasted time. This child is just a cheap tart. You'll never do anything with this child.

Apparently, 'this child' refers to Julie herself through one of her 'voices', directed at Laing.

Another of Julie's 'voices' had a perceptive quality, sometimes with more of a benign if somewhat condescending tone, which appears to embody the qualities Julie ascribed to her sister (Laing, 1969, p. 202):

> This child's mind is cracked. This child's mind is closed. You're trying to open this child's mind. This child is dead and not dead.... You've got to want this child. You've got to make her welcome. You've got to take care of this girl ... she's my little sister. You've got to take her to the lavatory. She's my little sister. She doesn't know about these things. That's not an impossible child.

In the big sister's 'voice' we find an island of coherence. Her message often seems reasonable, knowledgeable and rational. It incorporates a sense of responsibility. Laing suggests that these aspects of Julie's personality have been fragmented into her big sister component, but not other components.

Laing identifies two further components, both of which seem to represent earlier phases of Julie's own being (Laing, 1969, p. 200) – the good phase:

> I'm a good girl. I go to the lavatory regularly.

and the bad phase:

> I wasn't mothered, I was smothered ... stop it ... she's killing me. She's cutting out my tongue. I'm rotten, base. I'm wicked. I'm wasted time.

Laing argues that the 'voice' from the good phase, and indeed the entirety of the good phase, represents a false self, moulded by the mother, and presented in order to please her. He suggests that the bad phase represents Julie's real self trying but failing to establish itself. This is represented in the fact that Julie's 'voice' of her bad phase apparently is always interrupted by an onslaught from her inner wicked mother.

Apart from illustrating the developmental phases of good, bad and mad which Laing supposes are characteristic of the development of schizophrenia, the case of Julie also serves as a typical example of personality fragmentation. The earlier phases do not vanish without a trace, but instead components of them continue to compete for existence in Julie's persona, resulting in manifest schizophrenia.

So far we have been concerned with what schizophrenia is and how it develops through phases often beginning in childhood. We shall now turn our attention to why schizophrenia develops. Earlier I made the comment that schizophrenia might be a form of adaptation to a schizophrenogenic family. Now we shall consider Ronald Laing's view of the nature of that adaptation, and why it takes the particular form it does.

Laing's theory is based on the idea that schizophrenia is an adaptation to the feeling that the circumstances of living pose a threat to one's identity. The individual then has to find a way of trying to preserve his own identity. One way to do this is to become withdrawn and distant from the world, so that ordinary life experiences can no longer touch the individual. Ironically, however, the individual then comes to live in a world of his own making, and begins to lose contact with reality. Thus, the very strategies deployed to defend one's sanity have the effect of swamping that sanity. The strategies themselves come to obscure one's identity, but this might be considered preferable to the individual at the centre of the crisis: if his own strategies annihilate his identity, at least he will be protected against becoming an agent of someone else; at least he would not be an automaton controlled by another person's mind. So the inner defensive manoeuvrers cause self-destruction.

Let us consider the case of Peter, to examine in some detail how the individual's life experiences lead him on a path towards insanity. Peter, a man aged 25, was under the impression that an unpleasant smell was emanating from his genitals. Despite taking several baths a day, he continued to experience the pungent odour. He went to seek the advice of his doctor, who could not sense this smell, and suspected that Peter's problem was of a delusional nature. He then referred his patient to Laing.

Laing conducted an investigation into Peter's childhood and life history by interviewing both the patient and members of his family. With this method, he pieced together a picture of Peter's life experiences held to be relevant to his present delusional state. At the time of investigation, Peter was not schizophrenic – his symptoms were not sufficiently severe to warrant that label. Rather, he was schizoid, which Laing uses to mean that Peter was one step away from the syndrome of schizophrenia, but still on the right side of the precarious boundary between sanity and insanity. We shall now take a look at Peter's life story to see if it sheds light on his present predicament.

As a child, all Peter's material requirements were satisfied, but he was neglected psychologically. His uncle reports that he was well clothed and fed, but never cuddled or given attention. On the contrary, the uncle reports that Peter's parents behaved most of the time as though he did not exist. They completely ignored him, as though he was not there. When his father did acknowledge him, it was usually to reprimand and insult him: 'Useless Eustace ... just a lump of dough'.

It seems that Peter's mother was a rather conceited person who had never wanted a child because that posed an impediment to her own self-indulgence. It seems she perpetually held a grudge against Peter for occupying her time and damaging her figure. Peter's father, who doted on his wife, resented Peter for the same reasons.

This family climate provided no scope for the emergence of Peter's identity, according to Laing. Peter was treated as a nobody, and was not permitted to be anybody. As a consequence, the very existence of his identity was under threat. This case is very different from that of Julie in one respect: she was encouraged to have a certain personality, albeit the personality which matched the specifications prescribed by her mother. Nonetheless, Peter and Julie were in similar situations in that neither was given opportunity to allow their own personality to prevail.

Another of Laing's patients expressed an opinion which not only summed up her own feelings, but also captured the situation Peter found himself in (Laing, 1969, p. 172):

Everyone should be able to look back in their memory and be sure he had a mother who loved him, all of him; even his piss and shit. He should be sure his mother loved him for just being himself; not for what he could do. Otherwise he feels he has no right to exist. He feels he should never have been born.

These comments not only hold true for the patient who uttered the words, but also for Peter and Julie. Neither of them were loved for being what they were. Either they were ignored and treated as though they were nothing, or they were moulded against their will into something they were not.

However, there was a point in Peter's life when he did enjoy the experience of being valued for what he was. Peter was a child during World War Two. One night the house next door was bombed, killing the adults who lived there, but not their child. This was a girl aged 9 years, the same age as Peter. She did not escape unscathed, and was left blind.

Peter spent most of his time with this girl when she was eventually allowed out of hospital. He showed her kindness, and listened and talked to her patiently. He helped her to navigate the neighbourhood. Eventually, the girl regained some of her vision, and she started to become independent of Peter. Although we may rejoice in the girl's recovery, in one sense this eventuality might have been a blow to the tenuous status of Peter's identity. He was once again deprived of the feeling of being valued for what he was.

When Peter left school, his uncle managed to get him a clerical job in a solicitor's office. After a period of months he left due to lack of interest. He then took on a job in a shipping office, with the same result. He then spent an uneventful two years doing national service, following which he drifted from one unskilled job to another. It was at this point that he went to his doctor about the smell.

The smell anxiety seems to have arisen from a specific incident that occurred when Peter worked at the solicitor's office. He used to fantasize about female colleagues while masturbating in the lavatory. One day, he vacated the lavatory only to find himself face to face with the woman he had just been fantasizing about. He felt that she could see right through him, and read the fantasy off his face. He then became anxious that everyone would be able to smell the tell-tale clue of the semen. His anxiety was that people could recognize that his outward behaviour was just a facade, and could identify him as the fraudulent pretender that he was.

Peter subsequently chose to be a drifter out of a terrible sense of honesty. He viewed himself as a nonentity, as communicated to him by his parents, and decided that he should only do work that is suited to such a nonentity. By giving up any decent job, therefore, he was being honest to himself and to the world.

Peter reported that there was a time when he felt that perhaps he could find solace in a relationship with a woman. Here was a ray of hope that a member of the opposite sex could be his saviour. However, he then came to the sad conclusion that any woman who was stupid enough to love him must be equally pathetic.

Although Peter had chosen to live an honest life, as the useless person he believed himself to be, he also felt a strong urge to defend this citadel, this remnant of his personality. This was all he had to cherish. To do this, he made an attempt to become completely anonymous. He was interested in reading, but feared that he would be 'recognized' if he went to his local library on a regular basis. Therefore, he registered at many different libraries, all under a different pseudonym, and providing a false address each time. By doing this, he hoped to avoid being discovered. One of the things Peter hated most was a visit to the barber's shop. During such a visit he felt that he was a captive of the barber, who would ask questions and make discoveries about him. Peter's personality had become so fragile that he felt his being would be threatened by another person knowing trivial things, such as what he thought of the latest football results. He had come to feel that his personal preferences, opinions and tastes needed to be kept secret to preserve his identity and prevent himself being swallowed up by his environment.

Paradoxically, Peter also had a latent sense of omnipotence. He felt that he was on earth to carry out a mission on behalf of God.

Peter was a sane but schizoid individual. He did have delusions, though he did not suffer a complete breakdown of his personality. According to Laing, Peter had become this way through being treated as a useless nonentity during childhood. Peter viewed himself in the same light, but became anxious to preserve the remaining vestige of his personality, however useless that vestige might be. In defending what was left, in other words in defending himself against a world which threatened to overwhelm him, he cut himself off. He became anonymous and took low-status jobs to enable him to be honest with himself.

In the case of Peter, we can see that his 'false-self system', as Laing calls it, was suppressed by Peter's attempt to be 'honest'. In other words, he chose not to present to the world a personality that he was not worthy of, and which could have taken over his entire existence. He feared that if that had happened, his real inner self would have been destroyed.

Perhaps Peter should have allowed his false self to predominate. Perhaps his fear about the consequences of doing this were unfounded. However, the following case suggests that is not so. This is the case of David, who was referred to a psychiatrist by his university tutor at the age of 18 years.

As a young child, David had been inseparable from his mother. He acted as her agent, and seemed to embody many aspects of her personality. This even extended to a flair for embroidery which he shared with his mother. As it would with any child, it came as a crippling blow to David when his mother died. He was 10 years old at the time. However, David's mother lived on through his behaviour. He took on her duties and her style of personality, even more so than in the past. He subsequently became convinced that everyone is just acting a part, and that there is a distinction between the outer personality that is presented to the world and the inner self.

For a while, David seemed quite happy to act parts. Indeed, he used acting to his advantage. He was a rather shy boy deep down, but was able to overcome this by playing the role of a self-confident person. At university, he acted at being eccentric, donned a theatrical cloak and acquired a cane. His outward personality was just a series of impersonations.

However, David began to have difficulties. He had kept his dead mother's clothes, and frequently used to dress up in them, pretending to be a woman. He then became unable to stop acting this part, and found himself walking, thinking, talking, and seeing like a woman. At this point, an alien woman personality was beginning to intrude on his inner 'real' personality: the distinction between outer persona and inner self was becoming blurred as the outer persona threatened to overwhelm and engulf the inner self. In an attempt to defend against this, David presented competing personae, until he became reduced to a jumble of fragmented personalities.

David, like all of us, did have an inner self, but one which struggled for survival. He doted on his mother, and when she died, he preserved her personality by allowing her existence to continue through his behaviour. According to Laing, he felt a need to protect his inner self by keeping it detached from reality, never exposing it to the world. However, the more the self is withdrawn and hidden away, the less of a hold it has on reality, and therefore the more tenuous its existence. In David's case, this made it possible for the inner self to be subjugated by his impersonation of his mother. On recognizing this, and attempting to defend against it, David's personality started to lose all cohesion, and the inner defensive manoeuvres began to cause self-destruction. At this point David was referred to a psychiatrist.

Laing's theory is that during childhood in particular, it is crucial for the individual to have the freedom to be an individual, and not just an agent of another person's personality. In the unfortunate event of the latter occurring, the individual may deploy a variety of defensive strategies in an attempt to adapt to the situation, which can lead to a schizoid personality that can subsequently develop into a schizophrenic one. A family which does not permit the child to be an individual is a schizophrenogenic one. However, a schizophrenogenic family will not have the same effect on all individuals. Laing suggests that due to genetic factors, some people may lack the psychological strength required to assert themselves as individuals in all contexts. In the context of a schizophrenogenic family, such an individual is prone to develop madness. Here we see that genetic make-up combines with environment in determining developmental outcome.

Laing's account of schizophrenia is not the only one by any means. Other explanations raise the possibility of abnormal brain chemistry in schizophrenics. In this case, the idea is that abnormal functioning of the brain causes the patient to experience hallucinations and delusions, just as some drugs can have such effects. Indeed, one drug in particular, namely amphetamine, can produce a syndrome which is similar to schizophrenia if it is abused heavily for a prolonged period.

We cannot test Laing's account for it is an account which does not fall within the realm of scientific investigation, just as with Freud's theory, described in the previous chapter. Perhaps, then, its utility, like Freud's theory, relies upon how intuitively appealing it seems. There can be no doubt that many of Laing's arguments strike us as having a kernel of truth in them. Surely we have all been familiar with the experience at one time or other, perhaps particularly during adolescence, of a feeling that our individuality is liable to be wiped out by our acquaintance with another individual noted for their strong personality. It makes intuitive sense to suppose that the biggest threat would come from a family member, at a time when our fledgling identity is susceptible to domination by others. Also, there seems to be some intuitive sense in Laing's claim that the defensive strategies we deploy to prevent this might themselves threaten our sanity.

Further Reading

LAING, R.D. (1969) *The Divided Self: An Existential Study in Sanity and Madness*, Harmondsworth, Penguin.
This presents Laing's theory, along with many reports of the case histories of his patients. It makes for fascinating reading.

BIRCHWOOD, M., HALLET, S. and PRESTON, M. (1988) *Schizophrenia: An Integrated Approach to Research and Treatment*, London, Longman.
This provides a detailed overview of modern thought on schizophrenia. However, it is not from a psychoanalytic perspective, and there is no mention of Laing in it. This book provides the other side of the coin.

Chapter 12

The Development of Aggression

Humans can be highly destructive creatures, and have an apparent appetite for violence and aggression. Poignant testimony for this comes from the recent bloody battle of colossal destruction which raged between the military forces of the Iraqi president Saddam Hussein and the coalition forces led by the United States acting on behalf of the United Nations.

Alas, by human standards the recent conflict is to be expected. Any brief history of 'civilization' amounts to little more than a list of death, looting and pillage on a massive scale, perhaps reaching a pinnacle with the genocide conducted by Nazis against Jewish citizens unfortunate enough to come into contact with that abhorrent regime. Wars are a characteristic of civilization, and the only thing that changes through history in this respect is the sophistication and destructive potential of the weapons developed for combat.

Perhaps human aggression is a consequence of pathological bureaucracies or the psychotic and despotic tendencies of certain tyrannical leaders. This seems to be true to some extent in the case of Adolf Hitler's regime. His subordinates were trapped in a situation in which it was profoundly difficult for any individual to resist carrying out orders, even when those orders had hideous consequences. However, there is certainly more to the story than this, since it is clear that aggression occurs not just as a product of obedience to authority.

For example, consider mob violence at soccer matches, in which supporters of opposing teams meet in hand-to-hand clashes. There is no authority figure instituted by society commanding these hooligans to pick fights. On the contrary, they are explicitly told to refrain from such delinquent behaviour. Soccer violence is typically a group phenomenon, and perhaps it should be viewed as one 'tribe' seeking to conquer another.

An attraction towards violence is not just a phenomenon of collective behaviour, however. This is demonstrated by the popularity of boxing. Bouts screened on television often draw massive audiences. In many cases, people viewing alone sit enthralled as one man tries his very best to knock another man senseless. Anyone who has watched boxing knows that contests can be highly dangerous to the participants, often resulting in serious cuts and concussion, and sometimes, admittedly not very often, resulting in the death of one of the fighters. Seemingly, the potential of harm to the participants is one of the features of the sport which makes it appealing to spectators. This is demonstrated by the fact that when motions are put forward suggesting that boxers should wear protective headgear which would limit injury, boxing pundits are in uproar.

The human lust for violence is not restricted to other humans as victims, but can include cruelty to animals also. Consider the repulsive sports of fox-hunting and bullfighting. Any attempt to have these sports banned encounters fierce opposition.

No more need be said on the apparently unquenchable thirst for aggression which is characteristic of the human species. As developmental psychologists, we need to question how it is that violent people acquire that trait. Various thinkers over the centuries have taken different stances on this. The philosopher Rousseau argued that humans in their natural state are peaceful, non-aggressive creatures, and that aggression is a by-product of a social pathology inherent in our society. In particular, Rousseau believed that society can make us mean, selfish and hostile to our peers.

As you know from Chapter 10, Freud took the opposite view. He suggested that we are born with a death instinct, Thanatos, which lies behind all violence and destruction. Freud supposed that Thanatos was not only responsible for aggression on an individual level, but also for that at a societal or intersocietal level, as in international conflicts. In other words, Freud believed that the death instinct of individuals instils a violent undercurrent in society.

In contrast to Rousseau, Freud considered that society may serve to harness or at least neutralize much of the natural human aggression. So Freud took the view that in a natural state, humans are much more outwardly aggressive than in their civilized state. This is a theme that seems to have been adopted by Nobel prizewinning novelist, William Golding. In his story, *Lord of the Flies*, Golding depicts young boys who are stranded on a desert island. Initially, the boys are friendly and cooperative, but this altruism turns out to be a legacy of the civilized norms of the boys' culture which is rather superficial and soon wears away. After a short while the boys segregate into two opposing factions and rain death, destruction and terror on each other. At this point, they have reverted to their natural aggressive state.

Freud put forward ideas on how society might help dissipate our aggressive impulses. He took the view that violent tendencies cannot be curbed, but that they can be channelled into a harmless activity. For example, engaging in vigorous sport will provide an outlet for aggressive impulses which is socially acceptable. Freud's view was not that violence should be suppressed but that it should be expressed in a way that can do no harm.

Freud also suggested that violent impulses could be vented vicariously in a process he called 'catharsis'. An implication is that watching a violent sport such as boxing could have the therapeutic effect of reducing aggressive impulses in the viewer, given that the viewer's violent instincts are expressed vicariously by the fighter who beats the daylights out of his opponent. In general then, it seems Freud took the view that exposure to violence is a good thing. Had he been around in these twilight years of the twentieth century, no doubt Freud would have advised parents to allow their children to watch such violent television programmes as *The A-Team*. He would have believed that viewing programmes like this would be conducive to good psychological adjustment and nonviolent behaviour in children.

However, such a view is anathema to the social learning approach to child development. Basically, this school of psychology holds that a great deal of the child's behaviour is based on imitation, particularly when there is some incentive for that imitation. Social learning theory seems to make a good deal of common sense. If children witness aggressive behaviour, then that behaviour will become legitimized to the child by the very fact that there is now a precedent for it. Without seeing the act of aggression, perhaps the child would not have thought of behaving in that way, and even if he had, perhaps he would have dismissed it immediately from his mind for the simple reason that quite literally it is not the done thing.

For example, suppose a house in the child's neighbourhood becomes derelict, and he witnesses some other children throwing stones and smashing the windows. He might feel encouraged to do likewise, having seen that the others did not get reprimanded and that it seems a daring and fun thing to do. Common sense says that surely the boy who sees this kind of vandalism is much more likely to smash windows in the derelict house than a boy in a similar situation who was not exposed to a model of destructive behaviour. We might also add that if the scenario had been different, and the vandals were immediately punished for smashing the windows, the observing boy would not follow suit in throwing stones. The boy would learn from the models that in this case vandalism didn't go unpunished, though the observing boy may have made a mental note of the delinquent behaviour as an exciting thing to do in some future situation, providing the risk of punishment is minimal.

Support for this common-sense view comes from social learning theorists Bandura, Ross and Ross (1961, 1963). In their study, 3-to-5-year-old children observed through a special viewing window the antics of an adult in an adjacent room which was well stocked with toys. One of the toys was a giant 'bobo' doll. This is the kind of doll that always bounces back into its upright position when knocked over, due to its special shape and strategically located weights inside it. The adult behaved in an exceedingly aggressive manner towards the doll, punching it, kicking it, hitting it with a hammer and so on.

Eventually he ceased his onslaught and left the scene. Following this the children were shepherded into the room with the bobo doll. What would the children do? Freud would predict that they would play peacefully with the attractive toys available in the room, now that any aggressive impulses had been siphoned off by watching the adult's exhibition of violence. What happened in fact was just the opposite: the children went straight to the bobo doll and continued where the adult had left off. They assaulted it with a hammer, punched it and kicked it, and used aggressive language such as 'punch him, kick him, bash him'. The children's behaviour was not an exact copy of the adult's, but rather seemed to be an adoption of his general pugnacious persona. In this study we see that the children's inclination to follow the example of the violent adult outweighed any desire they may have had to play with the attractive toys also present in the room.

Under a second condition the adult was rewarded and praised for his acts of aggression by other adults, whereas under a third condition he was punished and severely reprimanded. If the adult had been rewarded, children became violent when they gained access to the bobo doll just as they had done when no consequences followed the adult's hostility. If the adult's acts were followed by punishment, children did not abuse the doll. However, the behaviour sequences and the attitude displayed by the adult apparently had been noted by the children, since they exhibited a repertoire of violent acts originally committed by the adult when later on they, the children, were praised for aggression. This alerts us to the possibility that even when children observed the adult being punished for his aggression, the behaviour patterns had been assimilated by the children and lay dormant, waiting to be triggered off by a suitable opportunity for their expression.

Two issues arise from the classic work of Bandura and his associates. The first concerns the screening of television violence in children's programmes such as *The A-Team*. In this programme, children witness adult actors behaving violently towards one another. Freud's view might have been that by watching this programme children's aggressive impulses would be dissipated away harmlessly, but Bandura's findings suggest just the opposite: that exposure to violence instigates violence in the children and therefore that violence breeds more violence. However, just because children will mimic an adult they are exposed to in real life, it does not necessarily follow that they will imitate actors in television programmes. Perhaps children recognize that what goes on in dramatizations has little to do with what goes on in the real world and therefore should not be imitated.

The second issue is that although the children were willing to imitate an adult abusing a doll, we do not know from Bandura's findings whether they would imitate if it meant being nasty to other people. In other words, it could be that imitation where aggression is concerned is limited to inanimate objects.

A longitudinal study conducted by Leonard Eron and his colleagues addresses both these issues (Eron, 1982, 1987). Eron's study began in the early 1960s, when the subjects were about 8 years old, and continued into the 1980s when they were in their thirties. This study was unlike Bandura's in one respect: Bandura studied children under the rather artificial conditions of a laboratory investigation, whereas Eron was more concerned with how children behave in their daily surroundings.

Eron asked children how much television they watched and which programmes they liked best, how similar to real life they thought these programmes were and how much they liked certain characters. Meanwhile, Eron commissioned a panel of independent raters to judge the level of violence in a variety of children's programmes, and the level of violence displayed by specific characters in them.

To find out which of the children were aggressive, Eron asked them to rate each other. For example, he asked, 'Who is it that is always pushing and shoving?' He also got children to rate their own aggression as follows: 'Steven often gets angry and punches other kids. Are you just like Steven, just a little bit like him or not at all like him?'

Equipped with these techniques of investigation, Eron was able to construct a profile for each child based on (i) their television viewing habits, including amount of violence watched and attitudes towards the violence (whether or not the child thought it was a reflection of real life); and (ii) their violent temperament, as rated by themselves and by their classmates. His next step was to examine the relationship between these two variables.

The findings were highly revealing, and precisely as predicted from social learning theory. There was a very strong relationship between watching violent television programmes and aggressive behaviour in the children. Those who stated that their favourite programmes were ones notorious for violence were the very same children who were judged by their classmates to be the most violent in the class, and who judged themselves to be violent. Those with the biggest reputation for violence were the children who judged violent programmes to be lifelike, and judged that they liked the most violent characters in those programmes.

The second phase of the study took place when the subjects were 19 years old. Those rated as highly aggressive at age 8 were usually rated by peers as aggressive at age 19. Interestingly, the violence on television watched at age 19 was not related with violent behaviour of the subject as rated by peers. Remarkably, however, the violence watched on television at age 8 was strongly related with violent behaviour at 19. It seems that the violent disposition acquired at age 8 became a legacy which adhered to the individual resulting in a perpetuation of violent tendencies. Yet this violent disposition acquired at the early age did not necessarily promote the continued watching of violent television programmes.

The third phase of the study took place when subjects were aged 30. It remained the case that individuals who had watched violent television at age 8, and who were rated as most aggressive by their peers during childhood, continued to be aggressive at age 30. This time, however, the researchers had more than just self-ratings and judgments by peers as evidence for aggression. First, compared with subjects who had not watched violent programmes as children, these aggressive individuals had more convictions for drink-driving offences, and had committed various other traffic violations such as speeding. Second, their marriage partners were more likely to complain of being bullied and beaten by their aggressive spouse. Third, these aggressive individuals were more likely, by their own admission, to inflict severe beatings on their children. Finally, most surprising of all and at the same time persuasive of the detrimental consequences of watching television violence in childhood, was the finding that of those individuals judged to be violent, the more violent programmes they watched at age 8, the more criminal convictions they had at age 30. This is very strong evidence indeed for a direct relationship between viewing television violence as a child and anti-social behaviour as an adult.

It seems astonishing that television viewing habits at age 8 should have such profound and enduring consequences. Eron suggests that there may be a sensitive period between 8 and 12 years, and that personality formation is highly susceptible to experiences at that time. In common parlance, we might say that the child is at an impressionable age. If the child is exposed to copious violence on television at this age, it may lay the foundations for an enduring disposition for violence.

Returning to the issues identified earlier arising from Bandura's research, we are now in a position to shed some light on these. It does seem to be the case that children will imitate adult models which appear on television, particularly when children perceive the events in the programme to be akin to what goes on in real life. Second, imitated violence is not limited to that directed against inanimate objects. Unlike the children in Bandura's study, those observed by Eron were frequently violent against their classmates.

However, perhaps we are being a little premature in supposing that watching violent programmes caused children to be aggressive. We have a chicken and egg problem in that we cannot be sure which came first, watching violent television or having a violent disposition. It might have been that children who were born violent preferred to watch violent television programmes. In this case, we would find a strong relationship between watching violence and behaving violently, but it would not be the case that the violent television caused the violent behaviour. Rather, the cause-effect relationship would be the other way round.

Naturalistic studies like Eron's are best suited to describing what happens in development, and any inferences about causes of certain patterns of development have to be tentative. To make stronger statements about cause and effect, we need to intervene and manipulate hypothesized causes to find out if they do indeed have the expected effect. Eron carried out one such intervention investigation with a group of 10-year-old children who were renowned amongst classmates for their violent tendencies.

Eron began with the idea that these aggressive children came to be aggressive by watching violent television and believing that the events depicted were just like real life. To combat this, he set about persuading the children that the events in violent programmes were unrealistic. He attempted this by exposing to the children techniques used by the film makers to achieve realistic special effects. He then got the children to write a paragraph on why television violence is unrealistic and why watching too much television is bad. Eron read the paragraphs, made comments and then asked each child to rewrite their paragraph in the light of the feedback provided by the comments. Having done this, children read out their paragraph and were videoed doing so. Finally, they watched themselves when the tape was played back to them.

A group of equally violent children went through a very similar procedure, except for one crucial difference. Instead of writing about the lack of realism of television violence, they wrote about what they did last summer.

The findings were that those alerted to the lack of realism in television violence showed a marked reduction in their aggressive behaviour over the ensuing four months. Also, the relationship between viewing television violence and violent behaviour in these children disappeared. In other words, even if these previously violent children continued to watch violent television programmes, they remained nonviolent in their behaviour. In contrast, children who were not alerted to the lack of realism of violent television programmes showed no change and were still violent.

Although insight into the lack of realism helped reduce aggression in children in general, a few remained violent. Interestingly, these children continued to rate violent programmes as portraying the kind of things that go on in real life, despite the tutoring they received to help them think otherwise. So the important factor appears to be whether or not the child can accept that television violence is unrealistic.

Eron's intervention study neatly demonstrates that coming to terms with the lack of realism in television violence can curb subsequent aggressive behaviour in the child. However, it does not show directly that exposure to violence on television promotes aggression in the child, even if the findings are highly suggestive of this. Rather, the findings only show that certain tutoring can reduce violence. For evidence showing directly that exposure to violent television promotes aggression, we turn to the findings of other researchers.

Stein and Friedrich (1972) arranged for 4-year-old children to watch selected programmes for a four-week period. Some children watched violent programmes, such as *Batman*, and some watched nonviolent programmes. Meanwhile, teams of observers watched the children in their play sessions. These observers were not informed about which child had been assigned to which television regimen, so any personal views they may have held about the effects of television violence could not have biased the results. The findings were exactly as predicted, in that children who watched the violent programmes became more aggressive over the period of observation.

Another study obtained essentially the same result. Liebert and Baron (1972) showed an episode of *The Untouchables*, a violent cops and robbers programme, to 5-to-9-year-old children. Another group of children watched a film of a sporting event, which was judged to be equally action-packed, but lacking in violence. Subsequently, the children were allowed to play. Predictably, those who had watched the violent programme were more aggressive in their play compared with those who had watched the nonviolent programme.

Just to make absolutely sure, here is yet another study showing the same results. Parke, Berkowitz, Leyens, West and Sebastian (1977) studied boys in a detention centre for juvenile offenders. Some watched a series of violent films over a period of a week, while others watched nonviolent films. As usual, those who watched the violent films were more aggressive, both in physical assaults against peers and in verbal hostility.

These studies conclusively show that exposure to violent television promotes aggression in children, but watching violence can also have a more insidious effect. Even if children watching violence do not become aggressive themselves, the exposure to violence could desensitize them towards aggression, and make them perceive violence as a legitimate activity. This was demonstrated in a study conducted by Thomas, Horton, Lippincott and Drabman (1977). Children aged 9 years watched either a violent police drama or an action-packed sporting event. After the film, children from both conditions witnessed a violent exchange between some younger children, which involved verbal abuse, punching and kicking. The scene had been staged by the experimenters, taking care to make sure nobody really got hurt. While the nursery children squabbled, the experimenter observed the onlooking older children who had just been watching the films. The findings were that those who had watched the high-violence programme reacted less emotionally (failing to squirm or make anxious comments) than those who had watched the nonviolent programme. Apparently, those who watched the violent programme had become hardened to aggression, reducing the emotional impact further violence had on them.

In sum, the evidence is overwhelming in support of the idea that watching television violence can promote violent behaviour in children. Moreover, Eron's findings suggest that the aggressive tendencies inculcated in children through viewing television violence can be very long lasting, and may nurture an aggressive personality.

All the studies I have reported so far were carried out in America, and it would be perfectly reasonable to question whether the findings are specific to an American culture. For example, perhaps American children are exposed to more violent television programmes than are children in other countries. However, studies conducted along the same lines as Eron's have replicated his results in countries as diverse as Finland, Poland, Australia, Holland, and Israel. Alas, the findings are not purely an American phenomenon.

Let us take stock of the findings reported so far, in relation to their theoretical implications. Freud's suggestion was that we have an innate inclination to be aggressive, arising from the hypothesized instinctual drive, Thanatos. Freud's view was that aggressive impulses can be vented, and thus reduced vicariously, by observing violence. So from this account we would predict that watching violent television programmes would reduce aggression in children. The findings show that this is not the case, but rather that the opposite maintains: watching violent programmes promotes violence in children. This finding is consistent with the idea that aggressive behaviour arises from the child's experiences, and that aggression is not instinctive after all.

However, violence on television is unlikely to be the only experience that can promote aggression in children. Aggression and violence are not new phenomena even though violent crime may appear to be on the increase in our society. Our species has indulged in bloody battles and brutality over the millennia, and all this cannot be attributed to television violence for obvious reasons. What factors might be responsible for such aggression? Presumably aspects of parental practice are important. We shall now examine this idea.

A common-sense view which seems to prevail from time to time is that perhaps violence is on the increase because parents do not keep their children under sufficiently strict control. For example, a popular view in relation to soccer violence seems to be that if hooligans received a sound thrashing occasionally their unruly behaviour would be brought under control, and they would become more civilized.

However, the available evidence suggests this common-sense view is wrong. Indeed, it seems not only that corporal punishment fails to curb aggression in children, but that on the contrary it may increase it. Once again, the pertinent data come from Leonard Eron's studies. In addition to finding a relationship between television viewing habits and aggression, Eron also found that children subjected to more corporal punishment in the home were the ones who were more aggressive at school, as judged by their classmates.

Eron argues vehemently that physical punishment causes aggression in children for the following reason. By lashing out at the child, the parent may provide a model of what is the appropriate response when one is frustrated. That is, the parent appears to the child to have become frustrated for some reason, and as a consequence acts in a violent and destructive manner. So although the parent could be punishing the child with the aim of curbing the child's aggression, the parent may inadvertently be providing the child with a model of aggressive behaviour in the face of frustration. As a result, when the child experiences frustration in other situations, he may react in the way he assumes is appropriate, by committing an act of violence.

Apart from this, punishment only indicates what the child should not do, and gives little indication of the alternative appropriate behaviour. Thus, one aggressive response of the child which is followed by punishment could simply be replaced by another aggressive response which has not yet been punished.

Eron's argument that physical punishment causes aggression, that aggression breeds aggression, is a highly plausible one, but the relationship between corporal punishment and aggression towards peers can be interpreted in other ways. It might be that aggressive children are born aggressive, and that their parents feel they have to resort to corporal punishment as a severe attempt to inhibit the aggression. We will never be able to find out for sure, since we are unable to carry out an intervention study on this topic for reasons of ethics. It would be unethical to subject a child to corporal punishment for the purpose of finding out whether aggression increases as a consequence. In that case, we have to rely on argument to help determine the cause-effect relationship, and the best that can be said is that Eron's argument is a highly plausible one.

Another factor we might suppose is involved in aggression is frustration. Perhaps aggression inevitably follows frustration, and therefore if we could reduce frustration we would witness a decrease in aggression in the world at large. In this case, 'frustration' refers to instances where the individual builds up an expectancy about receiving some reward, or some enjoyable experience, but then the expectation is thwarted.

Such a suggestion is sometimes put forward to account for acts of vandalism committed by the less privileged members of society. Television commercials and advertisements in newspapers and magazines often encourage us to hope for, and sometimes perhaps to expect, a more salubrious life style which in fact is out of our financial reach. Those poorer members of society who are repeatedly frustrated in their quest to attain societally defined expectations may ultimately resort to acts of aggressive vandalism as a natural response to the situation. Is this view of things accurate?

The pioneering study on this was carried out by Barker, Dembo and Lewin (1941). They led a group of young children to believe they would be able to play with some attractive toys, but then they were prevented from doing so by the experimenter, and were only allowed to look at the toys through a transparent screen. After a frustrating wait, the experimenter eventually allowed the children access to the toys, and observed their behaviour. The children behaved very violently, throwing the toys at the wall and generally abusing them. Another group of children who had immediate access to the toys played with them peacefully. We might have expected that children who had to wait would have had greater respect for the toys, valuing them more highly after being deprived of them for a sustained period. That was not the case, and it seems that instead the children's frustration at having to wait caused them to behave violently.

Evidently, aggression in response to frustration does seem to occur. However, it need not occur, as demonstrated by Mallick and McCandless (1966). In their study, children aged 8 years were thwarted from attaining a cash prize due to the awkward behaviour of a peer upon whom they were relying. In other words, an attempt to achieve a goal was frustrated by another child. Under one condition, children were told that the one responsible for the failure was sleepy and upset, whereas under another condition no explanation was offered. The findings were that when children had been given a good reason for the behaviour of the child who frustrated them, they directed little aggression towards him. In contrast, if no explanation was given, children were much more aggressive to the one who had been an obstacle to their goal. This shows that although aggression is likely to be targeted at a source of frustration, this need not be the case; aggression is not an inevitable consequence of frustration.

The same was demonstrated more powerfully in a study by Davitz (1952). Children aged around 8 years played in small groups. Members of some of these groups were rewarded for aggressive and competitive behaviour, while others were rewarded for cooperative and constructive behaviour. All children were then subjected to a severely frustrating experience. They were led to believe that they would be able to watch an entertaining film and that they would be issued with chocolates. The chocolates were handed out and the film commenced. Half-way through, just as the film was getting to an exciting point, the experimenter switched it off and claimed back all the chocolates from the children. Finally, they were given opportunity to play. Predictably, those who had been rewarded for aggressive and competitive behaviour expressed a great deal of aggression in their play session following this frustrating experience. In sharp contrast, those who had been rewarded for constructive behaviour were far less aggressive in the play situation, and instead engaged in some constructive play activites. Once again, the findings show that aggression is not an inevitable consequence of frustration, and that, in particular, prior learning experience can help curb aggression in the face of frustration.

Another common view of aggression in children is that it forms part of a more general corpus of naughty behaviour expressed by the child in order to get attention from adults. Perhaps children prefer to be infamous rather than anonymous. The implication is that if children do not get sufficient adult attention, if they are ignored by their caregivers, they will engage in behaviour which the adult simply cannot ignore. Such behaviour might be hurting other children or smashing toys: aggressive behaviour.

Brown and Elliot (1965) conducted a study pertinent to this issue. Teachers in a particular nursery agreed to ignore their 3-to-4-year-old children when they expressed aggression, but provide plenty of attention when children were engaged in peaceful and constructive behaviour which was incompatible with aggression. After a few weeks of the study aggressive behaviour diminished substantially in the nursery, suggesting that once aggression failed as an attention-getter, its expression no longer served any purpose for the children.

The findings support the idea that aggression could emerge as part of a complex of attention-seeking behaviour. It is tempting to suggest that when aggression is expressed as an attention-getter, it is an indication that the caregiver has been remiss in giving attention to the child when she is engaged in peaceful and constructive activities. On the other side of the coin, we see once again that a change in the child's experiences can reduce her aggression, and that the child can learn to behave nonviolently.

Psychological rejection seems to be strongly associated with aggressive behaviour in children. Eron (1982) questioned parents about their attitude towards their child, particularly whether they were satisfied with the child's table manners, whether they thought their child was too forgetful, or whether they thought their child was a poor reader for her age. Children whose parents had expressed dissatisfaction about them in response to these questions were the ones who were viewed by their classmates as being aggressive. In this case, Eron took disapproval of the child by parents as a sign of parental rejection.

A study by Dodge, Coie, Pettit and Price (1990) also identified a relationship between aggression and rejection, but this time the rejection was by the child's classmates. In this study, children who tended to be rejected by their classmates, those who had few friends, were the ones who exhibited most aggression in play sessions.

Once again we are faced with a chicken and egg problem. We cannot be sure whether children became aggressive because they were upset at being rejected, or whether they became rejected by parents and peers only after they had acquired a track record of aggressive incidents to their name. Whatever the cause-effect relationship, it is hardly surprising that social outcasts tend to be aggressive. Our everyday observations tell us that this is so.

One final matter we should consider is the gender of the child. A popular view is that girls are likely to be less aggressive than boys. Some of the studies on child aggression have used male subjects only, as in the research of Parke *et al.* (1977) looking at the relationship between television viewing and violence in boys detained in a centre for juvenile delinquents. We cannot be completely sure that the findings would have been the same had girls been the subjects in this study. However, from studies in which girls have participated, there is no reason to suppose that factors which influence aggressive behaviour are any different for boys and girls. For example, Eron's studies examining the relationship between viewing aggression on television and aggressive acts show that the relationship holds for both boys and girls.

In sum, girls seem to be just as susceptible to factors which influence aggression as boys. That is not to say females are equally aggressive as males. That is clearly not the case where adults are concerned, as is demonstrated by the differing crime statistics associated with the two sexes. However, the same processes apply for girls as they do for boys as regards aggressive behaviour.

Taking into consideration the overall picture generated by the findings reported in this chapter, the evidence is overwhelmingly in support of the idea that human aggression is strongly influenced by the environment. Perhaps the factor which stands out above all others is the child's tendency to imitate acts of aggression. When children see television characters behave violently, they are subsequently tempted to do likewise. When they observe their parents administering severe physical punishment, once again they follow suit by hitting classmates.

Just as children can learn to respond aggressively, so it seems they can learn to respond non-aggressively. The study by Davitz (1952) showed that this was the case, where children learned to react constructively rather than aggressively in the face of frustration.

In view of these conclusions, we are able to say with considerable certainty that human aggression is not exclusively due to a hypothesized instinctive lust for violence as suggested by Freud. Instead, Rousseau's suggestion seems more likely to be true, that humans are peaceful creatures by nature, but that society has the potential to mould them into violent beasts.

Further Reading

A good account of social learning theory can be found in Chapter 3 of Patricia Miller's book:

MILLER, P.H. (1989) *Theories of Developmental Psychology*, 2nd ed., New York, W.H. Freeman and Co.

A more general account of human aggression, going beyond issues of developmental psychology, can be found in Chapter 5 of Elliot Aronson's book:

ARONSON, E. (1988) *The Social Animal*, 5th ed., New York, W.H. Freeman and Co.

As for the relationship between television viewing and aggression, there can be no better source than the original:

ERON, L.D. (1982) 'Parent-child interaction, television violence, and aggression of children', *American Psychologist*, **37**, 197–211.

Chapter 13

The Development of Moral Consciousness

To some extent, what we are to examine in this chapter forms the other side of the coin of the content of the previous chapter. There we looked at the development of anti-social behaviour, but here we are going to look at the development of pro-social or altruistic behaviour which in many cases results from the development of a moral conscience.

The introduction to the previous chapter might make you think that there is not much to celebrate in the way of altruism in humans. However, that is not so, and under some circumstances we witness great sacrifices in the interests of the well-being of others. Consider the Band Aid festivals organized by Bob Geldof in the 1980s. These ventures benefited from overwhelming support from artists and fans alike, to raise substantial sums of money for famine relief in Ethiopia. In no way was this unique in terms of the generosity of the response it provoked. 'Children in Need' and 'Comic Relief' also enjoy considerable sponsorship from the general public. Apart from these high-profile 'show business' charities, very many more generate substantial funds with the help of volunteers with collection boxes in civic centres.

Altruism is not only manifest in terms of generosity in donating funds. People are also willing to devote time and effort in the interests of less fortunate members of society. For example, there are people who function as unpaid voluntary workers in hospitals, assisting nurses and porters. Additionally, people join the Samaritans to lend a sympathetic ear to those who have become suicidal, and who may benefit from expressing their difficulties to somebody with patience who will listen. Samaritans display considerable dedication in that they are willing to sit up all night waiting for distress calls from those with severe emotional difficulty.

Very often altruistic deeds are truly heroic. This was exemplified in the *Herald of Free Enterprise* ferry disaster, when the fully laden boat capsized in the English Channel with tragic consequences. Although there are gory tales of pockets of 'every man for himself' mentality, in sharp contrast there also emerged some cases of great altruism. For example, there was the man who straddled two structures with his body thus forming a human bridge, allowing others to climb over him to safety.

The most extreme case of altruism must be when an individual acts knowing that by doing so he will sacrifice his life to preserve that of others. One such case arose from the long-lasting conflict which prevails in Northern Ireland. Somebody threw a hand grenade into an open-top bus travelling around Belfast. In a barely comprehensible act of bravery, one of the passengers smothered the device by lying on top of it. In so doing, he sacrificed his own life, but preserved those of the other passengers.

Humans really are curious creatures. Callous deeds and terrifying destructiveness beggar the imagination, yet humans are also capable of extreme acts of self-sacrifice and altruism, as the examples above illustrate.

The concern of this chapter is to look at how pro-social behaviour develops in humans. One way of tackling this issue would be to suppose that altruistic behaviour is learned in much the same way that anti-social behaviour is learned. In other words, perhaps we need only look at the content of the previous chapter, and apply the principles which emerged to the case of pro-social behaviour. Indeed, this has been done to good effect by Eron, amongst others, but we shall not cover that ground once again in this chapter. Instead, we shall focus on belief structures to help us understand the development of a moral consciousness.

Beliefs and attitudes govern behaviour in humans. If an individual believes it is correct that self-interest should be sacrificed for the well-being of others, then the individual is likely to engage in altruistic behaviour. This could range from making donations to charity to laying down one's life for the sake of others. Thus, to understand altruistic behaviour, it is useful to understand the thought processes which underlie that behaviour.

The developmental psychology of Jean Piaget is highly relevant to the child's acquisition of the thought processes needed for a moral consciousness. As you will recall from Chapter 1, Piaget supposed that under approximately 6 years the child is egocentric. In other words, the child finds it difficult or impossible to empathize, to imagine someone else's point of view. If the child has no capacity to empathize, then it follows that the child is unlikely to sympathize. The idea Piaget put forward is that the cognitive limitation of the young child imposes a constraint on her capacity for concern about others, which is likely to be reflected in a lack of altruistic behaviour. The assumption is that once the child can empathize, altruism will automatically follow, and there is no need to go to great lengths to account for this. Looking at it the other way round, a lack of altruism could be the result of retarded cognitive development.

That might seem fine as an argument, and we might suppose that in so far as young children are egocentric they will lack a potential for altruism. Piaget was not satisfied with leaving it at that. He sought to devise a test directly related to moral issues to find out about the child's moral reasoning and judgment. He did this by telling the child stories involving moral puzzles. In these, a protagonist caused some damage, either with good or bad intent. In order to understand the moral issue at stake, the child had to focus on the intent of the protagonist. Of course, as Piaget repeatedly claimed, this is something which does not come easily to the young child, who, so Piaget supposed, has difficulty considering others' viewpoints.

Children listened to pairs of stories presented together. One was about a little boy who wanted to help his father by filling the father's ink-well. In doing so, he clumsily but accidentally spilled the ink over the tablecloth, making a very large and unsightly stain. Another story was about a little boy who wanted to play with his father's ink-pot just for fun, even though he was forbidden to do so. Whilst playing, a spot of ink fell on the tablecloth and made a small mark. Children listening to the stories were then asked which of the story protagonists was naughtier. Younger subjects, those about 6 or 7 years, often judge that the naughtier protagonist is the one who made the large stain, simply because the stain he made was big. Older children, in contrast, judge that the child who made the large stain was not naughty because he had good intent. What we find, then, is that younger children overlook good intent, and focus instead on the extent of damage caused when making moral judgments.

Piaget suggested that we should view the older child as a 'moral subjectivist', in that she considers subjective factors, such as the good or wicked intent of the protagonist, in judging whether or not he was naughty. Piaget calls the younger child a 'moral realist', since she neglects intent and simply focuses on the extent of damage. For these children, moral judgments are based on criteria relating to events in the real world, rather than on psychological factors.

Although younger children are prone to moral realism, and this is likely to have something to do with egocentrism, the age of transition to moral subjectivism is less tidy compared with other Piagetian phenomena, such as conservation. This is probably because adults sometimes punish children according to extent of damage, rather than intent behind the action, which is likely to hinder their grasp of the importance of intent in the moral evaluation of behaviour. This idea gets support from a study by Leon (1984), who discovered that children of parents who punish according to the extent of damage caused are more likely to be moral realists than are children whose parents punish according to naughty intent underlying the act. So it seems that even when children have the cognitive capacity to take into consideration the intent of others, it may take a while to bring this reasoning to bear on moral dilemmas, depending on how justice is handled in the home.

Piaget's pioneering work has been the subject of methodological criticism. As you might recall from Chapter 2, although Piaget had some highly stimulating ideas, his experimental techniques very often left a great deal to be desired. An obvious problem is that Piaget's stories place substantial demands on memory, demands which could be too great for the fledgling cognition of young children. A point made by Parsons, Ruble, Klosson, Feldman and Rholes (1976) is that information about good or bad intent of the story protagonist appears early in the story, whereas information about the extent of damage caused by the action appears at the end of the story.

Piaget reports the phenomenon as children's focus on extent of damage as opposed to intent, but Parsons *et al.*'s comment raises the possibility that due to memory limitations, perhaps the young children recalled only the most recently presented information, which happened to be the extent of damage caused, and focused on this when making their judgments. The point is that perhaps the immature morality in young children is more apparent than real, and that Piaget's test is no more than a demonstration of memory weakness.

This alternative explanation of Piaget's findings was investigated by Wimmer, Wachter and Perner (1982). They prepared a story which conformed to Piaget's formula, though it was different in its detail. The story was about a person painting a fence. In one version of the story this person was depicted as a boy who was lazy and put in very little effort. Although he was lazy, this boy actually painted quite a lot of the fence, because he was a big boy equipped with a large paintbrush. In another version of the story, the protagonist was a boy who put in a huge effort, but because he was small and equipped with only a small brush, he did not cover a great area of the fence. After listening to the story, children had to reward the protagonist by giving him cookies.

The important information, then, was how much effort the protagonist put into the job, and how much of the fence he covered. Piaget would predict that younger children would judge the boy who covered more fence to be the good boy, and reward him with more cookies accordingly. His prediction would be based on the idea that young children are moral realists, focusing on the outcome of the deed, rather than on effort. Parsons *et al.* would also predict that younger children would reward most highly the protagonist who covered more fence, but for a different reason. Namely, they suppose that younger children would forget about the effort the boy put in, and only remember how much fence was painted.

However, Wimmer *et al.* took the precaution of supporting memory of all the key information by introducing pictures to depict this. So when the experimenter explained that the little boy tried very hard, and was hard-working, accompanying this was a picture of the protagonist being diligent and energetic. In contrast, when the experimenter explained that the big boy was lazy, an accompanying picture portrayed this protagonist as tardy. Crucially, these pictures remained in view once the experimenter had introduced them, and thus were available to prop up the weak memory of the younger subjects.

The results supported Piaget's earlier findings, in that children aged 4 and 6 years tended to allocate reward to protagonists according to outcome, in this case concerning how much fence was painted. In contrast children aged 8 years were much more likely to take into consideration how much effort the protagonist had put into the job. This time, the outcome bias exhibited by younger children could not be attributed to memory failure, since all the relevant information concerning effort remained in view up to the moment children allocated reward. So it would seem Piaget was correct to view young children as moral realists.

Before we accept Piaget's conclusion as definitive, we ought to give consideration to one further objection, raised by Nicholls (1978). Nicholls suggested that young children's peculiar outcome-based moral judgments could be more to do with failure to understand cause-effect relationships rather than to do with failure to give sufficient weight to good or naughty intent. Nicholls correctly pointed out that in Piaget's stories there is no obvious cause-effect relationship between the intent of the protagonist and the extent of damage which resulted. In other words, neither the good nor the naughty boy intended to spill ink, rather it was just that one boy accidentally caused some damage whilst engaged in a forbidden activity. Consequently, we cannot say that the naughty boy's bad intent was responsible for the ink stain.

In Wimmer *et al.*'s story, things were different. The effort the protagonist put in presumably was related to outcome, except that one protagonist had the benefit of advantages independent of effort, in the form of a large paintbrush. Despite this, it might still be the case that the young subjects did not understand that all things being equal, greater effort would result in a larger area of the fence being painted. If so, young children's apparent moral realism would be due to a lack of understanding how effort features in outcome, rather than due to ignoring intention (in this case expressed as effort) as an important factor in making moral judgments.

To check for this possibility, Wimmer *et al.* asked children to estimate how much fence would be painted by a protagonist who put lots of effort into the job, and how much would be covered by one who put in only a little effort. Even many of the 4-year-olds seemed to understand that all things being equal, more effort results in more of the fence being covered, and therefore these children clearly did understand the relationship between effort and outcome. Most important, despite understanding the cause-effect relationship, younger children still allocated reward according to outcome rather than effort. So although Nicholls' criticism of Piaget could have turned out to be valid, in fact Wimmer *et al.* show that young children have a good understanding of the cause-effect relationship, yet still function as moral realists.

Let us now consider the wider implications of moral realism. We can see that not until about 8 years of age do children begin to attach great importance to the intent behind the act when reasoning about moral issues. Presumably there is some relationship between one's moral reasoning and one's moral behaviour. In that case, we might suppose that young children are not so much oriented towards 'trying to do the right thing', but rather are geared up to behaving in a way that is defined as good by others. In other words, young children may be unable to consider the difference between good and bad independently of the moral guidance they receive from parents and teachers.

However, an ability to recognize the importance of intention or effort is not all there is to moral development. According to Martin Hoffman (1970), the foundations of a moral conscience are laid in the first year of life. Hoffman points out that young infants find crying and laughing contagious: they cry when others cry, and laugh when others laugh. According to Hoffman, this forms a basis for empathy.

Both Piaget and Freud tell us that young babies cannot distinguish between themselves and their surroundings, including other people. Hoffman accepts this point, and therefore argues that the young baby who has a basis of empathy, thanks to a capacity for imitation, is lacking in another respect: the baby knows of nothing apart from the self.

Beyond the first year, a change takes place, according to Hoffman, when the youngster develops an awareness of the independent existence of people. Now the infant knows that when another child is crying, that other child is in a state of distress, even if he, the beholder, feels fine. However, the young child is not yet sufficiently aware of others as distinct from self to enable him to think of ways that could alleviate the distressful condition of the other person. For example, if Dad is upset because his employment has terminated, a young child might try to provide help by offering Dad a soft toy, whereas it would have been more apt to offer Dad his pipe.

By the age of about 10, Hoffman suggests that children come to understand not only the plight of individuals, but that of groups of people. This understanding undergoes further development into the teens and adulthood, as the individual forms a coherent set of attitudes and behaviour according to moral or political movements. For example, the individual may come to feel that it is immoral to pollute the environment with human waste, and begin by altering his own behaviour in accordance with that view, but then come to take active part in environmentalist rallies and protests to persuade others to adopt the same attitudes and behaviours. So as the individual approaches adulthood, behaviour of moral relevance can be strongly governed by attitudes and beliefs concerning the correct way to live one's life. These moral values need not be imposed upon the individual, as in the case of religious teaching, but rather they could be constructed by the individual.

Returning to young children, it follows from Hoffman's account that their pro-social behaviour will be highly susceptible to the influence of parents and teachers. We already know from the previous chapter that adult models can inadvertently encourage the development of anti-social behaviour, but what we have not considered so far is evidence suggesting that pro-social behaviour can be nurtured by the same processes. A study conducted by Yarrow, Scott and Waxler (1973) addressed this issue.

In Yarrow *et al.*'s study, 3-to-4-year-olds were assigned to a caregiver who modelled altruistic behaviour in various ways. She displayed a warm, nurturant attitude, offering help, sympathizing and protecting. The adult also modelled altruism in play sessions, when she offered assistance to disadvantaged characters in scenes involving the children's toys. Finally, the adult modelled altruism in a real-life situation by showing sympathy to a visitor to the nursery who bumped her head. The observing children witnessed their caregiver exhibit concern and offer medication.

Some weeks later, children went to visit the home of a mother with her young baby. The mother had difficulty managing the situation, and she dropped some of her sewing on the floor, and her baby dropped some of his toys. The investigators wanted to know whether the visiting children would come to the aid of the mother and baby in need. The findings were very clear. Those children who had witnessed their own caregiver behaving in a consistently altruistic manner spontaneously offered help to the mother and baby.

Things were different in the case of children whose caregiver had only been partially altruistic. For example some children had a caregiver who had been warm and nurturant towards them and to toy characters in the pretend play situation, but not to the visitor who bumped her head. These children were not so willing to offer help to the mother and baby in difficulty.

Yarrow *et al.* successfully demonstrated that under the right conditions, young children will adopt a nurturant and altruistic attitude displayed by an adult model. The adopted behaviour is not confined to direct imitation of the model. Had that been the case, children might have been sympathetic to a person who bumped her head, but not to the mother and baby in need because they had never seen pro-social behaviour modelled in that particular situation. It turned out this was not the case, and it seemed the children had acquired a generally altruistic disposition.

The possibility that young children can learn to be altruistic does not necessarily imply that their altruistic behaviour is merely mechanistic. On the contrary, Eisenberg, Fabes, Miller, Shell, Shea and May-Plumlee (1990) report that 4-year-olds observing another child in distress are affected on a physiological level, as indicated by speeding up of heart rate. When the observing child has the opportunity to provide assistance, thus reducing the difficulties of the child in distress, heart rate shows a decrease. This finding suggests that observing suffering in others, and helping to relieve that suffering, have a physical and emotional effect on young children.

Putting these studies into the more general framework of moral development, we can say the following. The work of Piaget and Hoffman collectively tells us that as children develop, their improved cognitive faculties make them better equipped to think about the intentions underlying the behaviour of others, and so they are better able to focus on this rather than just on the consequences of the behaviour of the other person. It might be the case, therefore, that young children are poor at making moral judgments because they are lacking in an ability to empathize. However, although a lack of empathy may adversely influence moral judgments and moral thought, it need not adversely affect sympathetic and altruistic behaviour. Young children are highly receptive to behaviour modelled by adults. As we saw in the previous chapter, if aggressive behaviour is modelled, children will themselves begin to behave aggressively. In contrast, as Yarrow *et al.* demonstrate, if children are exposed to a consistently altruistic model, they will adopt a general pro-social pattern of behaviour.

We shall now tackle the problem of moral development from a slightly different angle. For many centuries, an individual's virtue has often been judged according to how well that individual observes and adheres to laws and rules dictated by a higher authority. In the case of Christian societies, in times gone by the highest authority was the word of God, as stated in the Bible. Thus, a 'good person' was one who followed the laws of the Bible very closely.

Our society has become more secularized, but people are still often judged to be good or bad according to whether they follow the laws formulated in Parliament. Those who do not observe the laws are likely to be considered bad people, as in the case of the habitual drunk driver, or the thief.

However, it is not necessarily the case that the morally correct thing to do is to follow the law of the land. For example, the anti-semitic laws implemented in Nazi Germany were morally indefensible, as were the apartheid laws in South Africa. Most people recognize the turpitude of these laws, but things are not always so clear cut. For example, very many people in Britain, though certainly not all, felt that the Community Charge was a form of taxation that was no less than wicked.

A moral dilemma arises from these cases of controversial laws. We generally accept that the correct thing to do is to follow the laws of the government, particularly if we accept the constitution of that government, which most people seem to do in democracies like ours. Yet we may feel sometimes that the law is wrong, and decide to act according to another moral code, thus placing ourselves in an invidious situation. In this sense, it may take courage to act contrary to the law, even though we typically think of lawbreakers as having defective characters. This sentiment is expressed in a famous quotation from the novelist E.M. Forster, who said, 'if I had to choose between betraying my country and betraying my friend, I hope I should have the guts to betray my country.'

The pre-eminent figure in the field of moral reasoning is Lawrence Kohlberg (e.g. 1981), and he advanced a stage theory of thought processes related to externally instituted rules. The theory proposes three levels of moral development, each subdivided into two stages, thus making six stages in all. The three levels coincide with three of the main stages in Piaget's theory of cognitive development: Level 1, preconventional morality, coincides with Piaget's stage of preoperational intelligence; Level 2, conventional morality, coincides with Piaget's stage of concrete operations; and Level 3, postconventional morality, coincides with Piaget's stage of formal operations.

To demonstrate stage-like changes in moral thinking, Kohlberg, like Piaget, composed stories depicting moral dilemmas. Here is the most famous of them:

> A woman was near her death from a special kind of cancer. There was one drug that the doctors thought might save her. It was a form of radium that a druggist in the town had recently discovered. The drug was expensive to make, but the druggist was charging ten times what the drug cost him to make. He paid $200 for the radium, and charged $2,000 for a small dose. The sick woman's husband, Heinz, went to everyone he knew to borrow the money, but he could only get together about $1,000, which is half what it cost. He told the druggist his wife was dying, and asked him to sell it cheaper or let him pay later. But the druggist said, 'No, I discovered the drug and I'm going to make money from it.' So Heinz got desperate and broke into the man's store to steal the drug for his wife.

Following the story, Kohlberg asked a series of questions to assess the moral reasoning of the subject. He was not so much interested in whether subjects gave the right or wrong answers. Indeed, who is to say what is the right or wrong answer regarding these moral dilemmas? Instead, Kohlberg was concerned with the kind of moral reasoning people engage in when tackling the dilemma. Here are the questions:

> Should Heinz have done that? Was it actually wrong or right? Why? Is it a husband's duty to steal the drug for his wife if he can get it no other way? Would a good husband do it? Did the druggist have the right to charge that much where there was no law actually setting a limit to the price? Why?

These questions were designed to probe awareness of the conflict, that on the one hand stealing is bad but that on the other hand every effort should be made to preserve life. In particular, Kohlberg sought to establish whether subjects attached most importance to rules instituted by society, or to a personal sense of the difference between right and wrong, even if this went against societal rules.

The following is a description of the stages Kohlberg identified from the investigations he conducted.

Level 1, Stage 1. Actions are judged according to the physical consequences they have, and the intent behind the action plays no part in moral evaluation. In other words, young children are moral realists, as described by Piaget. Secondly, the child conducts herself purely according to anticipation of reward or punishment, and the intrinsic moral correctness of the act is not recognized. So, for example, the child might abstain from stealing not because she feels others' possessions should not be coveted, but because she fears she would be shouted at if she did steal.

Level 1, Stage 2. At this stage, the child understands correct behaviour to be that which satisfies her needs. During this stage, children appear to use their friendship as a form of barter: for example, 'I won't be your friend if you don't play with my doll's house', or alternatively, 'If you give me some of your sweets, I'll be your best friend'. Subsequently, we may see the child who stated the condition going round the playground boasting that Gemma is her best friend because Gemma gave her some sweets. In this stage, then, the child is purely geared up to approving or disapproving of others' behaviour according to whether that behaviour is to their own advantage.

Level 2, Stage 3. The transition to the new level is marked by an awareness of others' points of view and intentions, and an inclination to conform to institutionalized order. The child's morality seems to revolve around seeking approval from figures who wield power and represent authority. No assessment of moral worth of an act for children in this stage extends beyond the reaction of the authority figure. As such, the child is highly conformist, and the concept of the 'good boy' or 'nice girl' features prominently.

Level 2, Stage 4. In this stage, the child seeks to uphold and justify social norms, and identifies with individuals or groups who hold senior positions in the maintenance of social order. The child perceives the rules as fixed and sacrosanct, and judges moral behaviour according to the extent to which any individual adheres to these. So in relation to the story about Heinz, children in this stage would judge that Heinz was bad because he stole, given that there is a law against stealing. They are unwilling to accept that Heinz's act was good in the sense that he might have saved a life, simply because there is no law to say that a person should go to great lengths to save another person's life. Such an act is not recognized as morally good simply because there is no law pertaining to it.

Level 3, Stage 5. The individual no longer views rules and laws as fixed, and the product of an inevitable order of the universe. Instead, the individual has come to appreciate that rules are relative, and merely constructed by certain groups. The laws are viewed as phenomena which can be understood by examining the history of any particular group, with the corollary that if the historical background had been different, then the laws would be different. The individual is now able to adopt a legalistic mentality, with the attitude that if a law seems to be wrong or unjust, then that law ought to be changed. However, the individual may ultimately feel that morally correct behaviour is behaviour that falls within the predefined bounds of the law. So the individual may recognize that laws are unjust, yet nonetheless uphold the idea that laws are morally binding, and that it would be immoral for any individual to violate democratically agreed upon rules.

Level 3, Stage 6. This is the highest stage of moral development. according to Kohlberg. The individual may adhere to externally imposed rules much of the time, but now her behaviour may also be governed by her own moral principles, independently of rules imposed on her from an external source. For example, suppose a schoolteacher believes it would be in her pupils' interests to watch a video recording of a certain television programme. The teacher knows that a copyright law forbids her from doing this, and that she can get round this by requesting permission from the broadcasting company. However, the teacher chooses not to get permission, and proceeds with showing the film. It might have been that she did not get permission because of laziness, but in fact that is not the case. The real reason is as follows.

The teacher in question judged that showing the video to her pupils would in no way be to the detriment of the company which made the programme. She judged in contrast that the time and effort involved in getting permission to show the video could be greatly to the detriment of her pupils' education. The teacher has a fixed amount of time, and any effort she puts into seeking copyright permission would be at the expense of putting time into making comments on her children's essays. Additionally, the film presented important information that the pupils could use in their exam, which was in the not too distant future. By the time the teacher had obtained permission to show the programme, it might have been too late for her pupils.

It is not that the teacher thinks the copyright law is bad in any general sense. Indeed, she holds a very firm belief that authors who write important educational books ought to be paid more, and that one way that could be achieved would be to ensure that copyright laws are observed. Despite all this, our hypothetical teacher felt it to be imperative that her pupils should see the programme on video in good time for the exam, and that it would be morally wrong for her to be spending time sorting out copyright technicalities at the expense of time spent giving personal attention to her pupils. For these reasons, she came to the decision that the morally correct thing to do was to violate the copyright law, and show the video.

In this case, we can see that the teacher upheld the rights of the pupils over and above those of the law concerning copyright infringements. The individual functioning at Kohlberg's Stage 6 has the capability to perceive higher moral principles, those which transcend any specific laws. These relate to justice, equality of human rights, and respect for the dignity of other people.

According to Kohlberg, we gravitate towards Stage 6 as we develop, but not everyone gets to the top of the hierarchy of stages. Indeed, Kohlberg acknowledges that perhaps only a minority of the population progress all the way to the highest stage. So nobody can move down a stage, but on the other hand it is possible that a given individual would fail to move up into a higher stage. Another central point Kohlberg makes is that it is impossible for any of the stages to be skipped during the course of an individual's moral development.

Very many studies have been conducted to test the accuracy of Kohlberg's description of moral development. In a review of such studies, Rest (1983) concludes that moral development does proceed in the way Kohlberg suggests, and that the sequence of stages maintains across a variety of cultures investigated throughout the world.

One study in particular has generated an intriguing finding exactly as Kohlberg would have predicted (Nunner-Winkler and Sodian, 1988). Children aged 4 to 8 years listened to a story in which a protagonist stole some sweets she wanted. Child listeners were then invited to judge whether the protagonist thief felt good or bad about what she had done. Nearly all the 8-year-olds tested judged that the protagonist felt bad, and recognized that she would feel guilty about succumbing to her temptation to steal. In contrast, many children of 6 years and below judged that the protagonist felt good, reasoning that she had got what she wanted. In the older children, then, we see reasoning according to violation of a well-known rule that people should not steal. In contrast, in younger children, we see reasoning according to the 'feel good' principle. This finding is perfectly consistent with the kind of shift Kohlberg suggested occurs during moral development.

We can now bring the story full circle. We began this chapter with comments on human altruism, and proposed that moral reasoning is likely to play an important part in this. One point made was that once a child is proficient in attending to and assessing others' plights, she is better equipped to sympathize compared with the early stage when empathy is not so easy. That point seems to be a valid one, but Eisenberg (1986) has proposed ideas which complement Kohlberg's, specifically in relation to moral development concerning altruistic behaviour.

Eisenberg presented a story to children about a child going to a friend's birthday party, who comes across another child who has fallen and hurt himself. The moral dilemma is: does the child on the way to the birthday party stop and give assistance, thus jeopardizing his opportunity to have a piece of birthday cake, or does he proceed to the party thus not helping someone in need? The findings are consistent with what we might have predicted from Kohlberg's theory. Namely, children who we could suppose would be in Kohlberg's Level 1 apparently operate on a hedonistic principle of judging that the story protagonist should proceed to the party in order not to miss out on the cake. In contrast, older children, who we might suppose would be in Level 2, seem to operate on a principle concerned with the needs of others. These children put the needs of others before the self in some circumstances, given that they judge that the story protagonist should stop and give assistance even if it means missing the birthday cake.

Eisenberg's study neatly demonstrates the link between moral reasoning and pro-social behaviour. What we see is a general shift at approximately 5 years of age from holding the concerns of the self as foremost, to entertaining ideas about the well-being of others.

The findings and ideas we have looked at in this chapter strongly suggest that there is nothing inevitable about human aggression. Children can learn to be aggressive, as we discovered in the previous chapter, but equally, they can learn to be altruistic, or indeed they can learn to be both. In addition, in the present chapter, we have discovered that children's developing reasoning about moral issues and justice appears to have an important bearing on their general moral development. In terms of judgments about punishment and reward, this is reflected in a developmental shift from judgments based on outcome, such as extent of damage caused by action, to judgments based on intention or effort underlying the action. In terms of judgments about correct behaviour, this is reflected in a developmental shift away from hedonistic criteria, exclusively pertaining to what feels good to the child, to concern about adhering to rules, and ultimately to concern about deeper moral principles over and above particular rules.

Further Reading

Perhaps the foremost authority on moral development, particularly in relation to pro-social behaviour, is Nancy Eisenberg. This, coupled with the fact that her style of writing is highly readable, makes me recommend her book without hesitation:

EISENBERG, N. (1986) *Altruistic Emotion, Cognition and Behavior*, Hillsdale, N.J., Lawrence Erlbaum.

References

ACHENBACH, T.M. (1982) *Developmental Psychopathology*, 2nd ed., London, Wiley.

AINSWORTH, M. (1973) 'The development of mother-infant attachment', in CALDWELL, B.M. and RICCIUTI, H.N. (Eds) *Review of Child Development Research, Vol. 3*, Chicago, University of Chicago Press.

ANISFELD, E., CASPER, V., NOZYCE, M. and CUNNINGHAM, N. (1990) 'Does infant carrying promote attachment? An experimental study of the effects of increased physical contact on the development of attachment', *Child Development*, **61**, 1617–27.

BALL, W. and TRONICK, E. (1971) 'Infant responses to impending collision: Optical and real', *Science*, **171**, 818–20.

BANDURA, A. (1969) 'Social learning theory of identificatory processes', in GOSLIN, D.A. (Ed.) *Handbook of Socialization Theory and Research*, Chicago, Rand McNally.

BANDURA, A., ROSS, D. and ROSS, S. (1961) 'Transmission of aggression through imitation of aggressive models', *Journal of Abnormal and Social Psychology*, **63**, 575–82.

BANDURA, A., ROSS, D. and ROSS, S. (1963) 'Vicarious reinforcement and initiative learning', *Journal of Abnormal and Social Psychology*, **67**, 601–7.

BARKER, R., DEMBO, T. and LEWIN, K. (1941) 'Frustration and regression: An experiment with young children', *University of Iowa Studies in Child Welfare*, **18**, 1–314.

BATES, E., BRETHERTON, I., BEEGHLY-SMITH, M. and McNEW, S. (1982) 'Social bases of language development: A reassessment', in REESE, H.W. and LIPSITT, L.P. (Eds) *Advances in Child Development and Behavior, Vol. 16*, New York, Academic Press.

BEAL, C.R. and FLAVELL, J.H. (1984) 'Development of the ability to distinguish communicative intention and literal message meaning', *Child Development*, **55**, 920–8.

BENTON, D. (1991) 'Vitamin and mineral intake and cognitive functioning', in BENDICH, A. and BUTTERWORTH, C.E. (Eds) *Micronutrients in Health and the Prevention of Disease*, New York, Marcel Dekker Inc.

BENTON, D. and BUTS, J.P. (1990) 'Vitamin/mineral supplementation and intelligence', *Lancet*, **335**, 1158–60.

BENTON, D. and ROBERTS, G. (1988) 'Effect of vitamin and mineral supplementation on intelligence of a sample of schoolchildren', *Lancet*, **331**, 140–3.

BLOCK, J.H. (1983) 'Differential premises arising from differential socialization of the sexes: Some conjectures', *Child Development*, **54**, 1335–54.

BOUCHARD, T.J., LYKKEN, D.T., McGUE, M., SEGAL, N.L. and TELLEGEN, A. (1990) 'Sources of human psychological differences: The Minnesota study of twins reared apart,' *Science*, **250**, 223–8.

BOWER, T.G.R. (1965) 'Stimulus variables determining space perception in infants', *Science*, **149**, 88–9.

BOWER, T.G.R. (1967) 'Phenomenal identity and form perception in infants', *Perception and Psychophysics*, **2**, 74–6.

BOWER, T.G.R. (1982) *Development in Infancy*, 2nd ed., San Francisco, W.H. Freeman and Company.

BOWER, T.G.R., BROUGHTON, J.M. and MOORE, M.K. (1970) 'Infant responses to approaching objects: An indicator of response to distal variables', *Perception and Psychophysics*, **9**, 193–6.

BOWLBY, J. (1965) *Child Care and the Growth of Love*, 2nd ed., Harmondsworth, Penguin.

BRAINE, M.D.S. and RUMAIN, B. (1983) 'Logical reasoning', in FLAVELL, J.H. and MARKMAN, E.M. (Eds) *Handbook of Child Psychology, Vol. 3, Cognitive Development*, New York, Wiley.

BREMNER, J.G. and BRYANT, P.E. (1977) 'Place versus response as the basis of spatial errors made by young infants', *Journal of Experimental Child Psychology*, **23**, 162–71.

BREMNER, J.G. and MOORE, S. (1984) 'Prior visual inspection and object naming: Two factors that enhance hidden feature inclusion in young children's drawings', *British Journal of Developmental Psychology*, **2**, 371–6.

BROWN, P. and ELLIOT, R. (1965) 'Control of aggression in a nursery school class', *Journal of Experimental Child Psychology*, **2**, 103–7.

BROWN, R. and HANLON, C. (1970) 'Derivational complexity and order of acquisition', in HAYES, J.R. (Ed.) *Cognition and the Development of Language*, New York, Wiley.

BRUNER, J.S. (1983) *Child's Talk: Learning to Use Language*, Oxford, Oxford University Press.

BRYANT, P.E. and KOPYTYNSKA, H. (1976) 'Spontaneous measurement by young children', *Nature*, **260**, 773–4.

BRYANT, P.E. and TRABASSO, T. (1971) 'Transitive inferences and memory in young children', *Nature*, **232**, 456–8.

BUTTERWORTH, G. (1981) 'Object permanence and identity in Piaget's theory of infant cognition', in BUTTERWORTH, G. (Ed.) *Infancy and Epistemology: An Evaluation of Piaget's Theory*, Brighton, Harvester Press.

CARPENTER, G. (1975) 'Mother's face and the newborn', in LEWIN, R. (Ed.) *Child Alive*, London, Temple Smith.

CHENG, P.W. and HOLYOAK, K.J. (1985) 'Pragmatic reasoning schemas', *Cognitive Psychology*, **17**, 391–416.

CHOMSKY, N. (1975) *Reflections on Language*, New York, Pantheon Books.

CROMBIE, I.K., TODMAN, J., McNEILL, G., FLOREY, C., DU, V., MENZIES, I. and

KENNEDY, R.A. (1990) 'Effect of vitamin and mineral supplementation on verbal and non-verbal reasoning of schoolchildren', *Lancet*, **335**, 744–7.

CROOK, C.K. (1984) 'Factors influencing the use of transparency in children's drawings', *British Journal of Developmental Psychology*, **2**, 213–21.

DAVIS, A.M. (1983) 'Contextual sensitivity in young children's drawings', *Journal of Experimental Child Psychology*, **35**, 478–86.

DAVITZ, J. (1952) 'The effects of previous training on postfrustration behavior', *Journal of Abnormal and Social Psychology*, **47**, 309–15.

DODGE, K.A., COIE, J.D., PETTIT, G.S. and PRICE, J.M. (1990) 'Peer status and aggression in boys' groups: Developmental and contextual considerations', *Child Development*, **61**, 1289–1309.

DONALDSON, M. (1978) *Children's Minds*, Glasgow, Fontana/Collins.

EISENBERG, N. (1986) *Altruistic Emotion, Cognition, and Behavior*, Hillsdale, N.J., Lawrence Erlbaum.

EISENBERG, N., FABES, R., MILLER, P.A., SHELL, R., SHEA, C. and MAY-PLUMLEE, T. (1990) 'Preschoolers' vicarious emotional responding and their situational and dispositional prosocial behavior', *Merrill-Palmer Quarterly*, **36**, 507–29.

ELARDO, R., BRADLEY, R. and CALDWELL, B. (1975) 'The relation of infants' home environments to mental test performance from six to thirty-six months: A longitudinal analysis', *Child Development*, **46**, 71–6.

ERON, L.D. (1982) 'Parent-child interaction, television violence and aggression of children', *American Psychologist*, **37**, 197–211.

ERON, L.D. (1987) 'The development of aggressive behavior from the perspective of a developing behaviorism', *American Psychologist*, **42**, 435–42.

FLAVELL, J.H. (1982) 'On cognitive development', *Child Development*, **53**, 1–10.

FLAVELL, J.H., EVERETT, B.A., CROFT, K. and FLAVELL, E.R. (1981) 'Young children's knowledge about visual perception: Further evidence for the Level 1–Level 2 distinction', *Developmental Psychology*, **17**, 99–103.

FOX, N. (1977) 'Attachment of Kibbutz infants to mother and metapelet', *Child Development*, **48**, 1228–39.

FOX, T. and THOMAS, G.V. (1989) 'Children's drawings of an anxiety eliciting topic: Effects on the size of drawing', *British Journal of Clinical Psychology*, **29**, 71–81.

FREEMAN, N.H. (1980) *Strategies of Representation in Young Children*, London, Academic Press.

FREEMAN, N.H. and JANIKOUN, R. (1972) 'Intellectual realism in children's drawings of a familiar object with distinctive features', *Child Development*, **43**, 1116–21.

FREUD, A. and DANN, S. (1951) 'An experiment in group upbringing', in *The Psychoanalytic Study of the Child, Vol. 6*.

FRITH, U. (1989) *Autism: Explaining the Enigma*, Oxford, Basil Blackwell.

GARDNER, H. (1982) *Developmental Psychology*, 2nd ed., Boston, Little, Brown and Co.

GIBSON, E.J. and WALK, R.D. (1960) 'The "visual cliff"', *Scientific American*, **202**, 64–71.

GOLDFARB, W. (1943) 'The effects of early institutional care on adolescent personality', *Journal of Experimental Education*, **12**, 106–29.

GOLDIN-MEADOW, S. and MYLANDER, C. (1990) 'Beyond the input given: The child's role in the acquisition of language', *Language*, **66**, 323–55.

GOODWIN, J. (1982) 'Use of drawings in evaluating children who may be incest victims', *Child and Youth Services Review*, **4**, 269–78.

GOPNIK, A. and ASTINGTON, J.W. (1988) 'Children's understanding of representational change and its relation to the understanding of false belief and the appearance-reality distinction', *Child Development*, **59**, 26–37.

GREGORY, R.L. (1966) *Eye and Brain*, New York, World University Library.

HARRIS, P.L. (1974) 'Perseverative search at a visibly empty space by young infants', *Journal of Experimental Child Psychology*, **18**, 535–42.

HIRSHBERG, L. (1990) 'When infants look to their parents: II. Twelve-month-olds' response to conflicting emotional signals', *Child Development*, **61**, 1187–91.

HIRSHBERG, L. and SVEJDA, M. (1990) 'When infants look to their parents: I. Infants' social referencing of mothers compared to fathers', *Child Development*, **61**, 1175–86.

HOFFMAN, M.L. (1970) 'Moral development', in MUSSEN, P.H. (Ed.) *Carmichael's Manual of Child Psychology, Vol. 2*, New York, Wiley.

JENSEN, A.R. (1980) *Bias in Mental Testing*, New York, Free Press.

KAGAN, J., KEARSLEY, R.B. and ZELAZO, P.R. (1978) *Infancy: Its Place in Human Development*, Cambridge, Mass., Harvard University Press.

KOHLBERG, L. (1966) 'A cognitive developmental analysis of children's sex-role concepts and attitudes', in MACCOBY, E. (Ed.) *The Development of Sex Differences*, Stanford, Stanford University Press.

KOHLBERG, L. (1981) *The Philosophy of Moral Development: Moral Stages and the Idea of Justice*, San Francisco, Harper and Row.

KRAUSS, R.M. and GLUCKSBERG, S. (1969) 'The development of communication: Competence as a function of age', *Child Development*, **40**, 255–66.

LAING, R.D. (1969) *The Divided Self: An Existential Study in Sanity and Madness*, Harmondsworth, Penguin.

LAPSLEY, D.K. and MURPHY, M.N. (1985) 'Another look at the theoretical assumptions of adolescent egocentrism', *Developmental Review*, **5**, 201–17.

LEEKAM, S.R. and PERNER, J. (1991) 'Does the autistic child have a metarepresentational deficit?', *Cognition*.

LEIDERMAN, P.H. and LEIDERMAN, G.F. (1974) 'Affective and cognitive consequences of polymatric infant care in the East African highlands', in PICK, A. (Ed.) *Minnesota Symposium on Child Development, Vol. 8*, Minneapolis, University of Minnesota Press.

LEON, M. (1984) 'Rules mothers and sons use to integrate intent and damage information in their moral judgments', *Child Development*, **55**, 2106–13.

LEONARD, S.P. and ARCHER, J. (1989) 'A naturalistic investigation of gender constancy in three- to four-year-old children', *British Journal of Developmental Psychology*, **7**, 341–6.

LESLIE, A.M. (1987) 'Pretense and representation: The origins of "theory of mind"', *Psychological Review*, **94**, 412–26.

LESTER, B.M. (1974) 'Separation protest in Guatemalan infants: Cross cultural and cognitive findings', *Developmental Psychology*, **10**, 79–85.

LIEBERT, R. and BARON, R. (1972) 'Some immediate effects of televised violence on children's behavior', *Developmental Psychology*, **6**, 469–75.

LIGHT, P.H. and HUMPHREYS, J. (1981) 'Internal relationships in young children's drawings', *Journal of Experimental Child Psychology*, **31**, 521–30.

LIGHT, P.H. and MACINTOSH, E. (1980) 'Depth relationships in young children's drawings', *Journal of Experimental Child Psychology*, **30**, 79–87.

LIGHT, P.H. and SIMMONS, B. (1983) 'The effects of a communicative task upon the representation of depth relationships in young children's drawings', *Journal of Experimental Child Psychology*, **35**, 81–92.

LIGHT, P.H., BUCKINGHAM, N. and ROBBINS, A.H. (1979) 'The conservation task as an interactional setting', *British Journal of Educational Psychology*, **49**, 304–10.

McGARRIGLE, J. and DONALDSON, M. (1975) 'Conservation accidents', *Cognition*, **3**, 341–50.

MALLICK, S. and McCANDLESS, B. (1966) 'A study of catharsis aggression', *Journal of Personality and Social Psychology*, **4**, 591–6.

MARCUS, D.E. and OVERTON, W.F. (1978) 'The development of cognitive gender constancy and sex role preferences', *Child Development*, **49**, 434–44.

MARTIN, C.L. and LITTLE, J.K. (1990) 'The relation of gender understanding to children's sex-typed preferences and gender stereotypes', *Child Development*, **61**, 1427–39.

MENIG-PETERSON, C.L. (1975) 'The modification of communicative behavior in preschool-aged children as a function of the listener's perspective', *Child Development*, **46**, 1015–18.

MILLER, N.E. and DOLLARD, J. (1941) *Learning and Imitation*, New Haven, Yale University Press.

MILLER, P.H. (1989) *Theories of Developmental Psychology*, 2nd ed., New York, W.H. Freeman and Co.

MISCHEL, W. (1970) 'Sex typing and socialization', in MUSSEN, P.H. (Ed.) *Carmichael's Manual of Child Psychology, Vol. 2*, London, Wiley.

MITCHELL, P. and LACOHEE, H. (1991) 'Children's early understanding of false belief', *Cognition*, **39**, 207–27.

MITCHELL, P. and ROBINSON, E.J. (1990) 'When do children overestimate their knowledge of unfamiliar targets?', *Journal of Experimental Child Psychology*, **50**, 81–101.

MITCHELL, P. and ROBINSON, E.J. (1992) 'Children's understanding of the evidential connotation of "know" in relation to overestimation of their own knowledge', *Journal of Child Language*.

MITCHELL, P. and RUSSELL, J. (1989) 'Young children's understanding of the say/mean distinction in referential speech', *Journal of Experimental Child Psychology*, **47**, 467–90.

MITCHELL, P. and RUSSELL, J. (1991) 'Children's judgments of whether slightly and grossly discrepant objects were intended by a speaker', *British Journal of Developmental Psychology*, **9**, 271–80.

MITCHELL, P., MUNNO, A. and RUSSELL, J. (1991) 'Children's understanding of the communicative value of discrepant verbal messages', *Cognitive Development*, **6**, 279–99.

MOORE, C. and FRY, D. (1986) 'The effect of the experimenter's intention on the child's understanding of conservation', *Cognition*, **22**, 283–98.

NELSON, K. (1985) *Making Sense: The Acquisition of Shared Meaning*, Orlando, Academic Press.

NICHOLLS, J.G. (1978) 'The development of the concepts of effort and ability, perception of academic attainment, and the understanding that difficult tasks require more ability', *Child Development*, **49**, 800–14.

NUNNER-WINKLER, G. and SODIAN, B. (1988) 'Children's understanding of moral emotions', *Child Development*, **59**, 1323–39.

O'BRIEN, M. and HUSTON, A.C. (1985) 'Development of sex-typed play behaviour in toddlers', *Developmental Psychology*, **21**, 866–71.

PARKE, R., BERKOWITZ, L., LEYENS, J., WEST, S. and SEBASTIAN, R. (1977) 'Some effects of violent and nonviolent movies on the behavior of juvenile delinquents', in BERKOWITZ, L. (Ed.) *Advances in Experimental Social Psychology*, New York, Academic Press.

PARSONS, J.E., RUBLE, D.N., KLOSSON, E.C., FELDMAN, N.S. and RHOLES, W.S. (1976) 'Order effects on children's moral and achievement judgments', *Developmental Psychology*, **12**, 357–8.

PEARS, R. and BRYANT, P. (1990) 'Transitive inferences by young children about spatial position', *British Journal of Psychology*, **81**, 497–510.

PERNER, J., LEEKAM, S.R. and WIMMER, H. (1987) 'Three-year-olds' difficulty with false belief: The case for a conceptual deficit', *British Journal of Developmental Psychology*, **5**, 125–37.

PERNER, J., FRITH, U., LESLIE, A.M. and LEEKAM, S.R. (1989) 'Exploration of the autistic child's theory of mind: Knowledge, belief and communication', *Child Development*, **60**, 689–700.

PIAGET, J. and INHELDER, B. (1969) *The Psychology of the Child*, London, Routledge and Kegan Paul.

PLOMIN, R. and DEFRIES, J.C. (1980) 'Genetics and intelligence: Recent data', *Intelligence*, **4**, 15–24.

PLOMIN, R., LOEHLIN, J.C. and DEFRIES, J.C. (1985) 'Genetic and environmental components of "environmental" influences', *Developmental Psychology*, **21**, 391–402.

POPPER, K. (1972) *Conjectures and Refutations: The Growth of Scientific Knowledge*, London, Routledge and Kegan Paul.

PREMACK, D. and WOODRUFF, G. (1978) 'Does the chimpanzee have a theory of mind?', *Behavioral and Brain Sciences*, **4**, 515–26.

REST, J.R. (1983) 'Morality', in FLAVELL, J.H. and MARKMAN, E.M. (Eds) *Handbook of Child Psychology: Cognitive Development, Vol. 3*, New York, Wiley.

ROBINSON, E.J. and MITCHELL, P. (1990) 'Children's failure to make judgments of undecidability when they are ignorant', *International Journal of Behavioral Development*, **13**, 467–88.

ROBINSON, E.J. and MITCHELL, P. (1992) 'Children's interpretation of messages from a speaker with a false belief', *Child Development*.

ROBINSON, E.J. and ROBINSON, W.P. (1981) 'Ways of reacting to communication failure in relation to the development of the child's understanding about verbal communication', *European Journal of Social Psychology*, **11**, 189–208.

ROBINSON, E.J. and WHITTAKER, S.J. (1987) 'Children's conceptions of relations between messages, meanings and reality', *British Journal of Developmental Psychology*, **5**, 81–90.

ROSE, S.A. and BLANK, M. (1974) 'The potency of context in children's cognition: An illustration through conservation', *Child Development*, **45**, 499–502.

ROSENTHAL, D., WENDER, P.H., KETY, S.S., WELNER, J. and SCHULSINGER, F. (1971) 'The adopted-away offspring in schizophrenics', *American Journal of Psychiatry*, **128**, 87–91.

RUBLE, D.N., BALABAN, T. and COOPER, J. (1981) 'Gender constancy and the effects of sex-typed televised toy commercials', *Child Development*, **52**, 667–73.

RUSSELL, J. (1978) *The Acquisition of Knowledge*, London, Macmillan.

RUSSELL, J. (1981) 'Children's memory for the premises in a transitive measurement task assessed by elicited and spontaneous justifications', *Journal of Experimental Child Psychology*, **31**, 300–9.

RUSSELL, J. and MITCHELL, P. (1985) 'Things are not always as they seem: The appearance/reality distinction and conservation', *Educational Psychology*, **5**, 227–36.

RUTTER, M. (1972) *Maternal Deprivation Reassessed*, Harmondsworth, Penguin.

SCAIFE, M. and BRUNER, J.S. (1975) 'The capacity for joint visual attention in the infant', *Nature*, **253**, 265.

SCARR, S. and KIDD, K.K. (1983) 'Developmental behavior genetics', in HAITH, M.M. and CAMPOS, J.J. (Eds), *Handbook of Child Psychology: Infancy and Developmental Psychobiology, Vol. 2*, New York, Wiley.

SCARR, S. and WEINBERG, R.A. (1983) 'The Minnesota adoption studies: Genetic differences and malleability', *Child Development*, **54**, 260–7.

SCHAFFER, H.R. and EMERSON, P. (1964) 'The development of social attachments in infancy', *Monographs of the Society for Research in Child Development*, **29** (Serial No. 94, No. 3).

SCHOENTHALER, S.J., AMOS, S.P., DORAZ, W.E., KELLY, M. and WAKEFIELD, J. (1991) 'Controlled trial of vitamin/mineral supplementation on intelligence and brain function', *Personality and Individual Differences*, **4**, 343–50.

SHATZ, M. and GELMAN, R. (1973) 'The development of communication skills: Modifications in the speech of young children as a function of listener', *Monographs of the Society for Research in Child Development*, **152** (Serial No. 152, No. 2), 1–38.

SLATER, A., MATTOCK, A. and BROWN, E. (1990) 'Size constancy at birth: Newborn infants' responses to retinal and real size', *Journal of Experimental Child Psychology*, **49**, 314–22.

SLATER, A., MATTOCK, A., BROWN, E. and BREMNER, J.G. (1991) 'Form perception at birth: Cohen and Younger (1984) revisited', *Journal of Experimental Child Psychology*, **51**, 395–406.

SNOW, C.E. and FERGUSON, C.A. (Eds) (1977) *Talking to Children*, Cambridge, Cambridge University Press.

SODIAN, B. and WIMMER, H. (1987) 'Children's understanding of inference as a source of knowledge', *Child Development*, **58**, 424–33.

SOLLEY, C.M. and HAIGH, G. (1957) 'A note to Santa Claus', *Topeka Research Papers, The Menninger Foundation*, **18**, 4–5.

SONNENSCHEIN, S. (1986) 'Development of referential communication skills: How familiarity with a listener affects a speaker's production of redundant messages', *Developmental Psychology*, **22**, 549–52.

STEIN, A.H. and FRIEDRICH, L.K. (1972) 'Television content and young children's behavior', in MURRAY, J.P., RUBINSTEIN, E.A. and COMSTOCK, G.A. (Eds) *Television and Social Behavior, Vol. 2: Television and Social Learning*, Washington, D.C., US Government Printing Office.

THOMAS, G.V. and SILK, A.M.J. (1990) *An Introduction to the Psychology of Children's Drawings*, London, Harvester Wheatsheaf.

THOMAS, G.V., CHAIGNE, E. and FOX, T. (1989) 'Children's drawings of topics differing in significance: Effects on size of drawing', *British Journal of Developmental Psychology*, **7**, 321–32.

THOMAS, M.H., HORTON, R., LIPPINCOTT, E. and DRABMAN, R. (1977) 'Desensitization to portrayals of real-life aggression as a function of exposure to television violence', *Journal of Personality and Social Psychology*, **35**, 450–8.

WASON, P.C. and JOHNSON-LAIRD, P.N. (1972) *The Psychology of Reasoning: Structure and Content*, London, Batsford Press.

WIMMER, H. and HARTL, M. (1991) 'Against the Cartesian view on mind: Young children's difficulty with own false beliefs', *British Journal of Developmental Psychology*, **9**, 125–38.

WIMMER, H., WACHTER, J. and PERNER, J. (1982) 'Cognitive autonomy of the development of moral evaluation and achievement', *Child Development*, **53**, 668–76.

WOODWORTH, R.S. (1941) *Heredity and Environment: A Cultural Study of Recently Published Materials on Twins and Foster Children*, New York, Social Science Research Council Bulletin.

YARROW, M.R., SCOTT, P. and WAXLER, C.Z. (1973) 'Learning concern for others', *Developmental Psychology*, **8**, 240–60.

ZAITCHIK, D. (1990) 'When representations conflict with reality: The preschooler's problem with false beliefs and "false" photographs', *Cognition*, **35**, 41–68.

ZAJONC, R.B. (1983) 'Validating the confluence model', *Psychological Bulletin*, **93**, 457–80.

ZARBATANY, L. and LAMB, M.E. (1985) 'Social referencing as a function of information source: Mother versus strangers', *Infant Behavior and Development*, **8**, 25–33.

Note on the Author

Peter Mitchell was born in Southport, Merseyside, and was educated at Liverpool University, where he completed both a BA and PhD in psychology. Having worked for a spell at Birmingham University and Warwick University, he now lectures in psychology at University College Swansea. His primary research interests are in the child's theory of mind and children's verbal communication abilities, and his articles on these topics are published in the leading international psychology journals. Peter is also organizer of a conference on the child's theory of mind at Swansea in March, 1992, attended by some of the world's foremost authorities on this subject.

Author Index

Subject Index

A-B Task 4, 20–21, 103
Accommodation 12
Affectionless psychopathy 100–101, 104, 106
Aggression
  – attention seeking 140
  – frustration 139–140
  – gender differences 141
  – imitation 133–134
  – psychological rejection 141
  – T.V. violence 134–138
Ambiguous speech 86–88
Assimilation 11–12
Attachment during infancy 103–104
Autism 43–46
  – and communication 81–82

Babbling 71
Binocular parallax 59–60

Carpentered environment 68
Castration anxiety 114–115
Catharsis 111, 132
Class inclusion 8–9, 27–28
Concrete operational stage 9–10
Confirmation bias 34
Conservation 7–9, 13, 22–24, 118
  – compensation 9
  – identity 10
  – inversion 9
Correlation 51–52, 55

Defence mechanisms 112
Discrepant messages 85–86
Down's syndrome 45
Drawings
  – incest 97–99
  – intellectual realism 92–96

  – size 96–97
Dream analysis 111

Ego 112–114
Egocentrism 6–9, 24, 26–27, 35, 38–40, 42, 93, 96, 144–145
  – during adolescence 14–17
Egocentric speech 82–84, 90–91
  – collective monologue 82–83
  – individual monologue 82
  – repetition 82
Elektra complex 114
Equilibration 12–13
Eros 111

Free association 111
Formal operational stage 10–11, 31–35

Gambler's fallacy 44
Good continuation 64–65

Hieroglyphics 70, 92
Holophrases 72
Hypnosis 111

Id 112–114
Imaginary audience 15–17
Imitation of language 75–76
Inference as a source of knowledge 42
Introspection 111
IQ
  – definition and history 48–50
  – role of diet 54–55
  – role of heredity and environment 51–54
  – role of social environment 55–56

Language
  – deep structure 76–77